D1707996

To Phyllis,
May this book help to remind you of
the "warmth" we experienced while
growing up in Chisholm.
Warm regards,
Mike Kovach
11/12/05

*Growing up in*

# Chisholm

*on*
*the Mesabi Iron Range*

## The Story of an Immigrant Family

Mike Kosiak

## DEDICATION

*To our parents, John and Julia Billo Kosiak, as well as all those immigrant parents who settled on the Mesabi Iron Range of Minnesota at the turn of the twentieth century.*

# Contents

# Acknowledgments

This book would not have been possible without the assistance of several people. To begin, one must be provided with the impetus to undertake such an endeavor. This impetus was provided initially by immediate family members, including my wife, Helen, our four children, Uncle Harry Billo, and my three sisters Mary Ann, Irene, and Eve.

What began simply as an effort to review the lifestyles of our parents and grandparents as they existed in the "Old Country" and on the Mesabi Iron Range at the turn of the century progressed to a comprehensive review of the geographic, social, ethnic, cultural and educational forces in existence at that time and how those forces affected not only the Kosiaks but also all other Mesabi immigrants and their families.

Sister Mary Ann was responsible for the genealogical research, and she and Irene contributed much to the actual content of our grade school and high school education, daily home life, religious celebrations, and our ethnic food. Uncle Harry Billo was an invaluable resource concerning our very early childhood and life as it existed in the mining company locations at the turn of the century.

The computer and grammatical skills of Renee Marquis Kosiak, ranging from the simple transcription and editing of multiple hand-written chapters to the pre-publication modification of the entire manuscript have proven invaluable.

My gratitude goes to Traci Thompson and Jean Costello for their word processing skills and to Michael Moore for his help in writing a significant portion of Chapter 2, as it deals with the history of iron mining on the Mesabi Iron Range. Deserving recognition for his suggestions is Alex Kurak, a native of Chisholm and also the son of Carpatho-Rusyn immigrants.

I am especially indebted to my dear wife, Helen, who not only provided much of the original impetus to research this project but whose ongoing patience, encouragement, and moral support were so essential in bringing this effort to fruition.

# Preface

In a letter dated April 27, 1987, addressed to the Director of the Iron Range Research Center in Chisholm, our brother Willy wrote, "I think that as a group we in Chisholm have a unique story to tell, a story we can be proud of and a story I think other people will find interesting. Twenty years from now our grandchildren will also have a valuable resource to help them understand their roots."[1]

Unfortunately, because Willy died soon after, that unique story has never been told. This treatise will attempt to write that story, which even today, more than fifteen years later, should still prove very interesting and informative and might assist the children and grandchildren of other European immigrants who settled on the Mesabi Iron Range to better understand their roots.

Recalling one's life experiences must always begin with family and home. The concept appears simple enough where personal interaction with grandparents, parents, aunts, and uncles, as well as older siblings is possible. Information presented about our home, school, and family was dependent on the memories of the author and his younger sisters, Mary Ann and Irene. Fairly extensive research was required to better understand life as it existed in rural east-central Europe during the late nineteenth and early twentieth centuries as well as in Chisholm and the Mesabi Iron Range of Minnesota through the first half of the twentieth century.

Because of the uniqueness of the Mesabi Iron Range from a geographic, geological, demographic and cultural standpoint, one of the longer chapters of this review is devoted to the entire Mesabi Range and especially to our hometown of Chisholm. Of critical importance were the in-depth studies of John Syrjamaki, a 1929 graduate of Chisholm High School, who was born and raised in Jordan Location, one of several mining locations situated on the outskirts of Chisholm.

(Because so much information was obtained from the two Chisholm newspapers, the *Mesaba Miner* and the *Tribune Herald*, only direct quotes from these two publications are listed in the reference endnotes.)

As with all immigrant families living on the Mesabi Range, the language spoken in the home was the language of the immigrant parents. The language spoken by the Kosiak family and all other Galician Carpatho-Rusyns who settled in northeastern Minnesota in the early twentieth century could best be described as a modified Slavic dialect. The immigrants referred to their language simply as *po-nashemu*. When literally translated *po-nashemu* means "like us, of us, as us." When applied to the general population, *po-nashemu* means "our people." So it was in the language of our birth, that we always addressed our father as "Tato." Our mother was fondly referred to as "Mama" when we were very young and "Ma" in our later years.

Second only to family and home in the life of any child is the education available during those formative years. For the children of poorly educated immigrant parents totally lacking in their comprehension of the English language, and more often than not illiterate even in their own language, education was of critical importance. What role the educational process played in the lives of all the citizens of the Iron Range occupies a major segment of this presentation. Mention must be made concerning the importance of the information obtained from the *James P. Vaughan Papers 1904-1963*, as well as the studies of Timothy Smith.

Religion is mentioned not only to demonstrate its effect on our early upbringing but also to point out some of the basic differences between the Carpatho-Rusyns who were followers of the Eastern Orthodox faith and those who were affiliated with the Roman Catholic Church.

Those chapters concerning health care and foods are based primarily on family reminiscences. In all families where the employer did not provide pre-paid health care, this void was more than adequately filled by the care provided through the school system. Nutritional needs were satisfied through the cultivation of various-sized garden plots and the raising of several types of livestock. Of greatest importance, however, was the never-ending labor and ingenuity of the immigrant mother who continued to provide meals that were both nutritious and also very tasty.

Finally, it has been said that you have to know where you have come from if you are to know where you are going. Joseph Komidar, who graduated from Chisholm High School in 1934 and who was also born and raised on Poplar Street, had this to say in his memoirs published in 1996. ". . . Not wishing to take the chance of your not ever getting to know where you are going, I have put together this compendium of information about family, place and myself . . . more than you might ever have to know in order to determine where you are going."[2]

[1]William Kosiak, personal communication, April 27, 1987.
[2]Joseph S. Komidar, *As It Was: Family, Town and Growing Up*, personal memoir, unpublished, 1996.

# 1

# *Our People*

*. . . most Carpatho-Rusyns spent their whole lives within their native or neighboring villages, where their life cycle was dominated by the demands of the agricultural seasons and the church calendar. Indeed, as high as ninety-seven percent of the Carpatho-Rusyns were born and died in the same village.*

—P.R. Magocsi

Many scholars have placed the original homeland of the Slavic people of Europe within the area just north of the Carpathian Mountains between the Dnieper River in Russia and the Elbe River in Germany. These scholars cite the Greek historian Ptolemy who, writing in the second century A.D., refers to the Carpathian Mountains as the "Mountains of the Slavs" and to the Baltic Sea as the "Sea of the Slavs."[1]

While Christianity was spreading within the far-flung borders of the Roman world centering on the Mediterranean Sea, the Slavic people were moving from their original homeland north of the Carpathian Mountains into and throughout eastern and south-central Europe. Historians believe that by the late sixth century A.D. they had penetrated southward into the Balkan Peninsula as far as the borders of the Byzantine Empire.

The Slavic tribes or groups that had migrated southward and occupied the greater portions of the Balkan Peninsula and the southernmost reaches of the Pannonian Plain came to be known as the Southern Slavs (today's Slovenians, Croatians, Serbians, Macedonians, and Bulgarians). Those tribal people who remained behind were later to become differentiated into the Western Slavs (present day Czechs, Slovaks, Poles), and Eastern Slavs (contemporary Russians, White Russians or Byelorussians, and Ukrainians).[2]

Our Kosiak and Billo ancestors came from Central Europe, just north of the Carpathian Mountain crests in the far southeastern corner of Poland. This area, referred to as the Lemko Region, consisted of many

1

small villages within the mountainous foothills. Originally part of the Galician principality under the Kievan-Rus Federation, the Lemko Region came under Polish rule in the fourteenth century, and then was part of the Austrian-Hapsburg province of Galicia from 1772 to 1918. Since World War I, the Lemko Region has been a part of Poland.

Map 1

Origin of the Kosiak and Billo Families (circled area on map)

*Most of the people were employed as farmers, livestock herders (especially sheep) and in forest-related occupations. The mountainous landscape never allowed for extensive agricultural production. The socioeconomic status had remained basically unchanged from the medieval period until the twentieth century. Almost without exception, the peasants who inhabited these small villages had worked as serfs for their Polish landlords until 1848 and then as poorly paid, usually indebted agricultural laborers for several more decades. The lack of available land was caused in part by its continual subdivision and, together with population increases and inefficient agricultural practices, resulted in severe poverty. These conditions, combined with the threat of being drafted into the military, prompted many to emigrate to the United States. Approximately seventy percent of the emigrants from the Lemko area were young males, either single or recently married.*

*After the decision to leave was made, an often heart-rending departure was accompanied by weeping relatives and a final blessing by the parish priest under the wayside cross at the head of the village. A slow, bumpy ride on a horse-drawn cart provided much time to reflect about family, friends and loved ones left behind as the prospective immigrant traveled to the nearest rail station to board a train that would eventually transport him or her to the coast. There were also numerous cases in which villagers walked most of the way to major cities before boarding trains for the faraway ports. This was often the case with the large number of young men who, on the eve of World War I, feared induction into the Austro-Hungarian army.*[3]

Persons from the Lemko Region of the Austro-Hungarian Empire usually traveled toward the northwest and embarked from the German ports of Hamburg or Bremen to begin the long two to three-week trip across the Atlantic. Most had never seen an ocean before and in most cases had never left the immediate surroundings of their native village.

By the 1890s, steam-powered ships had modernized the business of ocean travel, cutting the time to make the Atlantic crossing from three months to two weeks. Steerage passage was so-called because it was located in the lower decks where the steering mechanism of the sailing ships had once been housed.

*Steerage was enormously profitable for steamship companies. The average cost of a ticket was only $30. Larger ships could hold from 1,500 to 2,000 immigrants, netting a profit of $45,000 to $60,000 for a single one-way voyage. The cost to feed a single immigrant was only about 60 cents a day!*[4]

For most immigrants, the experience of steerage was like a nightmare. The conditions were so dismally dark, so unsanitary, so foul smelling, that they were the single most important cause of America's early immigration laws. Unfortunately, because the laws were almost impossible to enforce, steerage conditions continued to remain deplorable almost beyond belief.

As late as 1911, in a report to President William H. Taft, the United States Immigration Commission said of steerage:

*Imagine a large room, perhaps seven feet in height, extending the entire breadth of the ship and about one-third of its length. This room is filled with a framework of iron pipes, forming a double tier of six-by-two feet berths, with only sufficient space left to serve as aisles or passageways. Such a compartment will sometimes accommodate as many as three hundred passengers, and it is duplicated in other parts of the ship and on other decks. The open deck space reserved for steerage passengers is usually very limited, and situated in the worst part of the ship and subject to the most violent motion, to the dirt from the stacks and the odors from the hold and galleys. The only provisions for eating are frequently shelves or benches along the sides or in the passages of sleeping compartments. Dining rooms are rare and if found are often shared with berths installed along the walls. Toilets and washrooms are completely inadequate, and the air soon becomes foul. The unattended vomit of the seasick, the odors of not too clean bodies, the reek of food and the awful stench of the nearby toilet rooms make the atmosphere of the steerage such that it is a marvel the human flesh can endure it. Most immigrants lie in their berths for most of the voyage, in a stupor caused by the foul air. The food often repels them . . . it is almost impossible to keep personally clean. All of these conditions are naturally aggravated by the crowding.*[5]

Due to the extreme crowding and the frequent lack of food, many immigrants were struck with illness. At one time, the average mortality rate was ten percent per voyage. Their endurance prevailed despite rumors about life in America, combined with stories about rejections and deportations at Ellis Island. They rehearsed answering the immigration inspectors' questions, and spent their time learning the new language. At trip's end, most were physically, mentally, and emotionally tired, but all knew they had just completed one more step to bring them closer to the New World.

Medical inspectors boarded incoming ships at the entrance to the lower bay of New York Harbor where quarantine examinations were conducted only for the first or second-class passengers. Cabin passengers who failed inspection would have to pass through Ellis Island for additional checks. However, very few cabin-class passengers were ever marked for more thorough examinations. In 1905, of the 100,000 cabin class passengers arriving in New York, only 3,000 had to pass through Ellis Island for additional checks. During this same time period, 800,000 steerage passengers were processed there.

After the privileged passengers had disembarked on Manhattan, remaining passengers were herded onto ferries for transfer to Ellis Island.

*Chartered by the steamship companies, these vessels were little better than open air barges, freezing in the winter, sweltering hot in the summer, and lacking toilet facilities and lifesaving equipment. Deaths caused by exposure to cold were not uncommon and one Public Health Service official estimated that of the children suffering from measles when they arrived, thirty percent subsequently died because of their trip across the harbor. Although the ferries were thought adequate for the short ride, busy days saw immigrants imprisoned on these vessels for hours while they waited their turn to land at Ellis Island. The harbor was often choked with steamships crammed with as many as twenty thousand passengers waiting to disembark and be ferried to Ellis Island. Sometimes new arrivals had to wait in steerage for days, prolonging the miserable journey, and making America's promise that much more elusive.*[6]

Admittance procedures began in the Registry with a medical examination during which those with suspicious health problems were marked with a white letter indicating their supposed condition: "L" for lameness, a circled "T" for possible mental defects, "H" for a heart condition, and "F" for rash on the face. Those bearing such a mark were separated from the others for a more extensive evaluation and possible deportation. Although the number of immigrants deported was not great, it was a fearful prospect for the new arrivals who, in most cases, had nothing to return to and in some instances were fleeing political persecution or military conscription. It was

5

for this reason that some immigrants bought cabin-class tickets for their relatives who might be unable to pass the more thorough physical and mental examination given to those traveling in steerage.[7]

Others, with no obvious medical problems, were questioned by an examiner with the aid of an interpreter. They were asked about their work, their destination, the amount of money they had and who had paid for their passage. In most cases the immigrant received a stamp of approval and was sometimes given a new name by customs officers unsympathetic or impatient with the strange-sounding Slavic, Italian and Finnish names.

Railroad tickets for travel from New York City could be purchased on Ellis Island, so if no difficulties had been encountered, the immigrant was free to leave after a processing time of three or four hours.

## JULIA BILLO KOSIAK

Our mother, Julia Billo Kosiak, was born on May 20, 1898, to Mike and Eva Uchal Billo in the small village of Balnica, north of the Carpathian Mountains close to the Czechoslovakian border in the province of Galicia, Austria-Hungary. Though the village no longer exists, Balnica was located about five miles southeast of the village of Smolnik where John Kosiak was born.

Unlike John Kosiak, who left his home alone at age sixteen, Julia was almost eleven years old when she and her mother began their trip to America. Except for the comfort provided by her mother, the trip for Julia must have been at least as trying as that experienced by young John Kosiak the following year. Whereas he would leave his home at the encouragement of his brothers, Frank, Aleck, Max, Mike, and Steve, who were already in America, Julia and her mother were leaving to join her father who was living in Monroe, a mining location about a mile southeast of Chisholm, Minnesota.

Leaving the only home one has ever known, even with a parent, can in itself be a very traumatic event. Julia's fear and anxiety on leaving home must have been somewhat allayed by the happiness and excitement she felt knowing she was going to America to be reunited with her father. For some unknown reason, a younger brother, Stephen, was left at home in the care of an aging grandmother.

After the usual carriage ride to the nearest railroad station and at least a twenty-four to thirty-hour train ride to Hamburg, Germany, Julia and her mother boarded the *S.S. Cleveland* as steerage passengers on March 26, 1909. Thirteen days later, on April 8, they arrived in New York City. Following the processing on Ellis Island and a two to three-day trip by rail, the two arrived in Chisholm.

Their home at 113 Tener Avenue in Monroe Location had no electricity, running water or plumbing. There was no basement, which was true of all mining location houses. Wood-burning stoves provided heat, and kerosene lamps provided light. The home originally had five rooms on one floor: a kitchen, dining room, living room and two bedrooms. According to Uncle Harry Billo, it wasn't until approximately 1917 that the homes were provided with electricity, running water, and indoor plumbing. At that time, in the process of adding a bathroom, an additional bedroom was added to the house. In 1948, when the Oliver Iron Mining Company sold the Monroe houses, the new owners moved the house to the neighboring city of Buhl where it can be found today at 114 Grant Street.

Monroe Location in 1910 was described as follows:

*The Monroe Location merits especial notice as one of the best of many provided by this corporation (Oliver Iron Mining Company) for the comfort and convenience of its employees. Many pleasant and attractive homes are to be found in this place. Several acres have been set aside for a park in which trees and shrubbery are cultivated. . . .There is a public school in which two teachers are employed and cultivation of the better qualities of human nature is given much encouragement.*[8]

Writing in *Survey* in April of 1916, C.W. Pfeiffer described Monroe Location as follows:

*There is a monotonous sameness of houses and rigid streets; but modern roadway, good yards and regular collections of garbage and refuse. On the far hills are the remnants of the old forests, which afford a tragic contrast to the treeless dwelling-place where the ideas of beauty are coming in with efficiency, but belatedly.*[9]

At that time, the main office of the Chisholm district of the Oliver Iron Mining Company was located in Monroe Location, which might explain the relatively upscale appearance of Monroe as compared to other mining locations.

Monroe Avenue - Monroe Location - 1916.

Helen May DeLorimer Ramage, who was born in Monroe in 1914, provides the following description of Monroe in the mid-twenties:

*My roots were in one of these locations, namely the Monroe. This well-kept little place was about a mile southeast of Chisholm. It began in 1901 with a main office building, a laboratory and an engineer's office. In about fifteen years, there were seventy-five houses of all sizes and shapes. Four well maintained streets had hitching posts here and there. Behind each house was a shed for wood and yard supplies.*[10]

(In the poorer section of the location, Tener Avenue, these sheds were actually shelters for cows, pigs and chickens.)

Ms. Ramage describes the locally-owned general store as a good gathering place for friends. Across from the store was the jail of red brick consisting of an office and two jail cells. The mining company paid their policemen to protect the location twenty-four hours a day.

Having arrived in Monroe in early April of 1909, Julia had all summer to acquaint herself with life in the New World. That she was not privileged to enjoy a typical summer vacation that first year is documented by the 1910 U.S. Government Census that lists ten boarders living at the 113 Tener Avenue address.[11] Obviously Julia's father, Mike Billo, was in

8

the boarding house business. Theodore Vuicich, a pioneer Serbian immigrant who arrived with his brother Paul in Chisholm in 1912, stated in his memoirs, "For the operation of a boarding house . . . the first and most essential requirement was a woman."[12] Mike Billo not only had that woman but also the help of a young, energetic eleven-year-old daughter, accustomed to long hours of hard work.

All boarding house proprietors, including Mike Billo, owned at least one cow since milk was an important part of the miner's diet. Helping her mother care for the cow, along with helping with cooking, cleaning and washing to meet the needs of ten miners did not leave Julia with much free time. We are sure she was more than ready for school in the fall of 1909.

The Monroe School was a two-room, wood-frame building that had been completed in 1907. Because of the rapid increase in student enrollment, two portable school buildings were moved to Monroe in both 1913 and 1914. Whereas there were only two teachers on staff in 1907, by 1914 there were nine teachers for 290 students.

Ms. Ramage, in describing the Monroe school wrote:

*Each room had five windows with shades and curtains. A big solid oak teacher's desk was at the front of each classroom. There were thirty children's desks in six rows. A table or two were at the back of the room with a pencil sharpener, paper cutter and other miscellaneous educational materials which could be used by the students. Also in the back of each room was a cloakroom with two doors and a window. It included a teacher's closet and wall hooks for the students' clothes. Above the hooks were shelves for those who needed them.*[13]

As with some rural schools, initially the teachers lived year-round in the school building. Such was the case when Julia first enrolled in the Monroe School. One of her first teachers was Miss Leathe B. Wright who would later become the wife of Superintendent J.P. Vaughan.

For some reason, Miss Wright took special interest in Julia and actually provided her with some additional one-on-one tutoring during after-school hours, frequently on weekends and even during the summer. We're not sure at what grade level Julia started school in view of the fact that she was already eleven years old. We do know that she never did further her education beyond the school in Monroe.

Julia's inability to pursue additional education was probably due to the increasing need for her assistance in the home. It appears that the boarding house activities were terminated within a year or two after she and her mother arrived, due in part to a rather rapid increase in the size of the Billo family. On March 2, 1910, sister Eva (Smolensky) was born and two years later on February 23, 1912, sister Mary (Simons) arrived on the scene. Finally, on August 25, 1913, brother Harry was born. By the time Julia was fifteen years old, she was helping to care for three siblings younger than four years of age.

The Mike Billo Family - 1918.
Julia, Eva, Mary, and Harry.

We are not certain when Julia sought employment outside the home, but Uncle Harry Billo remembers that her first job was at the Palmquist Boarding House, a short distance from her home on Tener Avenue. The hours were undoubtedly very long and the pay very low. She then found a job as a housekeeper at the O'Neil Hotel in Chisholm. We think she was still employed there at the time of her marriage to John Kosiak on September 15, 1919.

# JOHN KOSIAK

Our father, John Kosiak, was born on March 30, 1894, to Simeon and Palagia Ochnicz Kosiak in the small village of Smolnik in the province of Galicia, Austria-Hungary. The village still exists north of the Carpathian Mountains in southeastern Poland about twenty miles south of the larger city of Sanok, which can be found on most maps.

In his book, *Galician-Rusins on the Iron Range*, John Goman gives the following description of the area.

> *The foothills of the Carpathians are forested with a mixture of conifers and deciduous trees which provide an ample fuel source and abundant building materials. The high pastureland receives an adequate amount of rainfall and snow cover for forage crops while the low farmlands experience precipitation at regular intervals during the summer months sufficient for good harvests. Both forest and field-land contain nuts, berries and mushrooms in bountiful supply. Orchard-land for the raising of cherries, apples, and pears is available.* [14]

Most of the smaller villages were comprised of no more than thirty or forty families each. Paul R. Magocsi provides a stark assessment of the life these people led in their homeland.

> *Until the twentieth century, social and even geographic mobility was uncommon. Although some railroad lines passed through the region, most Carpatho-Rusyns spent their whole lives within their native or neighboring villages, where their life cycle was dominated by the demands of the agricultural seasons and the church cal-*

11

*endar. Indeed, as high as 97% of the Carpatho-Rusyns were born and died in the same village.*[15]

The immediate stimulus for John Kosiak to leave home, in addition to the fact that he would soon be eligible for conscription into the Austro-Hungarian army, must have been provided by letters as well as travel funds from his older brothers who were already working in America.

Because John Kosiak rarely spoke of his life in his homeland or his trip to America, we can only speculate as to the details of his journey to this country. Although there were railroads in the general area, perhaps John had to walk or travel by horseback or carriage to one of the larger neighboring towns. The train ride to Hamburg was primarily through parts of both Poland and Germany.

At age sixteen, he left Hamburg, Germany as a steerage passenger aboard the steamship Cincinnati and arrived in New York City on July 10, 1910. Processing through Ellis Island must have been relatively uneventful, following which he made his way to Youngstown, Ohio, where he stayed with relatives while working for about one year in the local steel mills. In 1912 he moved to Chisholm, hoping to make more money as well as to escape the noise and crowded city life to which he was unaccustomed. Jobs on the Mesabi Range were plentiful, both in underground as well as in open-pit mining.

On arriving in Chisholm, John was confronted with two immediate problems: finding housing and employment. Fortunately, he already had two older brothers, Mike and Steve, living in the area. Mike was married and had two children while Steve was a boarder at the Frank Smolensky home in Glen Location. Mike's wife was Mrs. Smolensky's sister and it was at the Smolensky home that John found lodging.

John Syrjamaki describes the company-run mining locations as follows:

*The company locations developed as clusters of dwellings near mine shafts or open-pits for employees of the operators. They were built and maintained by companies, who rented them at nominal rates to their occupants, and furnished various services, such as sewage disposal, in addition. In architecture they were monotonously alike, and often inadequate in construction. Yet in the early decades they were among the best residences available, particularly those which were reserved for the use of officials. It is certain that the immigrants who lived in them had left far worse homes in Europe. Apart from their construction, however, the locations tended often to be dismal, forsaken groupings of residences huddled near a mining operation. They stood against an open and dreary background of mine shafts, open-pits, dumps, railroad tracks and tree stumps and boulders. In many of them there was little attractiveness of any kind. The locations, if they were several miles from villages, tended to be isolated, since means of easy travel to and from them did not develop until comparatively late. Hence, the locations, as well as the villages, tended to be communities by themselves, sometimes with some degree of independent social activity. In the earlier years when means of travel were limited, and the mines were in some number more than convenient walking distance from the villages, the locations served a useful purpose for mine employees.*[16]

Glen Location was just such a collection of some fifty or so one or two-bedroom homes situated virtually on the southern edge of the Glen open-pit mine. To the south of Glen Location were the Godfrey, Leonard and Wellington underground mines.

The homes in Glen Location at that time had no indoor plumbing, electricity or running water. The houses were without basements and a centrally located, wood-burning stove provided heat. Because the stove was functioning continuously from four or five o'clock in the morning until the night-shift crew of boarders left for work at about ten o'clock, the homes were fairly comfortable during the day. However, during the harsh winter months, temperatures fell quickly in the uninsulated homes. This was especially critical in those homes where there were young children. In those situations the children usually slept in the same bed, often between their parents. Even though the boarders slept two or three to a bed, using a goose-down or chicken-feather comforter, wool stockings were worn on the feet and a stocking-like cap on the head.

Summers were only slightly more bearable considering the fact that temperatures during the day could exceed ninety degrees Fahrenheit. There were no air conditioners, no fans, no screens on the windows and no mosquito repellents.

The locations were essentially within walking distance of the mine site. However, simply walking a mile or so to the mine or working on the mine stockpile or in the open pit for ten hours when the outside temperatures ranged from twenty to thirty degrees below zero must have tested the heart and soul of even the hardiest of men.

Boarding houses for the accommodation of single men or those who had left their families in Europe existed in all the villages and in some of the large locations.

> *These were owned either by mining companies or private individuals. Among the Finns there were several cooperative boarding establishments. Men were able to secure room and board and the care of laundry and similar services in these houses. Boarding houses were usually large, rambling frame buildings two or three stories high. In the houses owned by the companies the nationalities of the boarders tended to be mixed. The private boarding houses were, however, operated on nationality lines and each minority group established a cluster of its own. Slavic boarding houses often included groups of more than one nationality, but this frequently led to strained relations and was avoided where possible. Of the Slavic minorities, Slovenians and Croatians tended to associate most easily. If members of the smaller groups could find no boarding houses kept by a member of their own nationality, they were often forced to "batch" in shacks of their own construction.*[17]

Theodore Vuicich states that a fee of three dollars per month was paid the owner of the boarding house for cooking, clothes washing and mending. He further explains:

> *The food was ordered from the grocer by the housewife. At the end of the month the whole charged monthly grocery bill was divided equally among all the boarders. The total cost for the cooking, washing and groceries usually approximated twelve to fifteen dollars a month per person.*

> *For the operation of a boarding house very little capital investment was necessary. The first and most essential requirement was a woman. One had to have a strong and capable wife to go into the business of running a boarding house. The wife simultaneously had to be the cook and the launderer. The furnishings consisted of beds*

*and bedding, a long rectangular table and two equally long benches, and several plain wooden chairs, some large cooking pots and other most essential cooking utensils. With these capital assets, a man became a boarding house boss. At that time (1912) it was far easier to find employment than to get good board and room.*[18]

John was fortunate to have found both good board and room.

Underground mining at that time was paying $2.40 for a ten-hour day while working in the open-pit mine paid only $2.10 for a ten-hour day. Work in the mines was generally seasonal, especially in the open-pit mines, while underground mining was usually limited to two or three days of work a week during the winter months. Because the Great Lakes were frozen during the winter months, there were no means of shipping the iron ore to the eastern steel mills.

A stagnant economy in 1913-1914 resulted in the actual closure of many of the underground mines. As a result of the low demand for labor on the Mesabi, some of the men actually returned to the Old Country. At that time, the Austrian government was offering free fare home plus $10 for traveling expenses to all the young Austrian men (Slovenians, Croatians, Serbians, Russians and Ukrainians) who had left Austria-Hungary. When the offer was first made, the Austrian government reported that the request was to relieve a labor shortage. Later, it became obvious that the primary reason for the recall was in anticipation of a future military manpower buildup.

The long-standing conflicts between Austria-Hungary and Serbia concerning the ownership of Bosnia and Hercegovina suddenly exploded on June 28, 1914, when Archduke Francis Ferdinand, heir to the throne of Austria-Hungary, and his wife Sophie were shot to death in Sarajevo by Gavrilo Princip, a young Bosnian student who had lived in Serbia.[19]

Because Austria-Hungary suspected that Serbia had approved of the plot to kill Ferdinand, war against Serbia was declared one month later, on July 28, 1914. Fearing Russian intervention in support of Serbia, Germany then declared war on Russia on August 1, and on France, two days later. Following the invasion of Belgium on August 4, 1914, Great Britain declared war on Germany.

By 1915, the economic stagnation of the previous years had begun to disappear as wartime demands for steel increased. The increase in mining activity was accompanied by increasing labor-management problems. Attempts at unionization were rebuffed by the mining companies through threats of layoffs as well as the deportation of all striking aliens. At that time, John Kosiak was still an alien.

One other deterrent to union organization was the mining companies' use of the blacklist. Although denied by the companies, once an employee was blacklisted there would be no hope of his ever being rehired by any mining company.

Because of the marginal pay as well as poor working conditions that included dangerous mining practices, unionization efforts were undertaken by several of the younger miners. This culminated in a Mesabi-wide strike that began on June 2, 1916. Joining in the strike were John Kosiak and several of his fellow workers from the Godfrey Mine. Even though iron-ore production was reaching an all-time high, the companies began firing strikers. John was one of the first strikers dismissed from his work with the Oliver Iron Mining Company.

Out of work and blacklisted by the mining companies, his chances of obtaining any form of gainful employment were virtually nonexistent. In spite of the fact that at that time he was actively courting Julia Billo, a young lady from Monroe Location, he was compelled to leave the Iron Range to seek employment elsewhere. After several unsuccessful weeks of job hunting in Gary, Indiana, he enlisted in the U.S. Army on June 26, 1916.

John Kosiak rarely discussed his military experiences. We do know that his unit was at one time under the command of General John Pershing and was involved in the pursuit of Pancho Villa, the Mexican bandit chieftain, who was responsible in 1916 for the deaths of sixteen Americans during a raid in Columbus, New Mexico. Though the U.S. Army actually pursued Pancho Villa into Mexico, he was never captured.[20]

John continued to correspond with Julia Billo during his military career as is documented by a card he sent to her from Camp Shelly near Hattiesburg, Mississippi. Having been exposed to the English language as part of his limited night school education while living in Glen Location, he combined Cyrillic alphabet spellings with English terminology making a literal translation complicated at best. Generally, the tone of the card was that he was well and hoping to come home soon.

Although there are several pictures of John in uniform, we're fairly certain that he never returned to Glen Location on a furlough. However,

Corporal John Kosiak
Co. G., 47th Infantry Div.. United States Army, 1918.

after the United States declared war on Germany on April 6, 1917, the chances of any furlough or early discharge were remote at best. It was at Camp Shelly that John was issued his Certificate of Naturalization on May 13, 1918.

John was sent overseas on October 4, 1918, where he served as a corporal with Company G of the 47th Infantry Division. Since he arrived in France only five weeks prior to the end of the war on November 11, 1918, we doubt that he was ever involved in any actual combat. John spent some time in Germany as is documented by several blank picture-postcards that he brought home. John is pictured in a photograph of Company G that has the following notation in someone else's handwriting, "Picture taken in Remagen, Germany, near Rhine River."

John did relate to our family and several of our relatives on multiple occasions a certain event that took place while he was stationed in Europe. In his desire to see some action, since Company G of the 47th Infantry was never in the front lines, he volunteered to serve as a "courier." Since no form of wireless was available, communication between the various combat units was carried out by means of couriers, men who transported the messages while riding in the sidecars of motorcycles.

The assignment was very short-lived in that John was disqualified after his initial test ride in the sidecar. He reported that his orientation took place over country roads and across farm fields and wooded areas, all at very high speeds. After some ten to fifteen minutes into the trial run, he was convinced the job was not for him. Because his simple requests to stop were ignored by the motorcycle operator, John became considerably more animated, shouting repeatedly at the driver, "Stop, you son-of-a-bitch! Stop!" In spite of his repeated requests, the ride continued for several more minutes, long enough to convince him that the job of courier was not in his future.

John continued to serve in Europe until returning to the United States on July 27, 1919. Discharge from the service took place at Camp Sherman, Ohio, on August 5, 1919. At the time of discharge he was provided with travel funds only to his point of enlistment, Gary, Indiana. From there he took the train back to Chisholm.


# JOHN AND JULIA

Social interaction for the new immigrants was provided at the boarding houses, grocery stores, local taverns, fraternal societies and, of course, the church, at least on Sundays and holidays. Magocsi wrote:

*Next to the church, however, the most important organizations were the fraternal societies and brotherhoods. Actually, they arose*

*not so much because of the potential social function, but rather for
very practical needs. In a foreign land where most immigrant workers had insufficient funds to protect themselves in case of industrial accidents or other mishaps, the fraternal organizations were
able to provide a minimal but nonetheless important source of
financial help in times of distress. Social gatherings sponsored by
fraternal societies contributed a measure of psychological security
for immigrants.*[21]

Goman on the other hand reported:

*By far the most significant roles, however, that the fraternal broth-
erhoods played were in the social and economic spheres. Here the
social needs were indeed great with the compelling yearning to cre-
ate in the New World something of the Old World. Marriage bro-
kering was one important matter which touched the lives of the
bachelor men, who made up a not insignificant part of the immigration (greater than two-thirds). A hard-working chap was often
given his first hopes by the contacts he made within the fraternal
society as a fellow countryman would offer to put him in touch with
a promising young woman who was either still in the Old Country
or who was living in one of the other towns or cities of America
where Galicians and other Rusins had gathered.*[22]

Although construction of St. Nicholas Russian Orthodox Church in
Chisholm did not begin until the summer of 1916, religious holidays and
activities such as baptisms, marriages and funerals still played a promi-
nent role in the immigrants' lives. These events provided an opportunity
for social interaction for most of the Galician immigrants. Perhaps it was
during one of these events that John Kosiak and Julia Billo first met.

On the good authority of Harry Billo, Julia's younger brother, we
have come to know that the courtship was not without some major obstacles. The Billo family, primarily because of religious differences, generally objected to John's interest in Julia. He was a believer in the Orthodox
faith while Julia's parents were strict followers of the Greek Catholic
teachings.

As stated earlier, John left Chisholm in early June, 1916, when
Julia was only eighteen years old. Leaving town was bad enough, but after

he enlisted in the U.S. Army later that month, Grandma Billo must have been beside herself. The war was on in Europe, and the United States' entry was only a matter of time. Julia was becoming of age and was probably not needed as much in the home. Marriage at age sixteen or seventeen years was the norm in those days and Julia's mother wasn't in any mood to wait for several years, or until the war ended, to see her daughter out of the home.

Julia Billo - 1918.

Of greatest concern to Mrs. Billo was the fact that she just couldn't imagine her lovely daughter marrying John Kosiak, a member of the Orthodox faith. Consequently, for the next three years, until John returned from the army, she worked overtime as a potential marriage broker, but to no avail. In spite of the numerous eligible, employed, immigrant men in the area who were followers of the Greek Catholic faith, Julia was content to wait for John. For this decision, all the Kosiak children are and will remain eternally grateful.

After John was discharged from the army on August 5, 1919, he returned to Chisholm where, on September 15, 1919, John Kosiak and Julia Billo were married in the St. Nicholas Russian Orthodox Church. According to Uncle Harry Billo and Uncle William Smolensky, the only two living eyewitnesses to this event, the wedding celebration lasted two days.

John and Julia Billo Kosiak - 1919.

We're not sure when John returned to work in the mines but it was perhaps several months after the wedding. In the interim, the newlyweds needed to find a place to live. Since Julia's parents still had three children at home, Eva, Mary, and Harry, living space in the three-bedroom home on Tener Avenue was limited. Arrangements were therefore made for John and Julia to move into the Russian Orthodox Church parsonage. Serving the parish at that time was an unmarried priest, Reverend Stefan Sipajda. In the U.S. Government Census report of January 12, 1920, both John and Julia are listed as employees of Reverend Sipajda, John as a laborer and Julia as a housekeeper.[23] Later that year John and Julia apparently moved in with her parents in Monroe Location where on July 2, 1920, our oldest brother Johnny was born.

Soon after Johnny's birth, our father was able to find not only employment with the Oliver Iron Mining Company but also living accommodations in Glen Location. This undoubtedly came about primarily through the efforts of Julia's father who at the time was a shift boss for the mining company.

The *Chisholm City Directory* published in 1922 lists John Kosiak as a miner employed at the Monroe Mine and living at 150 Glen Location.[24] It was at this address, on August 4, 1922, where our brother Willy was born.

Soon after the purchase of the home at 307 West Poplar Street, the family of four moved to Chisholm.

# 2

# Chisholm on the Mesabi Iron Range

*Lying some sixty miles inland and northwest of Duluth, Minnesota, a port city located at the farthest western point of Lake Superior, is the Mesabi Range, the greatest iron ore mining center in the world.*

—J. Syrjamaki

The region of northeastern Minnesota where John and Julia Kosiak raised our family is called the Mesabi Range. This name was taken from the Native American name Mis-sa-be, which described the low barren hills that used to be mountains and which were referred to as the *grandmother hills of them all.* Indeed these hills contain some of the oldest rock on Earth, some of it the iron ore that was to bring to the Range its prospectors, mining companies, and people.

Pine forests originally covered the Mesabi, notably the white and Norway pine that attracted lumbermen into the area. Today most of the original pine forest is gone, sacrificed to the mills that built Minnesota. Second-growth hardwoods, mostly birch and maple, have sprung up to replace the giant pine trees. Some cutover or burned areas have been taken over for farms. But the poor quality of the soil, which consists of stony loam, has made farming difficult except in scattered pockets of the Range.

The climate of the Mesabi Range is rigorous, with an average mean annual temperature of thirty-eight degrees Fahrenheit. January and February are the coldest months of the year, averaging five to eight degrees Fahrenheit, but high winds that prevail during the winter months greatly accentuate the cold. Lows have been known to drop to the incomprehensible fifty to sixty degrees below zero Fahrenheit.

July and August are the warm months on the Range. The average mean July temperature is about sixty-five degrees Fahrenheit, while

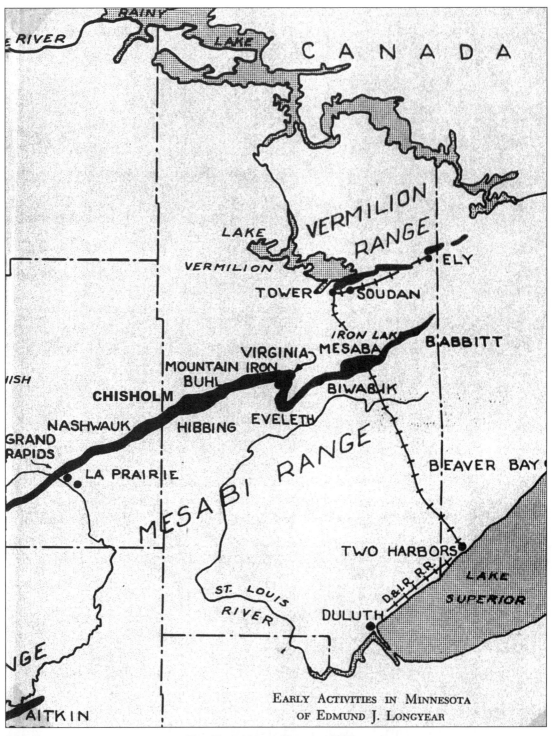

EARLY ACTIVITIES IN MINNESOTA
OF EDMUND J. LONGYEAR

Map 2.                    The Mesabi Iron Range - 1910

overnight lows from mid-June to mid-September rarely approach freezing. The growing season during the summer is about 100 days. The average date of the first killing frost is September 15, and the last killing frost about May 30. Precipitation for the year averages from twenty-five to thirty inches of rain, while annual snowfall can on occasion exceed sixty inches.

In 1940, in his Yale University Graduate School Ph.D. dissertation entitled, *Mesabi Communities—A Study of Their Development*, John Syrjamaki described the Mesabi Range as follows:

*Lying some sixty miles inland and northwest of Duluth, Minnesota, port city located at the farthest western point of Lake Superior, is the Mesabi Range, the greatest iron ore mining center in the world. It is reached from Duluth through a stretch of desolate cutover and swamplands, once covered by dense pine forests, and now sparsely settled by farmers. The Mesabi mines consist of vast open-pit and underground operations placed along the southern slope of a range of low-lying hills extending over a distance of eighty miles. Spaced among the gaping open-pits and rust-stained mine shafts and crowded by long ore and surface earth dumps, are some twenty villages and cities. These are the Mesabi communities in which live the miners and their families who secure their livelihood from the exploitation of the immense ore deposit lavished by nature upon the area.*[25]

George R. Stuntz, a U.S. Government surveyor who was searching for gold near Lake Vermilion in 1865, found instead a cliff of almost pure hematite, a high-grade iron ore that would be prized decades later by the steel company smelting furnaces.[26] Stuntz reported his find, which would later become part of the Vermilion Range northeast of the Mesabi Range, to his bosses, the mining companies back East. However, because the land northwest of Duluth was too remote and rugged to exploit easily, the mining companies were content to continue to extract ore just south of Lake Superior. So, for the next thirty years, the area was left to pioneer families to settle, explore and log.

One of those families, the Merritts, discovered the extensive iron ore deposits across what became the Mesabi Range. The father, Lewis Howell Merritt, led his sons in exploring and mapping iron ore sites in the 1870s and 1880s.[27] His sons later founded the Biwabik Mountain Iron Company with the help of local investors, but they lacked the capital to establish true mining operations. It wasn't until the early 1890s, after they started mining sites called Mountain Iron, Mis-sa-be Mountains, and the Biwabik, that the world took notice.

Geologist H.V. Winchell reported in 1892:

*More merchantable ore is already known to exist on the Mesabi Range than has been produced from all the other mines in the Lake Superior Region since they were first discovered.*

*The Merritt brothers, of Duluth and Oneota, were not to be discouraged by reports of explorers and miners added to those of experts and geologists who had condemned the range ever since 1875. To these Duluth pioneers the Mesabi was an attractive and promising district and their faith in it was never shaken. To them belongs the credit for persisting in the hunt for ore and the final discovery of it.*[28]

Realizing that their iron ore was worthless without a way to transport it to the Duluth harbor, the Merritts raised money, built seventy miles of railroad track and called it the Duluth, Mis-sa-be and Northern Railroad. In October 1892 the first trainload of high-grade (sixty-five percent iron) Bessemer ore reached Lake Superior from the Mesabi Range. To fund their mining operations, the Merritts leased their Mis-sa-be Mountain mine to Henry Oliver, a plow and shovel manufacturer from Pittsburgh, for a $75,000 bonus and guaranteed $250,000 in royalties on mined ore. The Minnesota Iron Company offered eight million dollars for all of the rights to the Merritts' mines and railroad, but the Merritts turned down the offer, aspiring to be barons themselves. Unable to secure financing and partnerships needed to expand their operations, the Merritts eventually lost everything.

To accommodate the mining operations, the St. Louis County commissioners authorized construction of a road, which became known as the Mesabi Trail. Communities of surveyors and miners sprang up along the trail: Merritt, Biwabik, McKinley, Mountain Iron, Virginia, Hibbing and Eveleth. In 1901, prospector Archibald M. Chisholm added the village of Chisholm to the Mesabi Trail communities. In the words of Edmund J.

Longyear, the first surveyor to use a diamond drill to confirm iron-ore deposits on the Mesabi Range, "I can truthfully say that I have seen the Mesabi Range develop from rocks and muskegs into a land of scores of communities constituting one of the most industrialized sections of Minnesota."[29] (Longyear Lake on the outskirts of Chisholm is named after Edmund J. Longyear, who helped Archibald Chisholm test his claims for iron ore.)

In geological formation, the Mesabi is a narrow strip of land some 110 miles long and varying from two to ten miles in width, having an area of about 400 square miles. However, ore has been mined in only about eighty miles of this length, and the Mesabi population lies within this distance, from Coleraine in the west end to Mesaba on the east.

By 1895 the Mesabi Iron Range passed all other iron ore ranges in the United States in annual shipments. In 1910 the Mesabi shipped thirty million tons, sixty percent of America's iron ore. Shipments grew to over sixty million tons in 1923, but dropped the next year to less than forty-four million tons due to declining demand. Surveyors of Minnesota's high-grade iron-ore deposits projected that the deposits would last at least through three-quarters of the twentieth century. However, they did not foresee the huge demands that would arise when the United States entered World War II. In 1939 the Mesabi Range shipped about thirty-six million tons of high-grade ore to the steel plants. In 1942, over seventy-two million Mesabi tons were shipped to help quench the war's appetite for steel.

This unexpected drain on the Mesabi's high-grade ore might have spelled the end of mining and the Range communities if not for decades of research by the University of Minnesota Mines Experiment Station. Led by Edward E. Davis, geological engineers developed processes to extract magnetic iron ore from the plentiful taconite rock that covers much of the Mesabi Range. Because the iron-ore content of taconite was too low to interest the steel companies, Davis and his colleagues developed machines that could grind taconite down to dust, extract the iron ore with magnets, and roll it into pellets to be baked and shipped. Although more expensive than mining high-grade ore, the taconite extraction and pelletization process created an end-product that had a higher iron-ore content and burned better in the steel company smelting furnaces.

Davis, in 1964, summarized the impact of the Mesabi Range iron-ore and taconite operations in his book, *Pioneering with Taconite*.

*It was the Mesabi Range which enabled the United States to become the world's largest manufacturer of steel and made Minnesota the largest producer of iron ore in the nation. Because of the rapid depletion of the Mesabi natural ores, United States steel firms in the 1940s and 1950s were looking the world over for new ore reserves. They were successful beyond all expectations. Great new deposits of natural ores, capable of supplying the needs of the steel industry for many years, were discovered in Canada, South America, and elsewhere.*

*If the University had decided to drop the taconite study, I believe that taconite would probably still be just an interesting possibility. As it was, an alternative was available to steel firms seeking greater ore reserves. That alternative was taconite, and it offered the hope of a domestic rather than a foreign ore reserve.*[30]

The Mesabi mining communities began as prospecting camps and became settlements as rich beds of nearby ore led to the opening of pit mines. Into these settlements poured the men needed to work the mines, a mostly immigrant population of more then thirty nationalities. Their multiplicity of languages and dialects and the diversity of their cultures melded in the communities and the mines where they worked side by side. They began to refer to themselves cumulatively as "Rangers" and to their region as "The Range." The Range or "The Iron Range," is known throughout Minnesota, although the lesser iron ranges, the Vermilion in St. Louis County and the Cuyuna to the southwest in Crow Wing County are generally included in the meaning of the term.

Most of the mining immigrants were the post-1900 movement who came largely from the countries of southern and eastern Europe. This movement was designated as the "new immigration" in contrast to the earlier or "old immigration," which had come mainly from northwestern Europe.

Syrjamaki described this population as follows:

*Greater uniformity existed among the Range ethnic groups, how-ever, than was true for the immigrant minorities in the country as a whole. The foreign-born of the Range were derived generally from the lower economic and social classes of their society. Persons in*

*the upper strata of these groups, and those equipped with indus-*
*trial or business skills, did not come to the Range. There was noth-*
*ing on the Mesabi to attract them: the Range was a sparsely set-*
*tled and somewhat wild region removed from the main centers of*
*population, and without other industries than mining. They*
*remained in the eastern and central sections of the United States,*
*therefore, where better opportunities existed for them.*

*The vast majority of the European immigrants who came to the*
*Range, probably more than 80 percent, were from a rural back-*
*ground. Less than 5 percent of the post-1900 immigration, it*
*appears from informants, were experienced in mining. Some of the*
*Slovaks, Slovenians, South Italians, Swedes, Norwegians, and a*
*few others had been employed in mines in their native countries,*
*but with the single large exception of the Cornish, the foreign-born*
*secured their experience in mining after they had settled on the*
*Michigan and Minnesota ranges. The number with prior industrial*
*skills in other types of industry were not much larger, in-as-much*
*as skilled laborers and urban industrial workers found employ-*
*ment elsewhere in the United States, and did not come to the*
*Range. In the main, hence, the Range immigrants possessed the*
*vocational aptitudes that are secured in rural existence work on*
*the soil and in the forests.*[31]

In 1940 when he did his research, Syrjamaki noted the changes
that had come over the Rangers and their communities.

*. . . few of the pioneers of the nineties are left, and the ranks of the*
*foreign-born who came after 1900 are thinning out swiftly. A sec-*
*ond-generation is coming into dominance, and the cultural and lin-*
*gual differences that characterized the first-generation are disap-*
*pearing. But long years of residence on the Range have not left the*
*foreign-born unchanged; they speak the English language, even*
*though it be with an accent often incomprehensible to a stranger,*
*they are dressed as Americans and no longer appear the strange*
*physical variants to the native type that they were upon their*
*arrival, and they feel and act with more or less familiarity in their*
*adopted environment. They are still Finns, and Slovenians, Poles*

29

*and Italians, but tolerant toward each other and toward the Old Americans. Their native-born children, educated in the Range schools, are taking their place in American society, and have become largely alienated from the culture of their parents.*

*While the Range communities have all of the public services of up-to-date cities, they are not otherwise attractive. Their very newness makes them stand out starkly against a barren and rough landscape; there are too few notes of redemption, such as tall street trees and lawns, to give them a touch of softness. The hinterland is dreary. Long stretches of cut-over lands upon which scraggly trees and bushes are struggling to grow, considerable areas festooned by a litter of boulders and rocks left by the glacial invasion of the district, areas burned over by fires or left mutilated by lumber operators, and swamps and bogs. Mine shafts and open-pits indent the land surface, and considerable displacement is taken by dumps, stockpiles, and a tangle of railroad tracks.*[32]

## CHISHOLM

*The mines and dumps flank the communities, and crowd them for space. Roads dodge around and about these mine operations. A paved highway runs the length of the Range, and along this the villages and cities are strung like beads on a string.*

—J. Syrjamaki

It was in one of those beads, Chisholm, on the string of the Mesabi Trail, where the Kosiak family grew up.

Chisholm was named after Archibald M. Chisholm, an early Mesabi prospector and land developer. It was incorporated as a village on July 23, 1901, eleven years before John Kosiak moved there. The population at incorporation was reported to be 496. Incorporation as a city, by public referendum, occurred on September 6, 1934.

The early years of the village are summarized in *The WPA Guide to the Minnesota Arrowhead Country* as follows:

Main Street - Chisholm, Minnesota - 1960.
Courtesy of H. Reynolds Studio - Hibbing, Minnesota

*The following year (1902), Chisholm established its first school, a frame building, and employed two teachers. During their first two years, the Catholics and Methodists erected log churches, the Methodists' being built in two weeks by men who contributed their labor. In six years, the population had grown to almost 6,000 and the town had an imposing city hall, four blocks of business houses, two banks, an electric lighting plant, sewers, two weekly newspapers, and it had been necessary to plot two residential districts. On September 5, 1908, a brush fire fanned by a shifting wind, swept down upon the village. In what seemed but a few minutes, Chisholm was practically destroyed. Fortunately, no lives were lost and rebuilding began immediately. Within nine months 70 fireproof brick buildings had been constructed as well as a municipal water plant and five miles of mains. Within a year, the town was flourishing, the population growing steadily . . . its buildings and residences were such as one would expect to find in an average village of that class and population.*[33]

A special edition of the *Virginia Enterprise*, dated September 1909, elaborated on Chisholm's recovery from the devastating fire.

*Few places of equal population have ever been so completely obliterated within a few hours' time as was this prosperous town of 6,000 people.*

*But the marvelous feature of Chisholm history does not pertain to its sudden and complete destruction so much as to the unprecedented vigor and determination exhibited by its inhabitants in the rapid and substantial rebuilding of the city. What the elements can destroy in a few brief moments usually requires many years of planning and labor and sacrifice before it can be replaced in as good condition as formerly. While the people in many towns which have suffered losses of far less relative extent, have been too greatly discouraged to even undertake the reconstruction of their homes and places of business, in this case however, the ashes of the demolished buildings had not grown cold before many of the former owners were making vigorous preparations for rebuilding on a more substantial and durable basis. The business and public officials of Chisholm are entitled to great credit for the determination and foresight which they exhibited in the face of disaster and discouragement, and the unanimous decision that a system should be adopted and adhered to which would make the reconstructed city one of the safest, most durable, comfortable and convenient in the state. An ordinance was passed, prohibiting the use of any but fire-proof building material on the main street. As a result of these measures, there was a uniform and spontaneous renewal of building activity such as had never before been witnessed on the Range, and which can find few parallels anywhere. In ten months this latest Phoenix of Minnesota had risen from its ashes and become a city of greater proportions than ever before. There was an increase during that period of at least 25 percent in its population, while the residences and other buildings not only increased in number, but there was a decided improvement in the character* *and appearance of the buildings of all kinds. The main business thoroughfare had just been graded, and new walks laid. There is a municipal water plant, with five miles of water mains and three and one-half miles of sewers. . . . Streets and buildings are lighted by electricity, and an electric power plant is contemplated. The splendid village hall, destroyed in the fire, is now being rebuilt, at a cost of $50,000.*[34]

Walter Van Brunt reported the following concerning Chisholm's status in 1910.

*It is beautifully located on a charming body of water known as Longyear Lake. Chisholm is now a community of five or six thousand souls, and is rapidly growing. It is already provided with perhaps the finest and largest city-hall building on the Range while a splendid lot of school and church buildings dot the town site. The business section is compactly built for a distance of four blocks and the businessmen are enjoying a fair share of the general prosperity. The demand for residence property is ever increasing and two additions were recently platted and added to the original village in order to meet this demand.*[35]

In 1915, the Commercial Club of Chisholm produced a brochure entitled, *A Brief Sketch of Chisholm's History, Industrial Life, Government and Educational Facilities*, to be distributed at the State Firemen's Convention in Pine City, Minnesota.

*The object of this illustrated booklet is to extend to the firemen of the state, their wives and friends, an invitation from the people of Chisholm to visit them on the occasion of the State Firemen's Convention to be held in the year 1916. The booklet gives a slight idea of the courage, resourcefulness, ambition and genuine American hustle that built a city from the ashes of the most disastrous conflagration in Minnesota in the present century. We bid you welcome and extend to you the key of the city with command of its ten thousand inhabitants.*

*Mining center, Lumber center, Railroad center, Agricultural center and Educational center of Minnesota's great iron ranges, Chisholm may well be designated the most progressive and aggressive commercial center of Northern Minnesota, excepting but one city, that the city of Duluth.*

City Hall.    CHISHOLM, Minn.

Chisholm City Hall and Fire Station, 1910. (Courtesy of the Minnesota Historical Society)

*The city hall, in which are located the fire hall with its perfect equipment, the municipal court, the recorder's office, water, light, power and building commission's chambers, poor commissioner's office, engineering department and the jail with police headquarters, gives an idea of the village's growth. This building cost around $100,000 and although but six years old is considered too small for the growing needs of the community.*

*The three school buildings situated right in the heart of the village and the four location and country schools are all shown, giving mute testimony to the care taken to educate thousands of children grow-*

34

*ing into first-class American citizens. The schools represent an out-*
*lay of close to $1,000,000 and employ no less than [sixty-seven]*
*teachers, of whom Superintendent J.P. Vaughan is the guiding*
*genius. In the years 1906-7, 584 pupils represented the total enroll-*
*ment. Today 1,884 seek knowledge. Night school classes were*
*opened in 1908 with small attendance. Today there are no less than*
*548 adult scholars engaged in bettering their education. The new*
*high school (later designated as Washington Grade School) complet-*
*ed this year is considered a model. The structure itself is stupendous*
*and beautifully finished. In the basement, manual training, domes-*
*tic science, housekeeping, printing, turning and general woodwork,*
*machine construction and repairing, millinery, sewing and mechani-*
*cal drawing are taught. On the same level a swimming tank, gym-*
*nasium, restaurant, a four-room flat and a physical training room*
*are situated. On the first floor are five grade rooms, a large kinder-*
*garten room, general office, library and superintendent's room; while*
*leading from the flat on to a balcony is a conservatory where plants,*
*vegetables and flowers grow.*

*Chisholm is lighted by electricity supplied by the Chisholm Electric*
*company, a privately owned corporation that is managed with so*
*much regard for the interests of the people that when a vote was*
*taken to empower the municipality to purchase it, the vote was so*
*overwhelmingly in favor of a continuation of the present system*
*that municipal ownership was killed for all time.*

*The Duluth, Missabe & Northern Railway and the Great Northern*
*serve the village. The Swan River Logging company, with head*
*offices here, operates a logging road running north to its lumber*
*camps in the tall pines growing on the banks of beautiful Sturgeon*
*and other lakes. An interurban Electric line (old street-car line) con-*
*necting Chisholm with other range towns to the east and west,*
*runs on an hourly schedule and gives most efficient service, open-*
*ing up the channels of commerce and, it is expected, soon the rich*
*agricultural lands surrounding the village.*

*Chisholm's chief industry is mining, and the group of mines lying*
*within its confines forms the chief basis of its present prosperity*

*and future prospects. There are twenty distinct mining properties extending in an almost continuous chain for several miles to the south and east. The proven deposits included in these properties aggregate more high-grade iron ore than can be found in any similar area in the world. These mines are being worked with more or less activity, and employ when active about 3,000 men. Some of the mines are worked by underground methods while others are worked by both the underground and open-pit systems. Most of the mines are operated by the Oliver Iron Mining Company, but many independents also have large holdings.*

*The following will give a comprehensive idea of the large iron-ore industry of Chisholm and the mine from which the shipments have been made. The mines currently in production include the Clark, Croton, Chisholm, Euclid, Elizabeth, Glen, Jordan, Leonard No. 2, Leonard Pit, Monroe, Myers, Pilsbury, Shenango, Pearce, St. Clair, Monroe-Tener, and Hartley. In addition to the above there have been lately opened five new mines, a record of the output of which is not available at this time.*

*The corporate limits of the Village comprise six sections of land of which 340 acres have been platted into village lots. The assessed valuation of the village is $16,690,213. The population given by the U.S. Census of 1910 was 7,684, but the village has steadily grown since that period until today it is conservatively estimated that 10,000 souls find peace and contentment within its borders.*[36]

By 1920, Chisholm had gone "healthily forward," as noted in *Duluth and St. Louis County, Their Story and People.*

*Chisholm (in 1920), has gone healthily forward, and many public works of recent establishment have added to the good repute of the place as an up-to-date municipality. Its public improvements include five and one half miles of concrete paving, and one mile of creosote block; seven miles of sewers; eighteen miles of water main, with hydrants on every block for fire protection, two city parks, with bandstand, and seating capacity for 1,000. One of the parks, the O'Neil, was dedicated on Soldiers' and Sailors' Home-*

*coming Day, September 1, 1919, on which day occurred the un-*
*veiling of the living memorial, donated by the Chamber of Com-*
*merce, a granite shaft on which is chiseled: "Erected in honor of the*
*men and women of Chisholm who served in the military and naval*
*forces of the United States of America in the World War, by the*
*Village of Chisholm, Township of Balkan."*[37]

The *Chisholm Tribune Herald* of September 1, 1919 reported:

*A beautiful soldiers' and sailors' monument was unveiled at O'Neil*
*Park following an excellent address to the service men by*
*Honorable Joseph Austin.*[38]

Joseph Austin was the mayor of Chisholm at that time. The monument is now located in the Veterans' Memorial portion of the Chisholm
Cemetery.

The decade of the twenties was, at least since the rebuilding after
the 1908 fire, the most dramatic in the short life of this vibrant community. The crowning structural accomplishment was the building and the
opening of what was to become the Junior High School. This structure,
located between Hemlock (Fourth) Street on the north and Poplar (Fifth)
Street on the south, occupied most of the blocks from Second to almost
Fourth Avenue South. Enrollment in the Chisholm schools at the opening of the Junior High School in 1925 was 3,688 students, the largest
number of pupils ever enrolled in the Chisholm school system.

A treatise entitled, *Chisholm: the Geographical Center of the World's*
*Greatest Iron Mining Region*, presents a comprehensive assessment of the
Village of Chisholm in 1925. Though the author is unknown, the promo-
tional tone of the report suggests that it originated in the office of the
Chisholm Chamber of Commerce.

*Few persons, beyond those who make their home in Northern*
*Minnesota, realized the great future ahead of the Mesabi Range or*
*the vast wealth the country holds. Here is the most active iron-min-*
*ing region in the world and here is one of the greatest dairying dis-*
*tricts in the making. Chisholm, which was incorporated as a village*
*July 23, 1901 with population of 250, has enjoyed a steady*
*growth until today its population is well over 10,000 and it is the*
*hub, the geographical center, of the world's greatest mining zone.*

*There are few if any great metropolitan cities in the world where civic improvements have been carried out on a more elaborate scale than in Chisholm. Wood sidewalks are being rapidly replaced with concrete and today there are [fifteen] miles of concrete curbs and gutters, eight miles of sanitary sewers, four miles of storm sewers, five miles of reinforced concrete paving and two miles of creosote wood block and Tarvia paving. There are [nineteen] miles of water main in Chisholm, and the water works, valued at $100,000 is referred to by officials of the Minnesota State Board of Health as among the most modern and best supervised in the state. The pumping and filtration plant of the water works has a daily capacity of 2,000,000 gallons.*

*Chisholm's system of public school buildings is most modern, and the methods of instruction employed here have been highly praised by the educators from all parts of the United States. There are seven large school buildings the aggregate value of which is $1,469,000. A new junior high school building, which cost $1,000,000 with equipment, equals, if not greatly surpasses in completeness and beauty the finest structures of its kind in the entire United States.*

*Forty-five mines in the Chisholm district have shipped 60,130,643 tons of iron ore up to January 1, 1922, and there still remained on that date, available for shipment 175,680,643 tons. At the rate of shipment in past years this supply of iron ore would not be exhausted for the next sixty years. The mines furnish employment to 1,500 men and the monthly payrolls aggregate $250,000.*

*Balkan Township, which completely surrounds the platted portion of Chisholm, is the second richest township in the world. Its real estate valuation is over $19,000,000 and its personal property valuation almost a half million dollars. Settlers are establishing in Balkan Township every year in great numbers and the country is rapidly taking form as a dairying locality.*

*Chisholm is the automobile tourist's paradise. From here the roads, all hard-surfaced, radiate to lakes where fishing is plentiful and camping sites are easily found. Beautiful Lake Vermilion is but an hour's ride by auto from Chisholm where high-class resorts, catering to the tourist's trade, are located and rates are very reasonable. The great Superior National Forest on the Canadian border, Nature's undefiled playground and the camper's and outing seeker's paradise, is only two hours ride by automobile from Chisholm, and there among the 1,268,000 acres of forest and 250,000 acres of water the lure of the wilderness beckons. Beautiful lakes within two hours' drive of Chisholm are too numerous to mention. Minnesota is styled throughout the world as "The Land of Ten Thousand Lakes" and the greater number of the ten thousand lakes are located in Northern Minnesota and but a short drive from Chisholm. Chisholm's hotel accommodations are first class, and a tourist's camping ground, with all modern conveniences, is maintained in the Chisholm park.*

*The true Western spirit of hospitality and the hustle and bustle of the East meet in Chisholm. Here the big iron mines are to be seen in active operation. The underground mines are a source of great interest to the tourist. Here the farms flourish and the great outdoor beckons. Chisholm has a welcome for you.*[39]

Chisholm continued to flourish throughout the twenties, until the stock market crash of October 29, 1929. The effects of the stock market crash were first experienced by the iron miners because of the total closure of many of the mines and at least a partial shutdown of all the rest. Men who had been working a forty-hour week were cut back to two or three days a week. Unemployment in Chisholm was at a historical high.

Dominated by a single industry and with the United States in the depths of the Depression, the outlook for Chisholm in the 1930s was grim indeed. Because it would be three years before any of the New Deal programs developed under President Roosevelt's leadership would even be proposed, immediate local governmental intervention was imperative.

Two major publicly-funded projects were inaugurated in Chisholm in the 1930s: the building of a new causeway across Longyear Lake, which was primarily a local and state-funded undertaking, and the construction of the Chisholm Memorial Park, a locally and federally-funded project.

The very first bridge across Longyear Lake, which was built in 1904, was replaced in 1918 by a wooden structure at a cost of $55,000. Though the wooden structure was apparently still quite serviceable and vehicular traffic was somewhat limited, on October 15, 1931, the State Highway Department submitted a proposal to Chisholm offering to assist in the building of a new bridge.[40] Because the entire country was in the depths of the Depression and unemployment in Chisholm was at its peak, the probability of creating new jobs was welcomed by the entire community.

Of the original estimated cost of $90,000 to $100,000, the state offered to contribute approximately $65,000, while Chisholm would be responsible for up to $35,000 of the cost. Several weeks later, the state increased its portion of the estimated bridge funding to $90,000.

While Chisholm residents would provide all the work not awarded to contractors, the work was to be carried out under the direction of an engineer appointed by the State Highway Department and in accordance with plans submitted by the state.[41] The Chisholm engineer at the time was George W. Anderson.

To meet its financial obligation, Chisholm submitted a bond referendum to the public in the amount of $50,000. Though soundly approved by the electorate by almost a five-to-one margin, both the Snyder Mining Company and the Auburn Mining Company, an affiliate of the Oliver Iron Mining Company, strenuously objected to the amount of the bonding. Since the mining companies would be responsible for a major portion of the taxes needed to repay the bonds, they questioned whether Chisholm could legally use municipal money to pay for work on a state highway.

Work on the landfill causeway began on January 2, 1931, and on January 7 a restraining order was served on the Village council to stop work on the project. The plaintiffs in that action were the Snyder Mining Company and the Auburn Mining Company. The restraining order was lifted one week later, on January 14, after the Village agreed to limit the amount of the project bonds to $30,000.

The causeway was to be 1,982 feet in length and fifty feet wide with two thirty to forty-foot spans at each end to accommodate boat traffic. It was estimated that approximately 300 men would be employed, 100 working full time and 200 working part time. The men working six-hour shifts would earn fifty cents an hour. Each man working fifteen shifts in a one-month period was able to earn three dollars per day or forty-five dollars each month.

Of approximately twenty trucks involved in the project, more than half were owned by private truckers who were paid twelve cents for each yard of fill moved. Since most trucks could carry up to three yards of fill each time, the truckers were paid thirty-six cents for each round trip from the Tioga properties near the Monroe Location to the causeway. Apparently no allowance was made for gas consumption or vehicle maintenance.

Fill for the project was to be obtained from the abandoned Tioga mine property located just north of the Monroe Road about halfway between Chisholm and Monroe. Though the fee owners of the Tioga properties strenuously objected to the price to be paid per yard of fill even as determined by the courts, on January 2, 1932, thirty men began work on the new causeway.

Since in northern Minnesota the ground in mid-January is always frozen solid to a depth of at least four or more feet, progress on the project initially was slow. The fill had to be dug by hand from where it could be shoveled into hoppers for transfer onto the trucks by means of several conveyors.

By February 18, the project became a twenty-four-hour operation, employing more than 160 men. Ten-man crews working four six-hour shifts were assigned to each loading area. Reportedly, using these methods, approximately 3,000 yards of fill were transported every twenty-four hours.[42]

The trucks doing the hauling entered the Monroe Road just east of the Tioga mine head frame. They then proceeded along the Monroe Road until turning to the right in front of the old ballpark, before traversing the entire length of Central Avenue to Lake Street. The trucks would then proceed onto the bridge as far as the assigned dumping area.

Because the vehicular portion of the old wooden bridge was only twenty-four feet wide, it was virtually impossible to enter onto the bridge and turn the loaded truck around prior to dumping the fill. Construction of a manually operated turntable or carousel ingeniously resolved this problem. The trucks then could drive onto the carousel and be turned around 180 degrees, making it possible to deposit the fill through slotted openings in the wooden bridge-deck.

Dumping of fill continued until March 10, 1932, when partial collapse of a small section of the bridge was detected. Thereafter, all fill was deposited at the west end of the lake. As the fill extended out into and essentially across the lake, the wooden bridge was gradually dismantled.

Construction of the causeway was generally uneventful with no reported construction or funding delays.

On December 31, 1932, while still just a dirt-fill structure, the causeway was initially opened for bus and automobile traffic. Contracts for spreading gravel on the surface were let in September of 1933, and the first oil surfacing was completed on August 28, 1934. Pedestrian traffic, at that time, was possible only by walking on the shoulders of the roadway.

It was not until almost four years later, on May 17, 1938, that the State Highway Department called for bids to complete the Longyear Lake causeway. Recommended at that time was a forty-foot-wide paved roadway with a six-foot-wide walkway on each side. Two thirty-foot spans at each end of the causeway were also suggested for boat passage.

Before any bids were let, and almost one year later, the state suggested that Chisholm consider paving a portion of the causeway using cast-iron corrugated plates placed on an underlayment of concrete. The plates would then be stabilized with a bituminous covering. The center twenty feet of the roadway would be of steel plating, with ten feet of concrete pavement on each side.

As bizarre as the idea may have seemed at that time, the Department of Transportation was convinced that such a surface would provide for a solid, long-lasting roadway. Widespread use of such a road surface would also impact favorably on the demand for steel, requiring an increase in iron-ore production.

Although both Mayor Wheelecor and Village Engineer George Anderson rejected the suggestion, the state continued to pursue the use of steel as a roadbed surface. Several years later, approximately eight-tenths of a mile of Highway 53, just south of Eveleth, was paved with cast-iron plates. This innovation did prove to have some merit, as was demonstrated during World War II by the extensive use of corrugated, cast-iron plates on overseas roadways and airport runways.

Bids for paving and completion of the causeway, at an estimated cost of $235,000, were finally requested by the state in early July 1939. The contract called for a forty-foot-wide roadway, 2,200 feet in length. A twelve-by-twelve-foot culvert was to be constructed on the west end of the causeway. Chisholm would be responsible for construction of the curbing and sidewalks using Public Works Administration funds.

Finally on August 24, 1939, finishing work on the causeway began with the building of the twelve-foot culvert. Though formal dedication would be scheduled for a later date, on October 18, 1939, the causeway was again opened for traffic.

The second major publicly funded structural undertaking during the 1930s involved construction of Memorial Park on the immediate western fringes of downtown Chisholm. The new park had been discussed for some time to replace the deteriorating old ballpark located at the intersection of Oak (Sixth) Street, South Central Avenue and the Monroe Road. Incidentally, the grandstand portion of the old park had been built in 1918.

Anticipating the possibility of obtaining federal funding from one of President Roosevelt's New Deal programs, the village of Chisholm in 1933 entered into an agreement with the Oliver Iron Mining Company for the acquisition of forty acres of land needed for the park. The purchase price of that land was $3,000.

Funding for the start of the project was originally obtained from the Civil Works Administration (CWA). This New Deal program was designed to supply funds to local authorities such as mayors of cities and governors of states, for the building of such public projects as streets, roads, bridges, and schools.[43] Receipt of these CWA funds resulted in eighty-three men reporting for work at the athletic complex on November 29, 1933. Three weeks later, an additional thirty-three men were put to work using funding provided by the St. Louis County Emergency Relief organization. All laborers, whether skilled or unskilled, were to be paid $100 a month. Because the original start-up work consisted mainly of the removal of rock and the digging of trenches to accommodate the proposed wall, skilled labor was not required.

Because much of the public and most of the business community viewed the CWA as simply another relief endeavor, the program was totally abandoned by the government in early April 1934. Consequently, on April 4, 1934, all 200 men employed on the new Memorial Park project were let go, and the project came to a dead halt.

However, some seven weeks later a grant from the Emergency Relief Administration (ERA) provided for the return of seventy men to the project with funding guaranteed until the winter. The ERA, established in 1933, was designed "to cooperate with the States in relieving hardships caused by unemployment and drought."[44] Following exhaustion of the original ERA funds, progress on the park project was again in a holding pattern until additional funding became available under the Works Progress Administration (WPA) on September 26, 1935. This Depression-era program was designed to get people off relief, put them to work and meet communities' infrastructure needs at the same time. The program not only provided much-needed employment from 1935 to 1943, but also provided towns with substantial multifunctional buildings they might not otherwise have been able to build.[45]

In addition to community centers, the WPA built or repaired schools, hospitals, stadiums, firehouses, dams, sewer and water facilities, athletic fields, swimming pools, airports, and fish hatcheries. The total cost of the program exceeded $10.8 billion nationally, $250 million of that in Minnesota where the WPA employed 63,762 people in its peak year, 1938.

On September 26, 1935, WPA funding of $186,000 allowed 160 men to return to work on the Memorial Park project. The basic salary of $60.50 was to be paid for 130 hours of work (less than fifty cents an hour). With the addition of thirty-one men on October 3, the payroll for all employees exceeded $13,000 each month. Progress on the park then proceeded at a fairly rapid pace.

The first baseball game played under the lights at the new park on July 21, 1936, ended with Chisholm winning over Virginia by the score of two to one. Some 2,000 spectators watched the first football game, which was played at the new park on September 18, 1936. The final score was Chisholm six, Greenway of Coleraine zero.

In October 1936, following depletion of the original WPA grant of $186,000, work on the park was again temporarily halted. In addition to the WPA grant monies, the City of Chisholm had expended $51,675. Of this total, $3,000 was for the purchase of the land, $9,800 for tools and equipment, and $36,000 for employee wages under the original CWA program.

Funding for the project was thereafter somewhat sporadic, resulting in substantial delays interfering with eventual completion. Benefiting from still another WPA grant on January 26, 1937, 130 men returned to work, primarily removing rock. Still another WPA grant in September 1938 provided work for an additional fifty men.

Inspection and approval of the Memorial Park project by federal officials took place on October 5, 1938. Even though construction of the Field House was not started until August 13, 1939, formal dedication of the sports complex was scheduled for August 31, 1939. As of the dedication date, federal monies expended on the project had exceeded $218,160, while Chisholm's share was almost $50,000.

When completed, the Memorial Park provided Chisholm with one of the finest sports complexes in all of Minnesota. Included was a lighted football field first used in the fall of 1936, a lighted major-league-class baseball field, a 220-yard straightaway running track (probably the only such track at that time in all of Minnesota including the University of Minnesota), a field house (locker room), many tennis courts and softball fields. Several tourist cabins constructed of stone and concrete were also built in the park. The post-World War II years have seen the addition of other structures, such as an ice arena, a curling facility, a National Guard Armory, the Minnesota Museum of Mining, and several bocce-ball courts as well as a trap-shooting range.

Credit for the completion of both Longyear Lake causeway and Memorial Park projects is due primarily to the technical skills and determination of City Engineer George W. Anderson, as well as to Edward Wheelecor, Chisholm's mayor through most of the 1930s.

Also deserving mention are the citizens of Chisholm who, during the depths of the Depression, initially approved the bonding measure for the causeway and then over the next ten years provided virtually all of the labor, skilled and unskilled, needed to complete these two major structural projects in the 1930s.

Incidentally, the federal monies provided Chisholm under various New Deal programs during the 1930s were exceeded in all of St. Louis County only by the city of Duluth.

In the 1940s, Chisholm would be witness to the most profound structural and social changes since the first decade of its existence. Changes impacting the citizens of Chisholm ranged from the numerical designation of all streets following publication of Ordinance #53 on January 1, 1940, to the forced relocation of 150 homes from the mining locations into Chisholm proper in the middle and late 1940s.

On March 7, 1940, Chisholm became the third town on the Mesabi Range to be provided with rotary-dial telephones. Dial phones had previously been installed in Biwabik in 1937 and in Keewatin in 1939. The installation of dial phones required a change in all phone numbers from three to four digits.

On June 10, 1949, the City Council determined that all city firefighters would be placed on a five-day workweek schedule. So after twenty-five years of working seven days a week, our father was finally entitled to a five-day workweek in addition to a two-week vacation each year.

Federal and state-funded construction included the Post Office, which opened on January 20, 1940, at a cost of $75,000, the new school garage built with $47,600 of WPA funds, and the new Shenango bridge funded by the State at a cost of $32,176. The bridge opened for traffic on November 23, 1940.

However, the greatest structural impact on the City was yet to be realized. Closure of the Monroe and Shenango Location grade schools in June of 1940 was soon followed by the structural but not spiritual demise of the Shenango, Meyers, Hartley, Dunwoody, Bruce and Monroe Locations. As early as August 17, 1939, the Pickands Mather Mining Company had served notice on the residents of Dunwoody Location that the settlement would soon be abandoned. Removal of all homes, most of them into Chisholm proper, was completed during the summer of 1940.

Shenango Location, despite the closure of the grade school, would continue to exist until early 1944, when all structures were moved, again most of them into Chisholm proper.

On March 4, 1948, in a letter to the families living in Monroe Location, the Oliver Iron Mining Company advised that abandonment of the location would be completed by November 1, 1948. All homes were for sale to their present owners for one dollar. It was suggested that all sales transactions be finalized by May 1, 1948.

Families living in mining company homes in Meyers and Clark Locations were also notified on September 16, 1948, that all homes would have to be purchased and moved by November 1, 1948.

Considering the fact that more than 150 homes would eventually be moved into Chisholm proper in less than ten years, one can appreciate the impact these moves must have had on the City infrastructure. The need for new streets, sidewalks, and curbing as well as water and sewer services was substantial.

The major social impact on the citizens of Chisholm during the 1940s was of course the war effort. Fortunately, manpower needs to accommodate the rapid expansion of the mining activities in the early 1940s were more than adequately met by the large pool of men still recovering from Depression-related unemployment.

However, especially after America's entry into World War II on December 8, 1941, the increased need for military manpower caused women to become an integral part of the mining workforce for the first time in history. Even high school students were needed in the mines, with

46

older students working on weekends during the school year and full time during the summer break.

Beginning with the enactment of the United States Selective Training and Service Act of September 10, 1940 (The Draft), Chisholm witnessed the gradual call-up of young men for active duty. Since the original draft call was determined exclusively by lottery, and because deferment guidelines were liberally interpreted, induction notices were sent only to unmarried men who were at least twenty-one years of age. However, after America's entry into the war, a dramatic increase was noted in the number of men reporting for induction.

Following the initial reports of Chisholm's first war casualties in March and June of 1942, for the next three years reports of fifty-six additional casualties as well as innumerable notices of servicemen wounded, missing in action, or prisoners of war were to dominate the front pages of both weekly newspapers.

A citywide Servicemen's Homecoming Celebration of October 10, 1946, was to be followed six months later by the steady return to Chisholm of the bodies of many of the fifty-eight servicemen who had made the ultimate sacrifice for their country. More than 1,600 young men and women, twenty-one percent of the total population, had responded to their country's "Call to Duty." Of the fifty-eight reported wartime casualties, four Chisholm families suffered the loss of two of their children.

Chisholm's fifth decade was also witness to additional far-reaching educational and demographic changes. To begin, after forty years of service, on July 31, 1948, J.P. Vaughan resigned as superintendent of Chisholm's schools. The departure of Mr. Vaughan signified the culmination of forty years of nationally recognized, quality education provided to the people of Chisholm under his direction.

The last half of the 1940s would also witness some of the most profound demographic changes in the young life of the community. Having long since been convinced of the value of education, and because of the monetary assistance provided by the "GI Bill" (federal legislation that provided funding for the continued education of former service personnel), the young veterans came to realize that their educational goals were now possible.

Just as their immigrant parents had left their homes and families in the Old Country a half century before, so now many young veterans, men and women, would leave Chisholm and all of the Mesabi Range, in search of a better life and advanced education. Unfortunately, a majority of these young, first-generation children of immigrant parents would never return to Chisholm or the Mesabi Range to raise their families and establish permanent homes.

# 3

# *307 West Poplar Street*

## Our Home
### 307 West Poplar Street
### Chisholm, Minnesota

Our home, located at 307 West Poplar Street (307 Fifth Street S.W.), was purchased on April 15, 1924, for less than $1,000. The purchase price estimate is based on the fact that the "True and Full Value" of the property as recorded in 1930 by the Chisholm assessor was only $800. The Total Assessed Value at that time was $320.[46] The stock market crash of October 29, 1929, may have contributed some to the depressed value of residential housing.

The home had neither a full basement nor central heating. However, the basement was soon dug, and the furnace was installed during the summer of 1924. Since our father was unemployed at the time, we are not sure where our parents got the money to purchase the home, build the basement and pay for a new furnace. We suspect our grandparents, Mike and Eva Billo, probably provided much of the money.

My three sisters and I were all born in Chisholm in the house still located at 307 Fifth Street S.W. Johnny was born in Monroe Location and brother Willy was born in Glen Location.

The original house was built on a lot that measured twenty-five feet in width and 125 feet in length. The house itself was only fifteen feet wide and thirty-four feet long. Because land in the city was at a premium, almost all the homes on the south side of town were constructed on single twenty-five-foot lots. However, the homes of both our neighbors, the Medveds to the east and the Champas to the west, were built on fifty-foot lots. On the east side, our house was situated less than three feet from the Medved home. The fact that the eaves of the Medved home overhung the edge of our roof by several inches was not a problem until it became necessary to paint either house. When painting our house, the ladders would be leaned against the Medved's house, and we would have to climb the ladder and paint with our backs against the rungs of the ladder. The Medved family resorted to the same method when painting their house. Because rain gutters had never been installed along the eaves of our home, which was not insulated, the two-foot wide concrete sidewalk on the west side was ice-covered during most of the winter.

The narrow lawn did not fare much better. Almost daily foot traffic caused by children at play was a major factor in producing a less than marginal appearing lawn. For that reason, the Kosiak family was never in need of a lawn mower. If the length of the grass ever caused the lawn to become unsightly, Tato would dispatch the greenery with the aid of his *kosa* (scythe).

Since we were the last family to move onto the block, fences on both sides of our lot were already in place. A reddish-colored barn/garage occupied most of the back of the lot, so that only a small gate was necessary along the back alley. A wire fence with a swinging gate was eventually installed across the front yard.

From front to back, the original building consisted of a glassed-in front porch, a living room, dining room, and a kitchen. A stairway, with a landing about two-thirds of the way up, occupied the entire west wall of the living room. Beneath the stairway was a small closet. Furnishings were very sparse. The hardwood floor was covered with a piece of linoleum. A naugahyde-covered davenport, which pulled out for sleeping, took up much of the space along the east wall, while an Atwater-Kent radio occupied the far northeast corner of the room. Several dining room chairs and a wooden rocking chair were located in the room, while on a homemade flower stand located in front of the living room windows was a potted fern plant.

A large archway separated the living and dining rooms. Ma's treadle (foot-powered) Singer sewing machine was always stationed in the northwest corner of the room. The round dining room table occupied the center of the room, and a buffet was located in the southwest corner.

The dining room and kitchen were separated by a two-way swinging door, which was always closed during the early winter mornings in order to conserve the heat generated by the kitchen stove.

The large wood-burning stove, the centerpiece of the kitchen, was located along the north wall. Next to the stove on the east side was the woodbin while immediately behind the woodbin was the "hot water" tank. Ma did not have the convenience of an electric stove until 1941, so, for the first twenty years of married life, she had to be content with a wood-burning stove. The stove was more than just a source of heat to be used for cooking. Because the whole-house heating system was a somewhat outdated, coal-burning furnace that provided only marginal comfort during the long, cold winters, the heat generated by the kitchen stove was of critical importance.

In the early morning, the kitchen was the only warm room in the house. After visiting the bathroom on the second floor, we would hurry down to the kitchen in our winter underwear to wash up at the kitchen sink. While waiting our turn at the sink, we would sit on a large towel draped over the open oven door, absorbing the heat radiating from the oven. As each one finished washing, he or she would sit down again on the oven door and begin getting dressed for school. Because of the wide range in ages, the boys were usually off the oven door and out of the kitchen before the girls were up for the day.

Another function of the kitchen range was to provide a source of hot water. Tato had ingeniously designed a system whereby a pipe from the hot water tank was directed through the firebox of the stove. The water was then heated as it went through the firebox before draining into the hot water tank, which at that time was located next to the stove. Because in the winter there was always a fire in the kitchen stove, there was always warm water available from the kitchen sink. During the summer, warm tap water was available only when there was a fire in the kitchen stove.

A few years later, Tato effected some important improvements. The hot water tank was moved into the basement, and the water pipes were run through the fire chamber of the furnace. Since the furnace was in operation both day and night during the fall and winter months, warm water was then in more abundant supply even in the bathroom on the second floor, including the bathtub.

The kitchen sink was a source of innumerable problems over the years. Because the walls of the home were not insulated and the water pipes to the kitchen sink were located along the outside walls, frozen water pipes were an ongoing problem. After an especially cold night, if Tato was at home, he would proceed into the basement with his blowtorch to start the thawing process. But if he was working the night shift and wouldn't get home until 7:30 or so, we would have to wait in line to use the bathroom sink. For coffee making and light dishwashing, Ma always kept a kettle full of water on the kitchen stove.

A pantry, which included a small window with a southern exposure, was located in the far southeast corner of the kitchen. A built-in cabinet along the south wall of the pantry included a large flour bin, which could easily accommodate a 100-pound sack of flour, as well as a smaller sugar bin.

Along the northwest wall of the kitchen, separated from the stove by the dining-room door, Ma had a small cupboard with glass doors where she kept her dishes and tableware. Dish towels and tablecloths were stored in the lower half of the cupboard.

The kitchen table was situated along the west wall, with a chair at the head of the table for Tato, one at the foot of the table for Uncle Mike and a wooden bench along the entire east side of the table where the kids were seated. Since Ma was always busy cooking and serving the food, she rarely got to eat with the rest of the family. As we picked up after the meal, she would generally sit down to eat.

Scatter rugs, one just inside the kitchen door and one in front of the sink, were the only floor coverings. On Saturday night after we had scrubbed the floor on our hands and knees, the entire floor was covered with newspapers, which were removed on Sunday morning. Needless to say, after more than a decade of such abuse the hardwood floor was literally bleached white as a result of frequent intense scrubbings.

We suspect that because the heavy kitchen stove would have had to be partially dismantled in order to install linoleum, commercial floor covering was not one of Tato's top priorities. However, in the early 1940s, at the time the kitchen underwent a major remodeling, linoleum was finally installed in the kitchen. We never did own an icebox, and our first refrigerator was purchased at the time of the kitchen remodeling in 1941.

The back door, which was located in the middle of the south wall, opened onto a stoop about eight feet in length and six feet in width. It was from this unenclosed stoop that Ma hung all the clothes to dry. Because family clothing was washed inside and dried outside, winter and summer, and because of the amount of clothing washed every week, Tato devised a rather ingenious method for drying the clothes. This consisted of a two-pulley system—one pulley was attached to the house above the back porch and the other pulley was attached to the barn/garage. The clothes were then hung with clothespins on the steel cable that ran between the pulleys. After each piece of clothing was attached to the line, the line was moved to make room for the next article. While taking in the wash, the process was just reversed. The primary benefit was the fact that Ma would never have to leave the stoop to hang the family wash.

The basement, which was made of stones of various shapes and sizes embedded in concrete, was rather dark and damp, especially in the summertime. A huge, coal-burning, gravity-circulating furnace, which was centrally located, took up most of the space in the basement, not to mention the large air ducts needed to dispense the heat throughout the house. There were only two small basement windows, both on the west side of the building. Part of the northwest corner of the basement was for the storage of coal while the northeast portion was for the storage of produce, especially potatoes, the forty-gallon barrel of sauerkraut, the five-gallon crock of pickles, and the entire gamut of home-canned fruits and vegetables.

The second floor of the house consisted of two bedrooms and a bath with a bathtub. The bedroom on the north end had a small closet built into the west wall. The bedroom on the south side had no closet, while an elongated bathroom was built along part of the east wall. A trunk, brought over from Europe, was stored just behind the bathroom door. The bathtub occupied most of the outside (east) wall, and the sink and toilet were located in the southeast corner. A small window was located on the southern wall of the bathroom.

Speaking of windows, there were only two windows besides this bathroom window on the second floor. One was in the north bedroom, facing north, and the other one was in the south bedroom, facing south. On the main floor of the original home, there were two side-by-side windows overlooking the glass-enclosed front porch, two side-by-side windows in the dining room facing west and two windows in the kitchen, one facing west and one facing south. There were no windows whatsoever facing east.

The first structural change involved the installation of two small windows over the staircase along the west side of the house. For that work Tato actually enlisted the services of a carpenter. However, from then on he was on his own, with help from the boys and Uncle Harry Billo.

The first major project tackled by this crew was to enlarge the basement by extending it underneath the glass-enclosed front porch. The actual excavation beneath the porch was strictly a family operation utilizing the pick and shovel needed to remove many wheelbarrows of dirt. A building contractor was hired to install the concrete block walls and pour the basement floor.

The completed addition was divided into two separate rooms, a coal bin with direct access to the outside for the delivery of coal and a contained root cellar for storage of garden-grown crops, especially the more than fifty bushels of potatoes harvested each year. The sauerkraut barrel and the pickle crock were also stored in this room along with numerous quarts of canned fruits and vegetables.

Even with the gradual increase in family size, it wasn't until the Russian priest became our star boarder for a year that Tato decided additional living space was essential. During the year that the priest lived with our family, he was awarded the south bedroom, while the three boys and my two sisters had the north bedroom. Our parents slept on the pullout davenport in the living room.

Since the family never kept financial records, there is no indication that the priest ever paid even one cent for his room and board, which is not surprising considering his wage at that time. The folks were probably content to write off his expense as a church contribution, although Tato never made enough money to file an income tax return until after the war years.

Finally, in the late 1930s, serious planning began for major remodeling of the house. Dormers with windows were to be constructed on both the east and west sides, and a bedroom was to be built on the south side over the existing kitchen, which was merely a one-story extension of the main structure.

The project began in the late spring of 1939 and by fall the structure was completely enclosed.

One year later, in the spring of 1940, work was started on building a new back porch to be located over an extension of the basement.

Excavation of the basement was again strictly a family affair. Professional help, primarily advisory in scope, was required for completion of the project. Part of this job involved creating a basement stairway with outside access from the back yard, as well as inside access through the porch. Also included was a space for a proposed, built-in refrigerator extending into the porch. Numerous windows made the porch a pleasant place to relax especially in the early spring and the late fall.

Finally, one year later, it was determined that a complete overhaul of the kitchen was in order. The pantry walls were removed, built-in cabinets were installed along the entire east wall and a large window, overlooking Medved's back yard, was positioned above the kitchen sink.

Once the old wood-burning kitchen range was dismantled and wall-to-wall flooring was in place, not only did Ma have a new electric stove, but she was also provided with a General Electric refrigerator. Our floor-scrubbing and wood-harvesting days had come to an abrupt end.

In addition to the structural changes in our home, mention must be made of the building of a new barn/garage in the backyard. The increasing size of the dairy herd as well as the fact that in 1937 Tato purchased a brand-new, eight-cylinder Chrysler Royal automobile for about $800 necessitated this project. It was the first new vehicle he had ever owned, and it deserved the finest accommodations possible. So, in the summer of 1937, we not only tore down the original structure but also completed the largest, finest barn/garage on our block. In addition to a narrow, one-stall garage for the new car, space was available for no less than four cows and a hayloft, which could accommodate almost all the feed necessary for the long winter.

# 4

# *Childhood*

L eisure activities played an important part in our early development. Most of the play took place in the back alleys, on the sidewalks and streets, or at one of the playgrounds. The activities were not structured other than what might result from the normal childhood pecking order; in other words, the games, the rules and the equipment to be used were determined by the older participants. Commercial sporting equipment was literally unheard-of and of course unaffordable. In spite of the lack of formal organization and fancy equipment, we were never lacking for things to do during our summer vacation periods.

Of greatest importance was the fact that there were virtually unlimited numbers of children from five to fifteen years of age looking for some action. Early involvement was usually with children of comparable age, playing games compatible with our developmental skills. Sandboxes were unheard-of, but who needed a sandbox? Although the entire backyard was covered with dirt, no one owned a toy dump truck. Digging was done by hand or with the aid of a small stick while the hands functioned as a grader, steam shovel, and dump truck.

As grade schoolers, the game of "Hide and Seek" was always popular, but the neighborhood imposed some rather serious restrictions in that all the yards were fenced with gates at both ends of the lot. This generally limited our ability to run and hide within the limits imposed by the one who was doing the seeking.

Early on, the boys were involved in unstructured pickup-team sports such as basketball, baseball, and football. Almost all games were played either in the back alleys or on some of the neighborhood streets.

The basketball could range in size from a tennis ball to a five or six-inch-diameter rubber ball, which could be purchased at the dime store. The baskets were simply the rims of various-sized coffee cans which had been nailed to somebody's garage door.

"Kitten Ball" was the simplest version of baseball. The ball was a small, round bundle of yarn held firmly in place by rubber binders or tape, while the bats were usually discarded tomato poles or broomstick handles.

The football varied in shape and consistency from a tightly rolled-up gunnysack held together by inner-tube rubber bands to an inflated pig's bladder. Soon after the pig was sacrificed, the bladder was removed and cleansed. After the ureteral orifices were tied off and after the bladder was inflated, the urethral orifice was then tied. Though the bladder could be passed, punting was not recommended. The original use of the pig's bladder is probably the basis for calling a football "the pigskin."

The most popular boys' pastime at the upper grade school and lower junior high level was "rubber guns." During this time, automobile tires were inflated by means of an inner tube so there was virtually an unlimited number of discarded inner tubes that were usually available. Cutting the inner-tube in a transverse direction provided one with generous quantities of rubber bands of varying elasticity. Elasticity was determined by the thickness of the band.

Guns were usually fashioned from the ends of discarded grape boxes. The form might vary, but usually the silhouette was that of a pistol. The trigger apparatus was a small lever fixed to the back of the handle, held in place by a rubber band. The rubber band being launched was hooked beneath the trigger apparatus and stretched over the barrel of the gun. Pulling the trigger caused the rubber band to be discharged toward the target. Using the rubber guns, games such as "Cops and Robbers" were the most popular. At times, we might just spend time shooting at targets.

"Tin Can Alley" was actually the back-alley version of cricket. The major difference was the fact that the wickets were usually two sets of empty condensed milk cans situated about twenty feet apart. The ball was usually a standard softball when available, and the bats were standard softball bats. There were two players on each team, one team would be at bat, and the other team was in the field.

The team at bat was free to swing at the ball as it was thrown or rolled toward the two small cans. If the ball was hit, the batters would then run back and forth between the wickets (milk cans) until such time as the ball was retrieved. One rotation of the batters counted as one point. If, however, the batter missed the ball when it was thrown and the cans were knocked over, that was counted as an "out." If only one can was knocked over, that counted as one out. If both cans were knocked over that counted as two outs. As in baseball, after three outs the players would change positions with the batters going into the field and the fielders going to bat.

Marbles was a popular early springtime sport. Unlike the standard game of marbles, which is played within the confines of a large circle, our version simply consisted of shooting (plunking) small hardened clay marbles (megs) while attempting to hit a larger, glassy, very colorful agate (snotty) which was set up some ten feet away on the ground. The person who owned the large glassy snotty would be sitting on the ground, his legs spread with the snotty in front of him. There might be as many as three or four boys plunking megs in hopes of hitting the snotty. Whoever hit the snotty would then take possession of it. The boy on the ground would then put up another target, and on and on.

The boy who had been sitting on the ground would eventually pick up all the megs and attempt to win back some of the snotties he had lost. Megs were very plentiful because fifty or more could be purchased for about five or ten cents. On the other hand, snotties were much more expensive, selling for about a nickel each. The idea of the game was, of course, to bring home as many snotties as possible.

Since most of the boys possessed a jackknife, a game called "Jackknife Baseball" was also very popular. The game had to be played on a wooden surface. To begin, the longest blade of the knife was positioned open, at a right angle from the handle. The small blade (most jackknives only possessed two blades) was fully extended. With the knife resting on the tip of the long blade and the base of the handle, the player would place his forefinger under the handle and gently flip the knife upward.

If the knife landed and stuck in the board in the same position, that was scored as a single. If the knife landed on the tip of the longer blade, that was counted as a double. Landing on both the tip of the long blade as well as the shorter blade was a triple, and a home run was scored when the knife landed only on the tip of the smaller blade. As in baseball, one had to keep track of the number of men on base and how they might be moved along with each subsequent hit. Whenever the knife did not stick in the board it was counted as an out and as in baseball, three outs and we changed sides. Then the other player took over flipping the knife until he too suffered three outs. The game might go on for nine innings, ninety minutes or all afternoon long.

Playtime activities involving the girls were similarly unstructured except when attending the summer playground programs, which were supervised by the city recreational department. In addition to the usual games of "Tag" and "Hide and Seek," one of the more physical forms of neighborhood play included jumping rope, which could be carried on by a single individual or with the aid of two persons who would twirl or twist the rope. Jumping rope was primarily a test of endurance as to how long one might continue to jump before fouling out or simply running out of energy. Rope jumping required both coordination skills and a high level of endurance. The equipment was readily available, as most households had a length of rope that could be spared.

The game of "Jacks" was also a popular summertime activity played almost exclusively by girls. The equipment costs were minimal; a set of jacks could be purchased at the local "Dime Store" for less than twenty-five cents. During the summer vacation, Jacks tournaments were routinely conducted at all the city playgrounds. Mary Ann still has two blue ribbons designating her as the City Champion for her age group in the City Jackstone Tournaments of 1940 and 1941.

Hopscotch, which required the surface of the city sidewalks and simple chalk, was also a popular activity. The only problem was that some of the older citizens frowned on this temporary "defacing" of the sidewalk, even though it was completely remedied by the next rainfall.

Next to the back alley, the street corner was the most popular play area. Unlike most other street corners, "Vuicich's Corner," Third Avenue South at Oak (Sixth) Street provided some unique play opportunities. First, the entire intersection was paved. Second, the street light was suspended exactly over the center of the intersection rather than being on a single pole. Thus, the entire intersection was well lit, allowing us to play some of the first nighttime baseball.

In spite of the fact that this corner was unusually well lit, much of the time was spent just sitting on the curb, planning our activities for the next day and reminiscing about the past day's activities.

60

Several empty lots on the southeast end of the street corner, about four city lots in size, provided space for a variety of sporting activities such as baseball in the summer, football in the fall, and some basketball in the winter. The family living adjacent to the empty field had erected a standard basketball backboard and hoop. Someone had even obtained a real basketball, which was used on a regular basis. That was the first standard-size basketball any of us had ever seen outside the confines of the school system.

Several of the vacant lots, which were strewn with boulders of various sizes, were also put to good use. Bonfires were built on almost a nightly basis during summer vacation. Wood for the fires was obtained by scrounging around the alleys or on several occasions by raiding one of the neighbors' firewood piles. Since most of the adults in the neighborhood worked in the mines, they usually went to bed quite early, so we didn't have to worry about them inspecting our firewood reserve.

We never took any firewood from the families of kids who were actively involved in building the fires, and we were careful not to remove too much wood from any one pile. Fires were usually built so as to be able to roast potatoes, which, because they were the primary food of all the kids involved, were in plentiful supply. Once the fire had essentially burned itself out and only embers remained, the potatoes were placed beneath the hot coals. Each participant kept track of his or her own potato, turning and repositioning it as needed. Baking time varied with the size of the potato, but since all of the potatoes were essentially the same size, they were all removed from the fire at about the same time. All were coated with a thick charcoal layer that had to be removed. Once the charcoal skin was removed, in spite of the fact that our fingers were completely blackened by now, the feast began without the benefit of either salt or butter.

It is difficult to understand why we enjoyed these baked potatoes so much, since we were served potatoes in some form at home at least once or twice a day, 365 days a year. We suspect the fascination was the fire, not the potatoes.

Finally, I would be remiss if I did not mention bicycling and the part it—or more precisely the lack of it—played in our early upbringing. Until the war years, no bicycle of any size, shape or form had ever darkened the doorway of the Kosiak home. We were the only non-Catholic family on Poplar (Fifth) Street between Second and Fourth Avenues, but there were three other Orthodox families on Oak (Sixth) Street. What did religion have to do with the sport of bicycling? The answer is simply, "Plenty."

Standard religious procedure in the early and mid-1930s was that as every Catholic child made his or her confirmation, most of the boys were virtually certain to be provided with a bicycle, the whole works—balloon tires, head lights, and even a horn. Apparently, the potential confirmant was able to choose a sponsor for this event, and only sponsors with some financial means appear to have been chosen. Undoubtedly, the sponsor would negotiate with the confirmant as to what an appropriate confirmation gift might be. Invariably, the boy would settle for a brand-new bicycle, which in those days ranged in price from twelve dollars for a stripped-down model, up to eighteen or twenty dollars for the deluxe edition.

Confirmation always took place soon after the close of school in June, so our Catholic friends had access to their bicycles all summer long. Not only could they ride out to Glen Pond to go swimming, they might even bike out as far as Dupont Lake (now called Carey Lake). An occasional trip as far away as McCarthy State Park was also possible for the bikers. All the while, we non-Catholics would sit at home or take the long walk to either Linden or Glen Pond to go swimming. Not to mention the fact that if our high school playground baseball team was playing at the Lincoln School playground or at Monroe Location, our Catholic friends would ride over and back while we would have to walk—a distance of at least one mile each way.

During summer vacations and actually year-round, a more structured recreational activity program was available for all the citizens of Chisholm. The schools first instituted a formal summer recreation program in the summer of 1917. The program was originally available only at the High School playground, but in later years it also functioned at the Lincoln and Roosevelt school playgrounds as well as at the Monroe and Shenango locations. While the program was under school system direction, supervisors were high school instructors who were employed during the summer months. Assistants were usually Chisholm graduates on summer break from their various colleges.

Team activities such as softball and baseball occupied most of the boys' time, while the girls were involved in a variety of arts and crafts activities, including the transferring and sealing of pictures onto pieces of wood that had been meticulously sanded. Designing, coloring and cutting out clothing for paper dolls was also a favorite pastime for the younger girls. Competitive girls' activities included running races and jumping rope or playing tetherball, hopscotch, or jacks. Except for tetherball, all these activities were also played in the neighborhoods. Bicycling and roller-skating, using clamp-on roller skates, were popular activities for those girls lucky enough to own the equipment. The Kosiaks had no bicycles or roller skates until the early 1940s.

Despite the offering of organized activities at the school playgrounds, the neighborhood back alley was still where most of the action took place.

# SWIMMING

Because of the large number of swimming holes in abandoned and inactive mine pits, swimming was a popular summer pastime on the south side of Chisholm. Not only did swimming provide relief from the summer heat, but it was also free. All one had to do was walk out to one of the ponds being used as a swimming hole.

Two ponds closest to the south side of town were Pipe Pond and Weedy Bottom, both located just a stone's throw from the north ridge of the Glen open pit. Pipe Pond got its name from the fact that two large culvert-type pipes were anchored along the south shore. Weedy Bottom, appropriately named, was located just west of Pipe Pond and was less desirable for swimming.

Not to be outdone by their male counterparts, some of the young ladies from Pearce Addition, the southernmost part of Chisholm, also availed themselves of these swimming holes. Included in this group was Ann Govednik, who was destined to become a member of the U.S. Olympic Women's Swim Team of 1932.

We began our swimming experiences in the Linden Pond, an open-pit extension from the Leonard underground mine situated just south of Glen Pit. In spite of the fact that to get to the pond required traversing the depths of Glen Pit, it was a favorite spot because of its proximity to our cows' grazing pastures. By going to the pond in mid-afternoon, we were able to swim for an hour or so, get dressed and then go out in search of the cows. Because wild raspberry bushes flourished along the entire south bank of Glen Pit, we managed to get some nourishment along the way.

Incidentally, our baptism into boyhood took place at the pond on Memorial Day. As soon as the parade was over, we would all take off for the Linden swimming hole. One needn't be a native of northern Minnesota to appreciate the fact that the water was usually very cool on the 30th of May. Consequently, there were times when all we did was remove our clothing, crawl into the pond and at least dunk our heads into the water.

Linden Pond was about thirty to forty yards long, fifteen yards wide and of an unknown depth. At the south end was a gradually sloping, sandy beach, while on the west side was a makeshift diving board. Because the beach was situated close to the mine shaft and the mining company road, we always left our clothes on the far end of the pond in case the mining company police might arrive unexpectedly.

One of the major drawbacks concerning Linden Pond was its close proximity to Leonard mine, which was inactive all during the thirties. However, the Godfrey underground mine, situated less than a half mile down the road, was still being worked two to three days a week. The ongoing activity at this mine resulted in frequent police visits to Linden Pond. In addition to the patrols, the diving board was routinely being destroyed within twenty-four hours of being erected.

One of the boys was always assigned as a lookout, and, whenever a company policeman was sighted, there was a mad scramble to get out of the water, grab our clothes and start running toward Glen Pit. Once we had reached a safe distance from the pond, we dressed in a hurry and either continued on our way home or went in search of our cows.

Transferring our swimming allegiance from Linden Pond to Glen (Pillsbury) Pond was not done without some regrets. Glen Pond, which was actually the Pillsbury open-pit mine, can still be found just south of Chisholm along the west side of Highway 169 as one leaves Ironworld.

The pond was approximately fifty yards wide at the narrow end. A small island was situated about forty yards from either side of the pond at its wider end. A sandy beach located in the northwest corner of the pit extended out some thirty feet to where the water reached a depth of about five feet. About ten feet from the shoreline was a large partially submerged boulder that served as a modified diving platform. Because the pond was strictly spring-fed with very little runoff from the sides of the pit, the water was always crystal-clear but never very warm.

One's swimming prowess was determined by one's ability to swim to and from the opposite shore or to and from the island. An even greater challenge was to swim from the beach to the island, then to the opposite shore and back to the beach, a distance of roughly 150 yards. None of the Kosiak boys ever accomplished the entire circuit, but both Willy and I were able to swim either across the pond and back or just to the island and back.

The buddy system now used at camps and beaches was not well publicized but was practiced at all times. The older boys were constantly keeping watch over the younger boys and accompanied them into the water at all times. There was no fooling around while in the water. The only drowning in the twenty-some years that the Glen Pond was used as a swimming hole occurred in 1934 when a boy, who was eight or nine years old, went to the pond by himself.

As mentioned already, one of the major advantages of swimming in Glen Pond was the fact that the mining company patrols appeared less frequently than they had at Linden Pond. When we did catch sight of them, we wasted very little time in getting out of the water, picking up our clothes, climbing up the side of the pit and heading for home.

The one-mile distance to the pond was never a problem. Those who owned bicycles completed the trip in less time but not with any less effort. Travel to Glen Pond by car was possible but not very practical. It was not until Johnny got his driver's license at age fifteen that we were privileged to complete the trip by automobile. The Kosiak family at that time possessed two vehicles, one of which was a touring, convertible-type, four-door Studebaker sedan. With boys hanging all over the vehicle, we would take off for the pond. The gravel road was no problem until we were confronted by the small dump of open-pit overburden at the northern edge of the pond, which rose above the landscape at about a thirty-degree grade.

All the passengers would disembark before the driver, Johnny originally and Willy two years later, began a high-speed running start, with the vehicle in high gear. Only on rare occasions was the vehicle not able to conquer the side of the dump. Failure usually resulted in allowing the car to roll back for another try. Once Tato got rid of the Studebaker, our car-riding days were over.

The pond ceased to be a swimming hole in the late 1930s because of the onset of war in Europe and the dramatic increase in area mining activities. Many of the inactive mines such as the Glen Pit and the Pillsbury mine were then placed into a production mode. Swimming in the raw came to an abrupt end for the young men of Chisholm's south side.

In spite of the close proximity of many of Minnesota's ten thousand lakes, family visits to any of the public beaches were extremely rare. Thanks to some old family photographs, we can collectively recall only one visit to what is now McCarthy State Park on Sturgeon Lake. Ma prepared a picnic lunch, and Tato accompanied us into the water.

On several occasions each summer, the Junior High School pool was open for swimming under the direction of the Summer Playground Program. Swimming on Mondays and Wednesdays was for boys only, while the girls used the pool on Tuesdays and Thursdays. Swimming was limited to students ages twelve to sixteen.

## WINTER SPORTS

Since the winter season in northern Minnesota usually extends over approximately a five-month period, winter sports in the 1930s and early 1940s played a very important part in our lives. Whereas Tato seldom purchased a single piece of sporting equipment associated with summer sports, he displayed relative generosity when it came to winter sports equipment.

Although there were no Gun Safety Programs, Tato did instill in us boys, at an early age, the basics of gun safety. The magic age for gun safety training was twelve, so about the time Johnny arrived at that age, Tato brought home a Winchester, pump-action .22-caliber rifle. Soon thereafter, Johnny had his first exposure to rabbit hunting in the nearby woods. Only on rare occasions did he bring home a trophy rabbit or any rabbit for that matter. A few years later, Willy also took up the sport. The competition for the use of the single family rifle was intense at times, and it only got worse when I entered the picture.

Initially, Johnny and Willy would share the gun on weekends. Fortunately I didn't get involved until Johnny's hunting interest began to wane. Then Willy and I shared the gun. Eventually Willy also lost interest, so I was pretty much free to use the gun whenever I wanted. I wasn't much more successful than my brothers, so that at no time had Ma ever depended on any of us boys to provide the next family meal.

The first pair of ice skates in the Kosiak household was discovered under the Christmas tree when Johnny was about ten years old. Since Johnny denied that he had ever tried on the skates prior to the purchase, we suspect that what Tato did was to take a pair of Johnny's shoes to either the local Mahne or Stonich hardware store to get some idea as to the shoe size of the skates.

Because children continue to grow, the same mentality of buying for the future prevailed even when buying a new pair of skates. It seems the skates were at least a size or two larger than Johnny's regular shoe size. Before one condemns Tato as being concerned only about cost, there probably was some method to his madness. Winters in northern Minnesota can be very cold, and the nearest rink to our home was outdoors. So perhaps Tato's primary concern was preserving Johnny's toes and feet. After all, with a skate two sizes too large, Johnny was able to wear not only one, but at least two pairs of woolen socks, thereby ensuring the warmth of his feet. Because there was only one pair of skates to be shared by three boys, it was obviously necessary to multiply the number of pairs of woolen socks Willy and I needed just to keep the skates on our feet.

Since it was impossible for any of us boys to adequately tighten the skates, they were always put on and laced at home. We would then walk through the snow along the edge of the sidewalk to the tennis-court rink about five blocks away. After skating for an hour or so, we would then have to walk home.

Even several layers of woolen socks did not offer complete protection, as evidenced by the fact that more often than not, we would suffer frostbite of the toes. Treatment for frostbite was to vigorously rub the affected appendages with liberal amounts of fresh snow. Frostbitten toes are essentially white, numb and pain-free. However, as they warmed, there was considerable pain, sometimes lasting for twenty-four hours or more. The situation was usually completely resolved within forty-eight hours.

Indoor skating was available at the Chisholm Memorial Building, free of charge during the afternoons on weekends and all week long during the winter break. In the 1920s and 1930s, Chisholm and several other Iron Range communities were the only cities in the entire state with indoor ice arenas. Because there was no refrigeration beneath the ice surface, the condition of the ice was dependent upon the outside temperature. Consequently, the temperature inside the arena was the same as it was outdoors. However, the skaters did not have to contend with the bitter winds, and snow was not a problem. Attendants were always available to assist with the lacing and removing of skates, as well as to check not only for frostbitten toes but also frostbite of the cheeks, fingers, nose, and ears.

Our first family sled was simply a neighborhood hand-me-down. If ever this sled had had any distinctive markings, they had long since disappeared. Instead of the usual shiny, varnished appearance, our sled was a dull gray. The steering apparatus was loose but still functional, and the runners were in fairly good alignment. Though rehabilitation of the superstructure would have required a major overhaul plus a paint job, the runners were brought up to par by simply running the blades back and forth in rapid succession through a pile of cinders. Cinders, the eventual end product of coal burning, were in plentiful supply because most people disposed of their cinders by simply throwing them into the alley.

As with the skates, the family's immediate concern was how to share the sled. Being the eldest, John had some initial priority. However, arguments always broke out since some sledding days were better than others. The problem prevailed until Johnny's interest in sledding waned as he got a little older. Then the problem was between Willy and me. Eventually, the sled belonged almost exclusively to me, to be shared on occasion with Mary Ann and sometimes with Irene. In the early 1940s, either Uncle Harry Billo or the Smolenskys presented the girls with a new sled.

Initially, Johnny and Willy would go out together, then Willy and I, and finally, I would go with one of the girls. Sharing, one of the important virtues of life, was therefore thoroughly ingrained into our psyche at an early age. That this philosophy was also an important factor in the minds of other sledders was demonstrated by the following anecdote.

Two young Chisholm boys, who were advised in no uncertain terms to share their sled, spent a cold winter afternoon on Two-Block Hill. On returning home, the younger boy was crying. When asked by his father what was wrong, he responded, "John wouldn't share the sled with me." When questioned concerning the accuracy of the statement, John (not John Kosiak) responded, "We did share the sled. I took it down the hill and he took it up the hill."

Excellent sledding was available on most local streets, which were generally snow-packed through the entire winter. Oak (Sixth) Street had a steeper grade and usually more vehicular traffic to pack the snow, so it was better for sledding than was our Poplar (Fifth) Street. However, the finest sledding hill in town was Two-Block Hill located on Fourth Avenue South, from Lake Street (Main Street) to Birch (Second) Street. The top of the hill was adjacent to the highest point in town, and the hill bottomed out at a centuries-old creek bed. The street was blocked off from traffic almost every weekend during the winter months. No cross traffic was allowed either, so sledding was both fast and safe.

Sharing also entered the picture after Tato had purchased a pair of skis for the boys. Because sharing one set of skis was virtually impossible, we resolved the problem by each using only one ski. Eventually, we developed into some of the best one-skiers from our end of town. Our persistent use of one ski may have had something to do with the present popular winter pastime known as snowboarding.

Improvisation in the early and mid-thirties was the name of the game. A popular homemade sporting apparatus was a device commonly known as a "skimmer." A skimmer consisted of a wooden barrel stave to which was attached a piece of birch firewood, three inches in diameter and about sixteen to eighteen inches in length. A seat about six inches wide and twelve inches long was then nailed to the birch log. The rider would then simply sit on the seat and be carried down the hill. The device could be controlled either by body movements, tilting in one direction or another, or by the use of one's feet positioned on the anterior portion of the barrel stave. Increased directional control could be obtained by grooving the underside of the barrel stave.

In the early to mid-1930s, the Village managed and supervised a toboggan slide on the northeast corner of Longyear Lake. The slide was essentially a sheet of ice, edged on both sides by a ridge to maintain the direction of the toboggan, similar to the bobsled tracks seen in the winter Olympics, except that the track was straight from the top to the bottom. The toboggan might reach speeds in excess of thirty to forty miles an hour and then would shoot out onto the lake surface for a distance of several hundred feet. Because of the potentially hazardous nature of the slide, it was discontinued sometime in the mid-thirties. As far as we know, Willy was the only Kosiak who was regularly involved in tobogganing.

The neighborhood mining dumps and abandoned open pits provided excellent terrain for a variety of downhill activities in addition to skiing. Homemade toboggans, usually sheets of metal with the front ends bent upward so as to better glide over the snow, were used. Because of the rapid rate of descent into the pit or down the side of the dump plus the fact that the homemade toboggan was virtually impossible to steer, the activity was generally frowned upon by our parents.

Street hockey could be played by anyone who could walk or run safely on a snow-packed road. The goals were merely two clumps of snow, about four feet apart situated at each end of the rink. The hockey sticks were homemade; two and one-half by two-inch laths nailed together comprised the handle and the blade of the stick was also made of short pieces of lath nailed to the handle at an appropriate angle.

The puck was always a one-inch thick slice of a three-inch birch log. Birch was the wood of choice because it did not easily splinter and its close-grain surface allowed for smooth gliding movement over the packed snow. Raising the puck or vigorous body checking was not allowed, although at times the game would get a little rough.

In spite of all the snow, ice, and snow-packed roadways available in Chisholm, back-alley basketball was still the most popular boys' winter sports activity for several reasons. Year after year, Chisholm was known for the high quality of its basketball teams. In fact, Chisholm High School teams had competed in the State Basketball Tournament every year from 1930 through 1934. The teams were always in serious contention, and in 1934 they were crowned State Champions. So, while still in the early grades, it was every boy's dream to someday be on the team and perhaps get to the State Tournament.

Back-alley basketball entailed a minimal financial investment. A small six or eight-inch diameter ball could be purchased at the local dime store or hardware store for about twenty-five cents. The basketball hoop was made from either the top ring of a large can, or better yet was constructed by riveting or welding together a strip of heavy-gauge metal.

Baskets were preferably installed above the garage doors of those few families who owned cars. Because the driveway was clean of snow at all times, and because frequent driving of the car in and out of the garage provided for a solid, packed base, on rare occasions the players could even dribble the ball. Appropriate winter clothing was part of our back-alley basketball attire. As the games progressed and the body warmed, clothing would be removed as needed.

The game of "Twenty-one" could be played with only two people; two points were counted for a long-range basket and one point for a lay-up. The goal was to score twenty-one points as fast as possible. The game could also be played with two or three persons on each side. There always seemed to be enough boys around to start up a game of basketball, whether it was one on one, two on two, three on three or, at times, even four on four.

Cold fingers or toes were managed by merely standing around for a while with our hands in our pockets or by just going into the house for awhile. Although the garage doors suffered greatly from the repeated contact by the boots of the combatants, Tato didn't mind having the basket on our garage because it helped ensure that the driveway would be kept clear of snow.

In the late 1930s, a standard basketball hoop was installed on a backboard behind one of the neighbor's buildings. A real basketball then appeared on the scene, reportedly taken without permission from the local high school gym. Needless to say, with the acquisition of both a standard basketball and basketball hoop, not only did our basketball skills improve, but we were also spending a great deal more time playing back-alley basketball.

# DOGS ON THE LOOSE

Pets are a big part of many children's lives, and for a brief period of time the Kosiaks did enjoy the friendship of a dog. In the mid-1930s, dogs in Chisholm were poorly trained, poorly supervised and usually not legally licensed. Though the Village employed one dogcatcher, the dogs were allowed to roam freely about town, giving the impression that there were more animals than there actually were.

There was never any question as to whether the Kosiak family would have a dog. It was more a question as to the desired breed. In addition to having a dog to accompany and protect us, we wanted one to assist in herding the cows, not to mention being able to pull us around on a sled during the long winter. After we had settled on the German shepherd breed, the search for our dog began.

We were soon alerted to the fact that a family living in the rural Bear River area, almost twenty-five miles north of town, had several German shepherds for sale. After viewing the available litter, we selected a good-looking male who was given the name Nero.

Nero left much to be desired when it came to herding cattle. While out in the pasture he would rather take off after chipmunks, squirrels, or rabbits, and while in town he entertained himself chasing stray cats. Our cows were all afraid of Nero, so he was not allowed to accompany us when chasing the cows to pasture or bringing them home. However, he saw no reason not to accompany us wherever we went, which was very distressing for the girls, whose friends were afraid of Nero.

What led to Nero's eventual demise was his bad habit of confronting young children as they were carrying orders of meat home from the corner grocery store. Once Nero smelled the meat, he would confront the child, begin to growl and refuse to allow the child to proceed on his way until the child had placed the meat on the ground. The child then started running for home, crying all the way. Nero had a meal of fresh meat, which he ungraciously never bothered to bring home.

The phone calls resulting from these meat heists rapidly became intolerable. Tato was then forced to arrange for Nero's demise. Nero was the only dog the family ever owned.

# 5

# Family Chores

## FARMING

Gardening for the Kosiaks was never a hobby. While living in Glen Location, the family was marginally sustained on Tato's mining pay and a small backyard garden, along with occasional financial support from Ma's parents. After losing his mining job in 1924, Tato, along with Ma, Johnny, and Willy moved to Chisholm. Not only was Tato unemployed, but he was faced with the house payments and the expected arrival of yet another child, me. Because the backyard garden could in no way provide even the barest of nutritional needs for the growing family, in the early 1930s, a small plot of public land just east of the present Northwest Airlines building in Chisholm was staked out and enclosed.

Since the better parcels of land had already been claimed by other immigrant families, it was necessary for us to clear some brush and remove a fair number of rocks before we were able to prepare the soil. Planting the crops, mostly potatoes and cabbage, was preceded by tandem hand spading as the ground was being fertilized. At about the age of six or seven years, I was responsible for spreading the manure while Tato, Johnny, Willy, and Uncle Harry provided the spading. Although the family was almost totally dependent on nature to provide the necessary moisture, hilling and hoeing of the potatoes were done by hand with Ma also assisting. Harvesting of the crop was more of a family affair with Tato and the older boys digging the potatoes and Ma and I picking them up.

Between the planting and harvesting of the crop, insect control was a problem. The potato bug or Colorado Beetle is still the most destructive insect pest to attack the potato plant. The beetles come out of the ground in the spring and lay their yellow eggs in small clusters on the underside of the potato leaves. After three weeks of feeding, the larvae drop off the leaves and burrow into the ground where, after ten days, they return to repeat the cycle.

Without the benefit of any hand cover such as rubber gloves, beetle control was done manually by removing the adult insects and crushing their egg clusters on the undersurface of the leaves. The beetles were collected in coffee cans for eventual incineration with the addition of small amounts of kerosene. The most frequently used commercial insecticide in powder form was Paris Green, a product whose main ingredient was arsenic. Because of the arsenic content, Paris Green has long since been banned.

The smaller crops such as lettuce, peas, beans, sweet corn, and tomatoes were always grown in our backyard. Other than the spading of the ground in early spring, most of the crop support was done by Tato. On occasion it was necessary to accompany him into the woods to stock up on tomato or bean poles. As young boys, we might be actively involved in hilling the tomatoes and potatoes and weeding the corn. Tato was in charge of watering the crop using the garden hose.

Because of the increasing nutritional needs of the ever-growing family, more sustenance from any source eventually became a concern of prime importance. The milk needs would be provided by enlarging the dairy herd. The increasing demand for more potatoes and cabbage as well as winter forage for the cattle could only be realized by expanding the farming acreage from the neighborhood garden plot to a farm.

In 1936, at a cost of six dollars per acre, the folks purchased from the State of Minnesota a forty-acre plot of land in Great Scott Township, about four miles south of Buhl. They also leased for one hundred dollars a year an adjacent forty acres of land.

Viewing the property for the first time was an eye-opening experience for us children. What we saw was not what we had envisioned. Where were the endless acres of rolling pastureland, the large garden area where we would raise potatoes and cabbages, or even a wooded area where we might be able to hunt rabbits or other small game? On both sides of the dusty township road, all one could see was brush, numerous boulders, a scattering of small aspen, birch, and evergreen trees, as well as countless tree stumps, remnants of the late 1800s logging era.

Aware of our obvious disappointment, Tato sought to console us by pointing out that the farm was adjacent to Clear Lake, a small lake reported to have an excellent swimming beach. We might even be able to go fishing in spite of the fact that none of us could recall that Tato had ever been on a fishing trip.

After the land was surveyed and the boundary markings were in place, clearing the land along the property line was necessary before fencing could begin. Brush and trees were chopped down and burned, rocks and boulders were removed and an occasional large tree stump was dispatched with the aid of dynamite.

Cedar fence posts were purchased by the trailer load for about fifty cents each from the McKusick Sawmill. Postholes that were spaced about eight to ten feet apart were all dug by hand using a posthole digger. Other tools included a #2 shovel, a pick, and a crowbar. Since each fence post was six feet in length, a two-foot-deep hole was necessary for solid placement. The circumference of the hole depended on the size of the intended post.

Tato was not necessarily a compulsive person, but he insisted on high-grade, excellent-appearing work. Consequently, each pole was positioned perpendicular to the horizon, even when located on the fringes of the property surrounded by dense brush and undergrowth. Tato also resorted to the use of a string guide to ensure that the fence was as straight as possible—no curves in his fence.

On a good day, even with the help of Uncle Harry Billo, we might place ten or twelve posts into the ground. Fencing could only be done in the summer months and only when Tato had a day away from work. We estimated that several hundred cedar posts were required to completely fence the property.

Four strands of barbed wire were then strung around the parcels of land, including along both sides of the township road. After firmly securing each corner post with angular supports, the barbed wire was nailed in place, positioned on the next post and stretched with a block-and-tackle apparatus to minimize any sagging in the wire. The wire was then secured on that post using a fence staple. On a good day, we might be able to secure four strands of barbed wire over the distance of about 100 feet. Because no livestock were kept on the property until early 1943, we often questioned the need for such extensive fencing.

After fencing in that part of the farm on which the garden was to be located, it was necessary to clear more land to ensure feed for the dairy herd. Armed with saws, axes, pickaxes, rakes, and shovels, we began the job with vigor and enthusiasm that waned somewhat as the process stretched out into weeks and months. The brush itself was usually attacked with the pickax so that the shrubs could be removed as close to the ground as possible. This was also true of the saplings and the smaller trees. Whatever was chopped down had to be picked up and stacked into large piles before the area was raked using the wooden hay rake. The wood chips and small branches were then placed on a large piece of burlap material, before being carried to the brush pile. The brush piles were then allowed to ripen or dry for several weeks before they were burned.

Removing stumps, some of which dated back to the turn-of-the-century logging, was considerably more of a challenge. Some of the smaller stumps could simply be levered out of the ground using a steel bar or, better yet, a long pole. Those stumps that could not be extracted in this fashion were removed by first securing the stump to the trailer hitch of the modified pickup truck, using a ten to fifteen-foot length of chain. Varying degrees of slack were allowed in the chain, after which the driver took a running start. More often than not, the stump did not budge on the first attempt, therefore requiring multiple runs. Once the stump did come loose, it was dragged to the brush pile to be burned later.

Those stumps that were not dispatched using the *jerk and run technique* were subjected to an even more violent procedure—dynamite. Dynamite was readily available in any of the hardware stores as were the dynamite caps and the fuses. For some unknown reason, Tato was unusually sensitive to the smell of dynamite. This was especially true whenever the dynamite had to be cut into pieces before inserting the blasting cap into the stick of dynamite. Consequently, after being instructed in the safe handling of the product, we boys were pretty much on our own. In fact, there were times when Tato would simply lay out the plan as to which stumps to attack, where to implant the charge and how many sticks of dynamite to use. We would then go out to the farm by ourselves. Johnny, who was only fifteen at the time, drove while Willy and I rode along, with a box of dynamite and a supply of dynamite caps and fuses in the box of the truck. One of us would usually stand on the road blocking traffic, while the other two completed charging the holes and lighting the fuses. Fortunately, we all survived without any injuries.

Rocks and small boulders were loaded onto the trailer to be carried off to one of the corners of the property. Leveling of the land was accomplished primarily by hand, but Tato did engage the services of one of the neighboring farmers for some extensive grading and disking of the land. Disking seemed to uncover even more various-sized rocks that had to be picked up and moved.

Crop management was about the same as it was in the Chisholm garden plot. Hoeing, weeding, as well as hilling the potatoes and controlling the potato bugs were always on the summer schedule. Because no special dexterity was required, picking potato bugs was an operation in which the whole family was involved.

Crop irrigation during dry spells consisted of removing water from the creek that passed through a culvert beneath the township road. The water was carried by the pailful up onto the road where it was dumped into several wash tubs situated on the trailer. The trailer was then pulled onto the field and the crops were watered as the trailer moved slowly along. The same method was used to water the fruit trees in our orchard. This was not a very efficient method but it did provide some relief for the crops.

Haying during the early years on the farm was a patchwork type of operation. Using a scythe (*kosa*), Tato cut all the hay by hand in those areas that had been cleared of brush and rocks. Because the hay lying in rows had to be spread to promote the drying process, one of us would always accompany Tato, spreading the hay as Tato went along. Once the drying process was completed, the hay was then raked into small piles, loaded onto the trailer and taken to town for storage in the hayloft of the barn/garage. Beginning in early July, haying was usually finished in two or three weeks, weather permitting.

Because space in the hayloft was limited when compared to the amount of hay being delivered, the whole family became involved in packing in the hay. As the forkful of hay was pitched through the hayloft door from the trailer, it was picked up by hand and carried to the farthest corner of the hayloft. We would then turn around and start to push the hay with our feet, *stomping the hay*. Because haying was always done in July when the outside temperature might range from eighty to ninety degrees, the temperature inside the building was at least ten degrees higher.

As the hayfield became larger and larger, Tato began to mechanize the operation. At one time he actually owned and used a hay mower as well as a power rake, both of which were pulled behind the pickup truck. During the pre-war days, the equipment was operated by one of the boys. Irene remembers operating the mower and the hay rake while Tato drove the truck. This was during the summers of 1943 and 1944, years when all the gardening and dairy work was done by the folks as well as Mary Ann and Irene.

Before we leave the farm, mention must be made of Tato's effort to develop a fruit orchard. With almost unlimited space being available, he decided to put it to good use. Once the fence was completed, a variety of fruit trees, which had been ordered through the mail, were planted.

Several varieties of apple as well as one cherry tree and at least two varieties of plum trees were planted that first spring. Although the colorful brochures from the nurseries virtually guaranteed cold-weather tolerance, the trees never did very well. In addition to the weather, Tato had never considered the local wildlife—ground squirrels, rabbits, and field mice that fed on the tree trunks in the winter as well as deer that fed on the upper branches. To our knowledge, not even one edible fruit was ever harvested from that orchard.

## DAIRYING

For as long as any of us can remember, our family always had cows. We don't remember exactly when Tato bought the first cow but cows were to become a part of our daily lives for many years. We made and hauled hay, chased cows to pasture and brought them home, hauled manure, made butter and delivered milk. When Ma wasn't feeling well, Willy even milked the cows.

Because we can remember owning only Guernsey cows, we think that our first cow must have been one of that breed. Guernsey cattle usually produce slightly more milk than Jerseys, and the rich milk of the Guernsey ranks second to that of the top-ranking Jersey in butterfat content. The growth of the herd then seemed to keep pace with the growth of the family so that at one time we had seven animals, four milkers and three heifers.

Housing the animals presented no major problem since a two-stall barn was already attached to the northern end of the original garage. Beneath the floor of the stall was a drainage sump, which was eighteen inches deep and about three feet in diameter. Even though the animals were confined to the barn from mid-October until late April, overflowing of the sump was never a problem. The solid waste, manure, was simply piled in the back alley to be removed after freezing during the winter months. Whatever remained in the spring was usually used in our garden and the gardens of our neighbors.

Families on the south side of town who owned cows used the pasture land that extended south beyond Linden (Ninth) Street through mining company property, which in the 1920s and 1930s was not being mined. The areas of grass, simple brush and swamp included all the land south of the Glen, Monroe and Pillsbury pits as well as the Godfrey, Leonard, Wellington and Monroe mines. Except for a fence on both sides of the Duluth Mesabi and Iron Range Railroad right-of-way, there were no enclosed areas.

To get our cows to pasture, we first released them down the alley to Third Avenue, then south toward the edge of town. Because we lived four blocks from the edge of town, it was necessary to traverse the streets or boulevards for that distance. Originally, Third Avenue South from Oak (Sixth) Street was not paved, so there were no curbs. However, there were paved sidewalks. Since several other families also owned cows and many of the other families were also raising hogs, no one ever openly objected to the cattle being herded along the streets.

As we walked south, we were joined by other herders and their cows. After crossing Linden (Ninth) Street, the cows were driven down a narrow path for the next several hundred feet through an area referred to as *the caves*, a section of land about six square city blocks in size, which resembled a moonscape. This was a result of the ground actually caving in over abandoned underground mine drifts (tunnels). Because the wooden timbers that had originally supported the ceilings and walls of the drifts had rotted, the drifts collapsed, causing the ground above to cave in. Hence the term *the caves*.

Also contributing to the unusual topography of the caves were the abandoned test pits at multiple locations. Prior to the availability of the diamond drill, widespread iron-ore exploration was usually performed by removing with pick and shovel the overburden to various depths at multiple locations. Though the mining companies had fenced off the caves when the underground system was collapsing, the end result was an unfenced area covered with numerous craters of various depths and diameters supporting a variety of rather dense vegetation—an almost impossible place to find a cow gone astray.

The terrain leveled off after we left the caves, and the path went past at least three small ponds, including Weedy Bottom and Pipe Pond, which we and our Pearce Addition friends used as swimming holes. That part of the trip was along the surface of a lean-ore dump upon which there was very little vegetation and no grass. We then continued between Glen Pit on the right and Monroe Pit on the left. About 100 yards farther was the Wellington Mine head frame, the northern border of our pastureland. The herders then left the cattle and headed for home.

On mornings when we had to attend school, we would usually just drive the cows past the caves and leave them, hoping they would eventually make it to the pastures. Fortunately, the cows generally stayed near each other and seemed to congregate in the afternoon, so locating them at that time was easy. Each of us then had to first confirm the fact that our cows were in the herd. Generally, we knew what cows belonged to each family and a concerted effort was always made to round up the entire herd. Periods of greatest concern were when one of the animals was due to calve. From our experience in herding, we were all pretty much aware of which animals were *due* and we kept a close lookout for them.

On one occasion, one of our cows, which was at term, did not return with the herd at the time of the afternoon roundup. All the fellow herdsmen were alerted to be on the lookout, but to no avail. On about the third day, after prolonged searches by car and on foot, Tato decided to call the Hibbing radio station and have them broadcast the information. To save Irene and Mary Ann some embarrassment, he asked that the family name not be given. The announcer complied with the request but did say that the cow belonged to a Chisholm fireman. This was essentially the same as reporting the family name. A few days later, both the cow and a newborn calf were discovered in the cave area close to home, an area we had neglected to explore carefully.

Once the gravel streets and avenues were paved and fewer people owned cows, there was some objection to having cows walk along the boulevards and streets. Because we were relatively young, we were not embarrassed or offended. Generally the people who did most of the complaining were the same ones who complained of noise whenever we played on the street or in the back alley.

Mary Ann had some herding experience in the early 1940s, meeting the cows as they approached Linden Street and directing them to our barn. At this time, when she was in her teens, chasing cows was embarrassing. We believe we were the last family to own cows on the south side of town and where we lived, close to several schools and churches, was not considered the outskirts of town.

Cows were useful for more than simply the production of milk. We churned our own butter in a small glass hand-churn, usually in the summer when milk production was high. All of us except Eve spent time making butter, sometimes alone and at other times with one person turning the crank and the other holding the churn. A batch of butter could be made in about thirty to forty minutes.

From a purely monetary standpoint, another benefit derived from keeping the cows was the fact that each cow would annually produce a calf that could be sold to either of the grocery stores, Bizal's or Gande's, where the family traded. Since our charge accounts at these stores were chronically in arrears, a credit of about twelve to fifteen dollars was applied to our account. Sometimes one of our aging milkers was also sold to be slaughtered. This invariably resulted in some sadness, especially for our mother.

Over the years, there had been a gradual decrease in the number of dairy cows being raised on the south side of town. This decrease became more pronounced after August 30, 1934, when state-wide testing for Bangs Disease was ordered on all dairy cows in northern Itasca and St. Louis Counties.[47] Although as early as 1896 it had been confirmed that humans could contract Bang's disease (or brucellosis) by drinking milk from infected cows, it was not until 1930 that scientists announced the discovery of an effective vaccine.[48]

Because all animals that tested positive were ordered destroyed, the state reimbursed the owners twenty dollars for each animal testing positive and fifty dollars if the animal was purebred. Though testing was responsible for more than a fifty percent decrease in the number of dairy cows on the south side of town, it had no effect on the size of the Kosiak herd since none of our animals had tested positive.

Because pasteurization of milk was also shown to prevent transmission of the disease, commercial dairies were required to pasteurize all milk products. However, private venders whose cattle had been successfully vaccinated were allowed to continue to use and sell raw milk. And so the Kosiak dairy was allowed to flourish for another ten years or so.

Due to expanding mining operations during the war, in the spring of 1943 the pastures south of town were completely eliminated. So in early May 1943, the entire Kosiak herd was transported to the farm in Great Scott Township where there was ample space for grazing. However, because the cows had to be milked twice each day, even during the school year, Mary Ann had to drive Ma to and from the farm every morning and evening whenever Tato was working.

The Kosiaks' experience with farming and dairying finally came to an end in the fall of 1944 when the Oliver Iron Mining Company purchased both farm properties to provide space for the dumping of overburden from one of the open-pit mines. In spite of the amount of work involved in the development, upgrading and maintenance of the farm, time has left us with many good memories. The farm was essential in providing most of our nutritional needs for more than ten years. Also, because successful management was so dependent on involvement of all family members, a work ethic and a family cohesion evolved which prevailed into our adult lives.

# WOODCUTTING

Because the kitchen stove was the only source of heat for cooking, wood was usually being burned 365 days a year. During the summer, the wood fire would be started on three separate occasions for the preparation of each meal. But from early fall to late spring, a fire was always burning in the kitchen stove, from five or six o'clock in the morning until ten o'clock at night. Consequently, a large amount of firewood was needed.

Even though trees were in great abundance, procuring firewood in northern Minnesota some seventy or eighty years ago was a major undertaking. First, one had to obtain the permission of a variety of landowners before one could start cutting. The federal, state or county governments controlled most of the rural property at that time. Though the mining companies frowned on any woodcutting on their property, they made no concerted effort to enforce any restrictions.

The aspen, or poplar tree, was present in virtually unlimited abundance as it still is today. However, aspen is softwood with very little heat-producing content. The birch tree, a hardwood with greater heat-producing quality, was not as abundant as the aspen. Although most of our neighbors used aspen as their chief source of firewood, only birch wood was ever burned in our mother's kitchen stove.

One of the reasons Tato could be so selective was because he was one of the few people who owned an automobile, allowing him to cover more territory in search of birch trees. His cars, always four-door, eight-cylinder vehicles—Hudsons were his favorite—allowed him to go deeper into the woods on poorer logging roads to harvest his firewood.

Early fall was always the start of the firewood-harvesting season. Of course, Tato had long since surveyed the local forests in search of firewood. Ma would always pack a lunch of sandwiches and coffee. Equipment included several axes and saws of various sizes and at least two small to middle-size bow-saws, all recently sharpened. Once we arrived at the cutting area, Tato would generally designate the trees to be harvested. Felling the tree was accomplished by chopping a wedge-shaped notch out of the tree as low to the base as possible and on the side to which the tree was to be felled. A second cut (wedge) was then made on the opposite side of the tree, slightly higher than the first. After the area was cleared of any personnel, a gentle or not so gentle push was all that was required to drop the tree.

Trimming the branches was done by the younger helpers using the smaller axes, cutting each branch with the grain, from the base of the tree toward the top. Once all the branches were removed and the tip of the tree was cut off, the log was picked up and placed on a pile. When Uncle Harry was along, he and Tato carried and stacked the larger logs. Rarely, even in later years, were we able to harvest in one day what Tato considered a trailer-load of wood. Consequently, we would pile the wood, pack our tools and go home to return another day.

I would be remiss if I did not comment on some of Tato's idiosyncrasies as related to his experiences with his cars and trailers, especially his need to load and pull the largest and heaviest loads possible of hay and firewood—not to mention frozen manure.

Tato built all his own trailers in the basement of our home on Poplar Street. All the lumber was sawed and drilled by hand. Except for the wheels and springs, the trailer was completely assembled in our basement before being disassembled and moved to the garage. From the local junkyards, he purchased the heaviest, most substantial materials. The springs were always heavy-duty, and the old wooden-spoked wheels were usually of maximum size. Steel bracing was used throughout and the wooden tongue of the trailer was reinforced by a three by one-half-inch-thick piece of steel plate.

There were no safety lights on the trailer. The hitch consisted of a metal flange through which a simple bolt could be inserted when connecting the trailer hitch to the vehicle. Because of the construction of the trailer, no load was too much for Tato. Consequently, more often than not, the trailer was probably overloaded.

Due primarily to simple luck, Tato was unusually successful in being able to move the fully loaded trailer with hay or firewood, winter or summer. On more than one occasion, one of the trailer tires on the fully loaded trailer would go flat. Spare tires, even for cars, were not standard equipment, much less for trailers. After unloading much of the firewood or hay, the tire jack was used to raise the trailer so that the rim and tire could be removed. After the trailer was disconnected from the car, the tire, inner tube and rim were taken home so that the inner tube could be patched. Then we went back to the trailer, put the rim and tire on the wheel, pumped up the tire using a hand pump, reloaded the trailer and again started for home.

One of the more memorable experiences occurred when one of the tires went flat on McNiven Road just north of Chisholm. Being within a mile or so from the edge of town, Tato decided to *go for it* even though the trailer was fully loaded. After we had proceeded a few blocks at a low speed, the tire, which was already shredded, simply fell off the rim. A block or so later, the rim fell off the wheel and by the time we crossed Lake Street all that was left of the wheel were the wooden spokes. Needless to say, since this happened in the early afternoon, we were the source of more than a little amusement to the persons walking by. We all slumped down in the car as far as possible but, as usual, it didn't seem to bother Tato. After all, he did succeed in bringing home the wood.

A problem more serious than Tato's tendency to overload his trailer was his apparent lack of concern when it came to safely connecting the trailer to the car. Because commercial trailer hitches had not yet been designed, the attachment was made by simply dropping a bolt through the hole in the vehicle hitch and the steel plate located on the tongue of the trailer. Ideally, one would use a three-quarter-inch bolt secured by an appropriate-sized nut. An additional safety feature was to incorporate a cotter pin through the stem of the bolt, guaranteeing that the nut could not be dislodged.

Because such a bolt was easily misplaced or lost, Tato more often than not was content to use any bolt available, whether or not it was attached to a nut and cotter pin. Though his lack of concern regarding this potentially hazardous practice never resulted in any disastrous accident, it did cause two rather embarrassing situations. On one occasion, driving south on Third Avenue South and approaching the bottom of the hill at Maple (First) Street, the trailer loaded with firewood suddenly disconnected and ran into a tree on the boulevard by the tennis courts. Logs were scattered on both the boulevard and the street, much to the amusement of the tennis players and others. Though we were thoroughly embarrassed in the midst of our friends, we proceeded to hook up and reload the trailer and continue on our way home. Again, the incident did not appear to embarrass Tato.

Several years later, in the early fall of 1941 when I was a senior in high school, the folks and I had spent the day on the farm harvesting potatoes. All the potatoes, about ten bushels, had been simply dumped into the trailer box for transport back to town. Considering the fact that the farm was some seven or eight miles from town and because the trailer, in retrospect, was connected to the hitch of the car only by an unsecured bolt, all went well until we literally *hit town*. While passing over the Great Northern Railroad tracks and the slight rise in the road at the far east end of Lake Street, the trailer suddenly let loose. As we were stopped, waiting to make a left turn on Central Avenue, the trailer passed by on the right side. It then turned slightly to the right and ran into a concrete mailbox post in front of the O'Neil Hotel. Not only was the mailbox post fractured, but potatoes were scattered over the entire half block of lower Lake Street.

After hooking up the trailer, we then spent the next hour or so picking up potatoes from the sidewalk, the street and from under several parked cars. Needless to say, the largest potato-picking audience in Chisholm history was available to encourage and cheer us on. Tato was embarrassed only because many of the potatoes were not of Blue Ribbon quality.

Getting back to the family wood-cutting operation, because of the width of our barn/garage, the firewood had to be stacked in our back yard, alongside the building. As the season progressed, the pile grew larger and larger. Cutting the logs into stove-size pieces was usually done after school and on Saturdays whenever we did not go into the woods.

*Tato never worked at home on Sundays and never allowed any of the family to perform any type of work on Sunday other than caring for the cows.*

Each log was placed on what we called a sawbuck. A sawbuck consisted of two x-shaped wooden frames, spaced about four feet apart and held together by 1 x 3 or 1x 4 inch-wide pieces of lumber. The logs were then placed on the frame where they were stabilized by one of us. With me usually holding the log, Johnny and Willy operated the bucksaw. If Tato was not at work, he was usually involved in splitting the larger pieces of firewood.

In order to facilitate the stacking of the wood in the basement, each piece of firewood was cut to an exact length, fifteen inches, as determined by using a measuring stick. As soon as the log was placed on the sawbuck, it was notched at appropriate distances using the measuring stick. This method helped to speed up the cutting process.

Whenever the sawing was being done on Saturday afternoons and the Minnesota Gophers were playing football, I was sent into the house at regular intervals for an update on the score of the game as it was being broadcast on the radio. There were no portable radios at that time. The need to be continually updated on the Gopher football scores was a constant but tolerable source of frustration for Tato. On Saturdays when Tato was working the day shift, we spent more time listening to Gopher games than sawing wood.

In later years, and whenever it appeared that the woodcutting season was behind schedule, Tato would contract to have a sawing machine brought in. The original sawing machines utilized the front end, including the engines, of either Model T or Model A Fords. The back half of the vehicle was replaced by a modified four-legged frame bisected by the vehicle's drive shaft upon which was mounted a large circular saw-blade.

The actual cutting of the logs was at least a three-person operation. The number-one helper was positioned closest to the engine, between the engine and the circular blade. The operator, usually the owner, was positioned on the outside of the blade, away from the engine. He was responsible for the length of every cut and also had control of the engine accelerator. Just before the log was pushed into the blade, the operator would push on the accelerator bar and then release the accelerator once each piece had been cut. Depending on the size and the length of the log, one or two other assistants might be required. The third person merely stabilized the end of the log.

Utilizing the sawing machine, one could saw up to a cord or more of firewood in an hour or two. A full cord of wood is four feet high, four feet wide and eight feet long, or 128 cubic feet. Tato and the three boys would require several Saturdays to cut that much firewood. The cost of renting the sawing machine was about five dollars an hour. But why spend five dollars when you had three strong boys at home?

Once the logs were cut into stove lengths, the pieces larger than three inches in diameter had to be split. Tato could usually accomplish this with a single swing of the ax. As boys, we might require two or three swings. Carrying the split wood and throwing it into the basement through the open window frame was a family affair. The girls would usually transport the wood on a wagon while the boys resorted to the use of a wheelbarrow that had been borrowed from one of the neighbors. Because the window frames were constructed of wood, care was required so as not to damage the frames.

Stacking the cut and split pieces of wood probably required more skill and patience than the actual cutting of the firewood. Literally a thousand or more pieces of wood of the same length, but of various sizes, shapes and weights, would be stacked to a height of eight feet in a relatively straight, unsupported line. Because the wood could only be stacked piece by piece, the job involved bending over, picking up one or two pieces of wood each time, carrying them three or four feet and placing them, one upon another, on the wood pile. The only consolation was that the work was done indoors, so we didn't have to contend with the weather. Keeping the woodbin in the kitchen full was an activity that involved all members of the family.

## URBAN RENEWAL THROUGH SALVAGE

Of major assistance in the construction of our new barn/garage in 1937 was Tato's knack for recycling materials from buildings abandoned by others. Though Chisholm had always been known for the fact that the residential buildings were usually in an excellent state of repair, the same could not be said for the outbuildings—the barns, garages, smokehouses, and animal sheds. The deterioration of these outbuildings correlated with the decline in the numbers of domesticated animals, especially hogs and cows. The type of shelter required when raising animals was considerably different from that needed simply for the storage of firewood.

The gradual deterioration of these buildings did not go unnoticed by the citizens of the community, and especially by the state fire marshall during his annual visit to Chisholm. Reports of deteriorating, unsightly structures became more and more commonplace as did directives to the property owner to either improve the structure or get rid of it. However, these official edicts were difficult to enforce, especially if the property owner resisted any of the changes recommended.

Whenever the structure became an obvious fire hazard due to its wooden construction and proximity to another wooden building, the state fire marshall was requested to review the situation. If he agreed with the decision, an edict co-signed by the local fire chief was served on the property owner: "Either take down the structure or we'll take it down for you." Since Tato was working for the fire department, he was alerted early as to what buildings were to be demolished. It became common local knowledge that, "We'll take it down for you," meant the Kosiak family would take over.

Once Tato had been notified as to what structures were available, he conducted his standard pre-demolition inspection. If there was any chance of salvaging even a few dozen solid 2 x 4s or 2 x 6s, some construction-grade shiplap, a few usable windows as well as nails which could be straightened and reused, the job was ours.

Armed with a trailer load of salvaging tools—hammers, nail pullers, crowbars of various sizes and lengths, ladders, wood saws, hacksaws, sledgehammers, and several pails to be used for a variety of nails, screws, and bolts—we were on our way. As usual, Tato would lay out the plan of attack since he might be called away to work on occasion or might have to work the day shift. We would then proceed to take the building apart, nail by nail, board by board, screw by screw. Each item was removed carefully by hand.

Special care was taken to remove the boards without breaking them, after which they were separated into different piles, the 2 x 4s or 2 x 6s in one pile, all widths of shiplap in another. Some sorting of the nails and screws was done on an ongoing basis, the spikes and large nails in one bucket, the smaller nails in another. Screws and bolts were also carefully removed and distributed.

Nails were even removed from those boards that had no salvage value but were destined to be used as firewood. Heaven forbid that, in the process of recovering the firewood, one might run into a nail while sawing the board. Each afternoon, the trailer would be loaded for transport home to prevent anyone from walking away with a stray 2 x 4 or a few pieces of shiplap. Even the nails were brought home each night for safe storage. Whenever rain would interfere with our work, we would spend the day in our garage, straightening nails. As one of our neighbors stated when recalling life in Chisholm, "We knew you Kosiaks when you had to straighten a nail before you could pound it."

The length of a salvage operation depended on the size of the structure. When most of the lumber could only be used for firewood, the job might be completed in a few days, including the cleanup. When the structure was larger and there was more salvageable lumber, the job might last for more than a week.

Perhaps our most interesting salvage adventure involved the old blacksmith shop located on the southwest corner of First Avenue North and Chestnut (First) Street. The unpainted wooden structure was black on the outside and completely covered with soot on the inside. From the beginning, though we questioned the value of the lumber, we were intrigued by what lay in the far corner of the blacksmith shop—a 200-pound safe in fairly good condition, but locked. We were convinced that the reason Tato had contracted to take down the building was because of the locked safe.

Regardless, the building came down. The amount of salvageable lumber and nails was minimal, and Ma's clothes-washing chores were increased exponentially. The safe was then carefully (as careful as one can be with a 200-pound object) removed to our home on Poplar Street where it was placed in the garage. Several years later, during which time we each imagined what treasures the safe might hold, a locksmith was hired. Much to Tato's chagrin and everyone's disappointment, the safe was empty. However, because it was still functional, Tato did eventually realize a small financial return, which may have compensated somewhat for the effort required to tear down the building and move the safe from the old blacksmith shop to our home.

The largest building we ever salvaged was the old Fitger Brewing Company building, a large two-story structure located just east of the Great Northern Railroad tracks, about one block north of Lake Street. Salvaging that building took more than a month because of the large amounts of usable lumber. Again, each nail and piece of lumber was removed one at a time.

Once all the lumber from the Fitger Building was properly sorted and the nails straightened, plans were then made to remove the building in our back yard and replace it with a larger barn/garage. The following year, during the summer of 1937, our old barn/garage was salvaged and a new structure was built which was still standing when the family home was sold in 1956.

# RABBITS

Though our father was never known for his business acumen, no one can ever say that he was not an enterprising individual. I would be remiss if I did not mention at least one of the less than marginally successful business experiences into which he entered in the early 1930s. At that time the family had not yet become involved in farming, so we suspect Tato felt he had a lot of free time on his hands, and there was not enough happening to keep the kids busy.

Although the trapping of fur-bearing animals such as mink and beaver provided a comfortable income for the trappers and adequate pelts for the furriers, the same could not be said for those looking for rabbit pelts. Because the color of the fur of wild rabbits was so variable, domestic rabbit pelts were usually used only for the trimming of cloth coats and hats. Rabbit fur could also be cut and dyed to look like mink, beaver or other more valuable fur.

During Tato's extensive readings while at the fire station waiting for the fire alarm to ring, he stumbled upon some advertising expounding on the possible fortunes to be realized through the raising of domestic Chinchilla rabbits. Man had domesticated European rabbits hundreds of years ago and had developed many different varieties, among them the Chinchilla, known primarily for its thick, white fur.[49]

After preparing several pens in a shed attached to the back of the barn/garage building, Tato ordered two pairs of breeding Chinchilla rabbits. Along with the shipment of the four rabbits were specific instructions relating to their feeding and housing, when and how they were to be sacrificed, and how the pelts should be stretched and dried. Several wire frames for this process were included.

Once the animals arrived, *the show was on the road*. Feeding and watering the rabbits was a twice-daily routine, while cleaning the pens was done daily. Since there was always a manure pile in the alley behind our barn/garage, disposal of waste was no problem. The same hay we used to feed the cows was also used to bed the rabbits.

Rabbits grow to maturity in less than a year and under ideal conditions reproduce several times a year. What started out as two pens at the beginning of this business enterprise mushroomed so that, after a year, the whole shed was full of pens.

Tato would determine which rabbits were to be harvested, while Uncle Mike, Tato's brother, was the executioner. Once the animal was removed from the cage, it was held up by the hind legs and struck behind the neck with a piece of wood about two or three inches in diameter. The animal was rendered unconscious and the integrity of the pelt was preserved. Once the animal had been dressed and the pelt removed, the pelt was stretched on the drying racks supplied by the company. Drying was always done in our basement before the pelts were shipped to the furriers out East.

At first, rabbit meat was a delicacy for a family who probably never had enough meat to eat. Ma even learned how to make delicious gravy to go along with the mashed potatoes. Eating rabbit meat every Sunday wasn't bad, but pretty soon it was almost every day.

Willy tried to get rid of one of the rabbits in another way. One day he brought home a two or three-week-old puppy, which he obtained from a friend in exchange for one of our baby rabbits. After an entire night of the dog's continuous whining and crying, Willy was instructed in no uncertain terms to return the dog. No attempt was made to recover the rabbit.

Tato achieved some degree of popularity during this time in our family history because of the fact that he not only made rabbit meat readily available to all our relatives but also to some of our neighbors. The operation eventually outgrew the family's and neighborhood's desire for rabbit meat. We also suspect that Tato's monetary return on the pelts was less than marginal.

All the animals were eventually sacrificed or given to some of the neighbors. The shed was cleaned out and all the pens were burned.

# 6

# *Our Schools*

Our earliest childhood activities were almost exclusively oriented toward family, school, and neighborhood. Because our grade schools were within walking distance of our homes, our neighborhood playmates were also our classmates.

Although our parents and our schools were to become the most important influences in our early development, we would be remiss if we did not mention the importance of our neighbors. As a family, we have always felt privileged to have been born and raised in our multiethnic neighborhood consisting primarily of European immigrant families of Slavic and Italian origin.

It was because of the support and encouragement of our family and our immigrant neighbors that we came to realize early on that the good life was possible only through honesty, integrity, compassion, hard work, and education. With neighbors whose names were Medved, Champa, Mihelich, Sterle, Vuicich, Bunjevich, and Smilanich as well as Pagliaccetti, Iannarelli, and Paleri, how could a child possibly go wrong?

In all homes, including ours, the primary language was the language of the parents' homeland. Most of the children were quite fluent in their parents' native language, and both Johnny and Willy were probably more fluent in Russian than in English when they started school. Language differences posed no real problems in our family since our mother was bilingual and spoke excellent English. She had attended the public school in Monroe Location for several years after arriving in this country at the age of ten.

Our father was multilingual in that he had mastered to a high degree of fluency the languages of all our Slavic neighbors: Slovenian, Croatian, and Serbian. Having been in this country for more than ten years, including two years in the U.S. Army during World War I, his ability to communicate with any English-speaking person was more than adequate. To our knowledge his only formal schooling in this country was his sporadic attendance of the English program as offered at the Chisholm Night School in about 1913 or 1914.

We are especially indebted to our two immediate neighbors, the Medved and Champa families. Though basic education was viewed as the key to a better life, financial constraints made advanced or secondary training out of reach for most children of the average family. In spite of the fact that very few adults pursued higher education, the Medved's younger son, Anton, and two of the Champa family's four sons completed college. Frank Champa, the eldest son, eventually completed law school.

The successful completion of a college education by two of our immediate neighbors under less than ideal financial conditions convinced our parents that a college education was not only possible but also an essential part of our long-term upbringing. Once those important basics of life—honesty, integrity, hard work, and compassion—were thoroughly ingrained in our minds, all we had to do was to get an education.

Before entering into a lengthy dissertation concerning the academic and social benefits of attending the Chisholm schools, I must mention several factors, which contributed to the uniqueness of our educational experience: the virtually unrestricted availability of quality educational materials at all grade levels, disciplinary measures not normally seen even at the finest private schools, a unique grading system that followed throughout our entire school experience, a structured recreational program designed to promote student well-being, both medical and dental health care provided to all students free of charge, and finally, the availability of a variety of in-depth resources as provided by our well stocked, centrally located public library.

## SUPPLIES AND EQUIPMENT

Throughout our entire school experience, from kindergarten through the twelfth grade, all educational materials were provided free of charge. This included pencils, pens, papers, notebooks, and even "flashcards." Crayons (artistic, not the "sixty-four-in-a-box" variety), as well as watercolor supplies, and all other necessary art-related products were also available.

Current textbooks covering all subject matters were provided to all students. Dictionaries, atlases, maps, and globes were located in every classroom.

Although on occasion there might be a suggested nominal charge for programs presented at the Junior High School Auditorium, rarely was any child left behind. All athletic equipment, including shoes and socks for the track, basketball and football teams was provided free of charge. Hockey players had to provide their own skates. The school also provided all the larger, more expensive musical instruments.

## DISCIPLINARY MEASURES

Grade school was never a major challenge for any of us, at least from a purely academic standpoint. Regimentation and discipline, especially for the boys, was another matter.

Minor social infractions such as being caught chewing gum in class often resulted in immediate and sometimes rather drastic corrective measures. The child might merely be asked, in front of the whole class, to deposit the gum in the wastepaper basket next to the teacher's desk. Solitary confinement for up to fifteen minutes in the cloakroom appeared to be in accordance with the standard recommended school-wide sentencing guidelines at every grade level. Though the teacher might suggest that following a second offense the child must provide chewing gum for the entire class, this was never enforced. Though a pack of Wrigley's gum was selling for only five cents or a penny a stick, to provide gum for the entire class would probably have had a serious impact on any child's total school-year allowance. That children continued to chew gum in class has been documented on many occasions by the large quantities of gum found adhering to the under surface of students' desks.

The simplest form of punishment for talking or whispering in class was to be sent to the cloakroom, which was a walled-off extension of the classroom where all the children's clothing was hung on plain hooks during school hours. The major problem with being confined was the fact that there were no chairs in the cloakroom. The child *serving time* was limited to sitting on the floor, walking very quietly about the cloakroom or just standing still until a classmate would come into the room and signal one's release from confinement.

Because much of the playground athletic equipment was stored in the cloakroom, during long periods of confinement the condemned student might grab a softball, football, or basketball, toss it into the air and try to catch it. Heaven forbid if one missed the catch. The teacher would then come storming into the room, and the period of solitary confinement would be extended for several more minutes.

The second level of punishment was a shaking of various degrees of severity, ranging from a gentle push to multiple tooth-rattling jerks. Needless to say, the girls were usually subjected to the gentle pushes while the boys were always the recipients of the tooth-rattling shakes. Teachers even slapped students across the face but only on very rare occasions. Unfortunately, it appeared the same boys were always being subjected to the slapping.

Being requested to leave the room to stand in the hallway was potentially the severest form of punishment, especially if the principal were to walk by. Then one was guaranteed a stroll to the principal's office while being held firmly by one ear. Because we all had had Miss Jessie Chase, the principal, as our first grade teacher, we were already well acquainted. We had all heard her lecture on good citizenship and scholarly behavior on so many occasions we suspect the confrontations were more frustrating to her than they were traumatic to us.

Although our parents never kept count, it appeared that I had more difficulty adjusting to the grade-school routine than either Johnny or Willy. This may have been more apparent than real, due to the fact that our next-door neighbor Tina was in my class all through grade school. Without exception, whenever I was disciplined at any level, Tina would come over and tell Ma all about the encounter. So, I always had some explaining to do by the time I got home.

After we had all finished our high school and college education, Tato informed me that when I was in the first grade, he told the principal, Miss Chase, "You can do anything you want to control that kid."

Once Miss Chase informed the rest of the Roosevelt schoolteachers, I became unrestricted, fair game.

Though undoubtedly all of the boys had at some time been subjected to the ultimate concern of Miss Chase, the family, thanks to our neighbor Tina, was only aware of two such encounters. In both instances, I apparently was the recipient of the ultimate measure of punishment—paddling.

I did confess to at least two such encounters when I was escorted by Miss Chase into the nurse's office and was told to lie prone on the small cot with my arms over my head. Miss Chase then commenced the beating process with the aid of a lightweight, wooden paddle, about twelve to eighteen inches in length and about three inches in width, similar in size to a racquetball paddle. Incidentally, the school nurse never remained in the office during these encounters.

One soon learned that stoicism and bravery were no virtues in that the sooner one started to cry and the louder one cried, the fewer the number of lashes one had to endure. Because of the fact that at such a young age a child has virtually no soft tissue padding over the buttock area, we soon became acutely aware of one of the distinct, unpublished benefits of long underwear, which we wore usually from November through March. The underwear served as another layer of protective padding, thereby softening each blow. Even though Tina in her report to the parents could not be completely sure of what had transpired in Miss Chase's office, a full confession was always forthcoming soon after my arrival home. Punitive measures of somewhat greater severity were reportedly utilized in the grade schools that were directed by male principals.

Punctuality was also taught to the students beginning on day one. We did not enter the building until the school bell rang, except on those days when the temperature was near or below zero or there was a heavy rain. Otherwise, regardless of the time of year, whether it might be raining or snowing, we were required to wait outside until we heard the bell. What made the ordeal even more stressful was the fact that other than the few trees around the school, there were no natural shelters. Although the few trees located on the school grounds could have provided some shelter, walking on the lawn was strictly prohibited. In fact, if anyone walked across the lawn and was observed by a janitor or a teacher, the child would have some explaining to do.

In the winter months, while waiting for the bell to ring, we would usually gather against the heating-plant wall on the southeast corner of the school, away from the brisk northwest winds. When entering the school building after a fresh snowfall, we were always subjected to the close scrutiny of one of the janitors. Not only did he make sure we shook off as much snow as possible, he always had a broom available to assist in the snow removal. *The boys were also expected to remove their hats as soon as they entered the building.*

The importance of punctuality and regular school attendance was wholeheartedly supported and strictly enforced by our parents. This parental support was present not only because they appreciated the importance of their children's education, but they also came to realize that the child who reported to school with even a minor medical problem might have the benefit of an evaluation by the school nurse or perhaps even the school physician. This fact was especially important for those families who had no other access to medical care.

Whereas average, above average or even exceptional grades at times may have been most reassuring to the parents, perfect attendance was the goal most strived for by the student. Though no tangible awards or recognition were forthcoming for intellectual achievement, each child with perfect attendance was awarded a certificate at the end of the school year.

In spite of the fact that the whole country and especially the Iron Range was in the very depths of the Great Depression throughout the entire thirties, the student dress code was strictly enforced. Footwear was perhaps of greatest importance since shoes were fairly expensive and, unlike clothing, could not be made or easily altered in the home. During the winter, four-buckle galoshes were the footwear of choice, at least through the third grade. High tops, leather boots, with a small jackknife insert along the outside of the boot, were in style for the fourth and fifth grade boys. Rubber-toe boots similar to the present-day Sorel boot, but without a felt lining, might be worn for a day or two on rare occasions.

Winter footwear for the girls consisted almost exclusively of four-buckle galoshes, which extended to about the lower one-third of the leg. Since all galoshes came in only one color, black, the only way children could identify their boots at recess time or when leaving school was to meticulously position them beneath their winter clothing in the cloak-room. Zippers for winter boots, though available in the middle thirties, never became fashionable or popular with even the high school student. In later years, variously colored, pullover boots referred to as "snow boots" replaced the black, four-buckle galoshes.

Because Tato had invested in some basic shoe-repair equipment, a minimal amount of shoe maintenance was possible. Rubber soles of various sizes were always on sale at the local dime store and could be easily glued to the bottom of any shoe in need of repairs. A simple, hand-cut, cardboard insert was the solution for any nails that might be protruding through the soles of the shoes.

Neckties from the first through the sixth grade were standard and required everyday wear for the boys, winter and summer. The fact that a child might wear the same tie every day was of no apparent concern to the teachers. Since the tie was worn at lunch as well as breakfast, one

Grade School Dress Code
Chisholm, Minnesota, 1932
Mike, Willy, Johnny, and Mary Ann

98

can imagine the food stains decorating the tie by the end of the school year. Our mother tied our ties only on the first day of school. After that, my brothers and I would merely slip the tie over our heads and gently tighten the knot.

Trousers varied in the weight of the material, heavier in the winter and lighter during the warmer months. No blue jeans were ever allowed in winter or summer, even during high school until some time after the war years. Clothing fashions did vary somewhat to the extent that knickerbockers, such as worn by some present-day golfers, were the trousers of choice for the second and third-grade student. Once the boys got to the fourth and fifth grade, long pants became the standard attire.

The girls may have had a little more flexibility concerning the dress code. However, no form of slacks was ever allowed in the classroom. In the winter, the grade-school girls usually wore winter underwear and long cotton stockings.

## GRADING SYSTEM

While in grade school, we were first introduced to the Chisholm schools' grading system. Instead of the usual A, B, C, D, and F method of grading, the Chisholm grade schools utilized a letter grade system designated by the letters E (Excellent), V.G. (Very Good), G (Good), F (Fair), and U (Unsatisfactory). Numerical ranges for each letter grade were as follows: Excellent (94-100%), Very Good (88-93%), Good (82-87%), and Fair (75-81%). Any numerical grade below 75% was considered unsatisfactory.

Letter grades were also assigned each student concerning the child's social behavior in class (Conduct) and his or her level of motivation (Effort). Over the years, it appeared that the letter grades assigned a student in Conduct and Effort were much more important than his or her performance in any specific subject matter. A child's conduct was graded depending on his or her ability to relate to one's peers and teachers as well as to adjust to the discipline and regimentation of daily school life.

Because of the fairly-wide range of intellectual abilities, only by evaluating the child's efforts could the administration realistically determine if a child had special needs. Knowing a child was exerting a maximum effort was a source of consolation to both the parent and the teacher regardless of the child's purely academic shortcomings.

Ideally, the student might have a straight "E" report card, which my sisters achieved on multiple occasions. Though my brothers and I usually did quite well in the various subjects, our grades in conduct and effort were more likely in the Very Good or Good category.

There were no teacher conferences as such, but parental visits were encouraged on a designated day in both the fall and spring. The spring-time visits by the parents usually were associated with Mother's Day. Mothers were invited to visit the classes of all their children, but because of language problems, there were rarely any prolonged personal interactions between the teacher and any of the mothers. Though our mother attended these sessions quite regularly, none of us can ever remember our father visiting the school.

## SUPERVISED RECREATION

Supervised recreational activities were not a major part of the grade school curriculum. Inter-school competition, in both touch football as well as basketball, was available at all schools only for boys in the fifth and sixth grades. Because of the difference in age and athletic skills, sixth-grade students represented most schools. This was especially true at the Washington and Lincoln schools where there were at least two or more classes of sixth graders in each school. At all the remaining schools, Monroe, Shenango, Balkan, and Roosevelt, because there was only one sixth grade class, the chances of a fifth grade student becoming a member of the school team were greatly enhanced. Consequently, Johnny, Willy, and I were all involved in interscholastic sports while still in the fifth grade at Roosevelt School.

Second in prestige only to the children's involvement in the Memorial Day parade was the annual grade school gymnastics tournament which was first organized in 1930 by Miss Esther Romarine, the grade school physical education supervisor. With the assistance of several of the school system's physical education instructors and coaches, the event prevailed for some eight years.

The popularity of the gymnastics tournament was due primarily to the fact that virtually every fifth and sixth grade boy and girl of every school in the entire system became an active participant. The competitive nature of each separate activity also added to the program's prestige.

Reporting on the grade school gymnastics tournament of 1933, the *Chisholm Tribune Herald* noted, "Junior high school gymnasium will be filled to the rafters this evening when the fourth annual grade school gymnastics tournament starts at 7:30 P.M. The tournament is a moving spectacle of constant action, a regular three-ring circus of gymnastic events, drills and documented events. . . . The tournament has color and plenty of it. Each school has its cheering section and cheerleaders, all dressed in school colors."[50]

Each event was judged in various categories and trophies were awarded to the schools achieving the highest aggregate scores. Highlighting the entire program was the grade school championship basketball game.

Unfortunately, for some unknown reason, the gymnastics tournament was discontinued in 1938. Consequently, Mary Ann was the only girl in our family who was able to participate in this event. The tournament was replaced in mid-May 1940 by a May Day event, which was held outdoors on the football field of Memorial Park. That event was terminated after only two years.

## Health care – medical and dental

Unique by today's standards was the fact that the Chisholm schools provided free medical care for the students at all grade levels. In 1917, Chisholm engaged the services of a full-time physician, Dr. Archibald W. Graham, and in 1930, Dr. William A. Jordan was hired as the full-time dentist. By the early 1920s, both the Hibbing and Virginia schools also employed a full-time physician. Chisholm, however, was the only school district to provide free dental care for grade school students.

The Roosevelt School and all other grade schools did have a nurse's office and the services of a school nurse who provided care on a part-time basis to each of the grade schools. That is, she was employed full-time by the school district but rotated through each school on a timely basis.

Each grade-school child received a pre-school medical evaluation and was re-evaluated clinically twice each year through the fifth grade. All children received diphtheria inoculations, small pox vaccinations, and Mantoux testing. Hearing and visual acuity testing was also conducted annually and eyeglasses were frequently provided to some students free of charge.

Dr. Graham was also the primary treating physician for those students enrolled at both the Junior and Senior High School. He performed all the athletic physicals and evaluated students requiring restrictions in their swimming or physical education classes. Athletes suffering injuries in varsity sports including girls' and boys' swimming as well as track and field, football, basketball, and hockey, were required to report to Dr. Graham for treatment and care.

As early as 1917, the internationally acclaimed Toothbrush Drill was first introduced into the Chisholm schools. The program, which was somewhat more aggressively promoted following the hiring of a dental hygienist in 1926 and Dr. Jordan's hiring in 1930, was continued well after Dr. Jordan's retirement from the Chisholm schools in 1944.

Beginning in 1917, the schools provided toothbrushes as well as toothpaste twice each year for every child from the first through the fifth grade. Long, narrow fountains for brushing teeth were located along one wall of the hallway on each floor of the building. Each day, upon returning to school after lunch, the children would have toothbrush drill. After lining up four students abreast, we would approach the fountain and start brushing our teeth. This activity was not done in any helter-skelter fashion but was rather well coordinated and rehearsed.

At the beginning of the school year, after each child had been issued a toothbrush and toothpaste, a rather intensive, in-service, tooth-brush-training program was instituted. Since many first-grade children had never even seen a toothbrush before beginning school, our introduction to the toothbrush drill was indeed an eye-opening experience. Not only were we instructed as to how to hold the toothbrush, but also how to squeeze the toothpaste onto the brush. Then we were ready for the toothbrushing drill, *by the numbers*. This meant that the teacher or one of her favorite students called out the cadence during the multiple rehearsals as well as during the actual drill. Though memory fades some with time, the routine was pretty much as follows:

On count "one" the student brushed the medial and lateral surfaces of the right upper and lower molars. On count "two" the student began repeating the process on the left side. Counts "three" and "four," each for about thirty seconds duration, called for a back-and-forth motion designed to cleanse the molar surfaces. By incorporating a simple up-and-down brushing on our incisors, count "five" marked the end of the actual brushing.

Toothbrush Drill
(being supervised by Dr. W.A. Jordan)
1940

Count "six" was supposed to be limited to merely rinsing out the mouth and the toothbrush. However, because the toothbrush drill was always the first activity of the afternoon program, and because at least in the late spring and early fall months we had just come in from the playground, we used that part of the drill to sneak in a drink of water. This was very important because access to a drinking fountain would not be possible until recess time, some ninety minutes or so later. Consequently, the rinsing portion of the drill was invariably accompanied by highly audible *slurping* sounds as we all attempted to get enough water to quench our thirst.

Mention must also be made concerning the almost military-like precision that allowed the class to address the toothbrushing fountain, four abreast. Whereas the usual marching routine when moving about the building or to and from the playground was to walk side by side, when leaving the classroom for the toothbrush drill, the students exited the classroom in single file, one row at a time. We then proceeded down the right side of the hallway until we were directly opposite the toothbrushing fountain when, in true military air-corps fashion we would *peel off*, four abreast and proceed across the hall to the fountain. It was then that the teacher or her designated drillmaster would commence the toothbrush-drill count. After completing the six-count drill, each foursome would return to the classroom again walking single file.

Students kept their own toothbrushes and toothpaste in their desks. At the time the toothbrushes were first issued, we were instructed in the design of a toothbrush holder, which was constructed from some form of wax-like paper held together with paper clips. Because the toothpaste possessed a somewhat sweetened flavor, children tended to use excessive amounts on their toothbrushes just because they enjoyed the taste. Consequently, many students ran out of toothpaste before the end of the year.

Incidentally, beginning in 1930, after the school system had employed a full-time dentist, we also had the benefit of biannual dental checkups. In addition to the extraction of both deciduous and permanent teeth, Dr. W.A. Jordan also advised us on good dental hygiene and care. If any extensive dental intervention was necessary, a referral to one of the downtown dentists was recommended.

## THE CHISHOLM LIBRARY

Though technically not a part of the school system, the public library played a critical role in the educational process of all the citizens of Chisholm. Because of their limited size and their emphasis on educational resources, the school libraries could in no way fulfill all the educational and recreational reading needs of their students, much less the needs of the adult population.

Although Chisholm was blessed with two excellent weekly newspapers during the first few decades of the 1900s, readership was probably very limited because most immigrant families as well as their children were generally unfamiliar with the English language.

For the children, educational progress was further compromised by the fact that school was in session for only a part of the year. Even though the system provided all necessary learning materials, grade-school children were not allowed to take their textbooks home. Consequently, for many students even during the school year, their only experience with the printed English language was limited to the classroom.

The problem was further compounded during the summer vacation when children might have no exposure at all to the printed English language, and all verbal interchange within the home was limited to the language of their immigrant parents. The purchase of children's books would have been prohibitive for the immigrant family. For the adult population, subscribing to newspapers or acquiring books was not a high priority. Sometimes several families, usually relatives, shared the cost of a newspaper subscription.

A library was clearly the best way to provide the children and adults of Chisholm with access to educational and recreational printed information. So, in 1913-1914, the Chisholm Public Library was constructed.

Public Library. CHISHOLM, Minn.

Chisholm Public Library, 1930 (Courtesy of the Minnesota Historical Society)

As described by Van Brunt in 1921:

*The Chisholm library is a distinct credit to Chisholm. It is not so large as those of some other incorporated places of the Range, but is, nevertheless, an artistic and well-constructed building, is well furnished, and in library service compares favorably with other libraries of the county. It is not a Carnegie library, the people of Chisholm preferring to establish one with their own money, and so have an institution that could be adapted, without restriction, to needs of the residents, as such needs developed.*

*The building, which is situated on the corner of Lake Street and Third Avenue, was built in 1913-14 at a cost of $37,000. It was opened to the public on May 15, 1914. In the first year, the library had 4,679 volumes, including works in seven languages: Swedish, Finnish, Serbian, Italian, Croatian, Slovenian, and English. Periodicals of many languages are filed. There are now about 12,000 bound volumes available for circulation, and the general opinion is that the institution furnishes a well-planned and adequate service. Miss Margaret Palmer has been librarian since the building was opened and has a good place among librarians of St. Louis County, being well read, experienced and interested in the work.*[51]

The Chisholm library has many unique structural features, including a master staircase leading up to the main library entrance. Ornate pillars flank either side of the main entrance, while an elaborate crest is situated above the doorway. On either side of the staircase are winding stairs (not enclosed in original structure) descending to the children's reading area. Except for replacement of some doors and windows and the resurfacing of the main staircase, the exterior of the building has been subjected to very few structural changes since 1913.

The library was also unique from a functional standpoint. The lower level, designed exclusively for the grade school and junior high student, included a single all-purpose meeting room as well as a much larger storytelling room. It was in this room where storytelling sessions were held every Saturday morning during the school year.

L.H. Weir, in his report of 1915 concerning recreational or leisure programs for the people of Chisholm, had recommended engaging the services of a trained children's librarian and storyteller. "The possibilities in the field of story-telling are large, and the efficiency of the Public Library will be wonderfully increased this coming year by this one forward step," he wrote.[52]

Fortunately, for the children of Chisholm, the role of children's librarian was more than adequately filled in the fall of 1930 by Miss Frances Klune, who, without the aid of electronic props, was not only the Captain Kangaroo but also the Mr. Rogers of the Depression era.

While the lower level of the library was primarily for the grade and junior high school child, the upper level served the needs of the senior high school students as well as the adult population. A wide variety of reference materials, periodicals, and daily newspapers was available for review.

An article in the March 6, 2001 edition of the *Hibbing Daily Tribune* reported on the popularity of the library in the late 1920s.

*By 1927, 25,000 volumes were on the shelves and 45% of Chisholm's citizens were patronizing the facility. In 1928, 44% of Chisholm's population patronized the library with a total of 137,534 books in circulation. First among the borrowed books were Slovenian nationality with Finnish second and Italian third.*[53]

Because the books in the library could open whole new worlds for the reader, owning a library card was one of every child's goals. A child could obtain this card simply by being able to print his or her name. So even before we were able to print all the letters in the alphabet, we could print those letters that made up our names. Any person possessing a library card, including the five-year-old kindergartner, could check out as many as two books at a time for a period of two weeks. A fine of one cent was charged for each day a book was returned late. Though nominal, the penalty tended to serve as a stimulus to the borrower to finish reading the books as soon as possible.

School homework never seemed to take up much of our free time. In fact, my brothers and I never took books home from school until we were in high school. With less than marginal radio reception—the Hibbing radio station, WMFG, did not come on the air until 1935—and very few or no programs aimed at the teenage audience, plenty of time was available for reading. Johnny was probably the most avid reader, reading two or more books, mostly Western novels or adventure stories, every two weeks throughout the school year.

Reading and library use for all the family tapered off as the winter waned. Most of the summer reading was done by the girls who took part in the Vacation Reading Club organized and promoted by Frances Klune, the librarian. It provided the stimulus for the grade-school and junior-high students to read and report on at least ten books during the summer. In some years, members of the club were rewarded with a trip to Bennett Park in Hibbing for an afternoon of games and refreshments. In 1938, for example, 450 children were transported to the park where they took part in an extensive sports program conducted by the Chisholm Recreation Department, followed by a treat of ice cream and cookies. While 450 children attended the outing, over 550 children had read their quota of ten books. The summer reading program was a great success.[54]

Winners of races at the park were allowed to choose their prizes of new books from a special collection in Miss Klune's office. Mary Ann still has the two books she won at these events. In 1938, at the age of ten, she chose *East of the Sun and West of the Moon*, a book of fairy tales. Jack London's *The Call of the Wild*, which is signed by Miss Klune, was her choice in 1940.

In addition to providing all types of reading materials, the library functioned as a social gathering place especially during the school year for the junior and senior-high students. The library was centrally located, warm, and was open until nine o'clock in the evening. Although silence was golden, on many a cold winter evening more conversation than reading took place. One, of course, at least had to be holding a book or newspaper. If at times a person or group repeatedly disturbed the quiet with loud talk or laughter, they were asked to leave. Chronic offenders might be denied admission for a week or two at a time. Promptly at nine o'clock, the librarian would literally clear the premises. It was time to go home.

As we reflect on our childhood and early upbringing, we realize that the passage of time and the advent of radio, television, and computers have not measurably dimmed the pleasant memories we have of the warmth and charm, both literal and figurative, associated with our library.

Completing the Chisholm Public Library system was the Men's Reading Room, which was first approved by the Library Board on January 18, 1918.[55] Originally occupying a store front at 127 West Lake Street, the Men's Reading Room was:

> . . . *as the name suggests, for the use of men only, giving them a place where they could smoke and have access to a first-rate collection of periodicals and current newspapers from across the*

*country. It was moved from its first location after a short time to a building strategically located between the Candy Kitchen on one side and a pool hall on the other. It was a well-maintained room with the current issues of the major newspapers of the country all neatly laid out on long tables and current issues of the most popular, and the best, general and special periodicals displayed on wall racks around the room. About one third of the way into the room sat the caretaker at the desk on a slightly raised platform, there to keep the newspapers and the periodicals in good order, to maintain peace and quiet, and to see to it that the room was being used properly. It was not a hangout; it was a place to read, a great place to spend an afternoon or an evening, and it was well used, especially during the Great Depression when the men in the community had a lot of time on their hands.*[56]

The Men's Reading Room continued to function well into post-World War II era.

# 7

# *Education*

*To this day, correct English, spoken without an accent, is a hallmark of those who were educated in Chisholm Schools.*

*—The Ranger*
Chisholm High School Annual, 1922

## GRADE SCHOOL

NOTE - ANY ATTEMPT TO RECALL MANY OF THE DETAILS OF OUR GRADE SCHOOL EDUCATION WOULD HAVE BEEN IMPOSSIBLE WITHOUT INFORMATION PROVIDED IN THE JAMES P. VAUGHAN PAPERS, 1904 - 1963.

In 1925, when Johnny entered kindergarten, there were three grade schools located within the village of Chisholm: Washington School, built originally as the High School in 1907 and converted to a grade school in 1916; Lincoln School, which opened its doors on January 8, 1912; and the Roosevelt School, which was built in 1920. The Washington and Roosevelt Schools were located on the south side of town, while the Lincoln School was located on Third Avenue North between Cedar (Fifth) and Willow (Seventh) Street.

Grade schools were also located in Balkan and three of the adjoining mining locations. The Myers School was built in 1903, the Monroe School in 1906, the Shenango School in 1910, and the Balkan School in 1911. The original Shenango School building, destroyed by fire in 1926 while being remodeled, was rebuilt by the following year.

Children residing in the locations were enrolled in their local grade schools. Billings, Hartley, and Jordan Location students were bussed to the Myers School until the school was closed in 1933. Then all first, second and third grade students were transported to the Shenango School, while all fourth, fifth and sixth grade students were bussed to Monroe. Students from Fraser attended the Shenango School, those from Dunwoody and Bruce locations attended the Monroe School, while the Balkan children attended their own school.

Except for a few students living north of Lake Street and east of First Avenue, all others living north of Lake Street attended Lincoln School. Grade school students living south of Lake Street attended either the Washington or the Roosevelt schools. Students living in Lakeview—that is east of Longyear Lake—were all bussed to either the Washington or the Roosevelt schools.

School boundaries on the south side were never clearly demarcated. In fact, one family member might attend Washington School while another child from the same family would be enrolled at the Roosevelt School. Except for those children living in Lakeview, all children living within the Village limits, including all kindergartners, walked to and from school.

All the Kosiak children attended Theodore Roosevelt Grade School. The three-story brick building, which was built in 1920 at a cost of $300,000, contained eleven classrooms, a large kindergarten classroom, a small (by today's standards) auditorium/gymnasium, a principal's office, and a nurse's office.

The Roosevelt School building and adjoining playground covered almost an entire city block between Central and First Avenue South and from Hemlock (Fourth) Street on the north to Poplar (Fifth) Street on the south. In addition to both morning and afternoon kindergarten classes, there were two separate classes at every grade level from the first through the fourth grade. However, there was only one fifth and one sixth grade class.

As with all the other Iron Range schools, one year of kindergarten was required before being accepted for the standard grade school curriculum. Kindergarten was where many of us had our first comprehensive exposure to the English language primarily through the verbal exchange with our instructors. Identification and the ability to verbally name a variety of objects and materials were reinforced through the use of pictures.

A structured classroom routine provided us with our first experience in self-control and regimentation. We were taught to listen, behave and follow simple directions. Basic coordination skills such as hopping and skipping were also mastered—to music no less.

But above all, we were started on the path designed to assist us in understanding, speaking, reading, writing and eventually mastering the English language. Precise enunciation and correct grammar were to become an obsession at every grade level. "To this day, correct English, spoken without an accent, is a hallmark of those who were educated in Chisholm schools."[57]

In Chisholm, according to Smith:

*Children in the first grade memorized nursery rhymes before they learned to read or write. Repeating these before class gave them the confidence in their ability to talk English. This led naturally to making up and telling stories of their own, based upon a simple picture which the teacher wrote down for them. Then followed, year by year, sentences, paragraphs, poems, essays and continuous experience in extemporaneous speech.*[58]

While "Flash Cards" were important in improving our reading and printing skills, verbal skills were mastered only as a result of many hours of memorizing and reciting simple children's songs, poems and nursery rhymes. One of our first grade favorites was "One Misty, Moisty Morning."

*One misty, moisty morning, when cloudy was the weather,*
*I chanced to see a little bird that sat with ruffled feather.*
*I looked hard at that little bird and thought I heard him say,*
*"I wish the sun would shine again and chase the clouds away."*

It was in the second grade that both our writing and verbal skills were put to the test. Written composition on an almost daily basis was to become an integral part of our curriculum for years to come. We would also be called upon to verbally express ourselves in front of our class, either extemporaneously or with the aid of pictures as provided by the teacher. Quotations served as the primary exercise utilized not only to tax one's memory but to also demonstrate our verbal skills. Some of our favorite second grade quotations included:

*If you can't help, don't hinder.*

*A merry heart goes all day.*

*The world is so full of a number of things,*
*I'm sure we should all be as happy as kings.*

A portion of the second-grade lesson-plan as outlined by Mrs. Vaughan included the following:

*Do not be satisfied until every child in your room can tell an excellent original story. . . . Make every language lesson an excellent lesson. A poor lesson does harm. It would be almost better to have no lesson at all.*[59]

The emphasis on our mastering the English language continued into the third grade and all grades thereafter. In the third grade, we were first introduced to the pen and ink. A small, partially embedded inkwell occupied the upper right-hand corner of each desk. Each child was also provided with a pen as well as a penholder. The pen and ink were used only when writing our compositions or during spelling tests. Oral language exercises in the third grade again included original stories as told with the aid of pictures and of course more quotations of the third grade variety.

*Who will remember the skies are gray*
*If he carries a happy heart all day.*

*A cheerful spirit gets on quick,*
*A grumbler in the mud will stick.*

By late September, we had already mastered all seven verses of "How The Leaves Came Down" by Susan Coolidge.

*"I'll tell you how the leaves came down."*
*The great tree to his children said.*
*"You're getting sleepy Yellow and Brown,*
*Yes, very sleepy little Red.*
*It is quite time you went to bed."*

113

In October we began to memorize that familiar Halloween song, "Jack-O-Lantern." We still remember not only the words but also the music.

> *Jack-O-Lantern, Jack-O-Lantern,*
> *You are such a funny sight,*
> *As you sit there in the window*
> *Looking out at the night.*
>
> *You were once a yellow pumpkin*
> *Growing on a sturdy vine,*
> *Now you are a Jack-O-Lantern*
> *See your candlelight shine.*

Quotations, by the time we were finishing the fourth grade, were only slightly longer and somewhat more thought-provoking.

> *Be sure you're right, then go ahead.*
>
> *He is a coward who will not turn back*
> *When first he discovers he's on the wrong track.*
>
> *If at first you don't succeed, try and try again.*

In the fourth grade we memorized several verses from "Hiawatha's Childhood" by Henry Wadsworth Longfellow. The beginning lines we still remember are:

> *By the shores of Gitche Gumee*
> *By the Shining Big-Sea-Water,*
> *Stood the wigwam of Nokomis,*
> *Daughter of the Moon, Nokomis.*

The fourth grade lesson plan outline suggested:

*Correct mistakes in English always at the time they are made. If on the other hand, a teacher neglects necessary corrections, mistakes increase. Bad English habits are formed and the need for correction grows. The frequent repetition of mistakes in any room is due only to poor teaching.*

*Pupils should be prepared at every language lesson to give a topic composition. Do not let the custom of being unprepared establish itself in your room. A pupil should respond as soon as his name is called.[60]*

The fifth grade curriculum was little changed, with more emphasis on composition and verbal expression. Quotations appeared to be of less importance but we still were expected to memorize poetry. A favorite poem in the fifth grade was "The Arrow and the Song" by Henry Wadsworth Longfellow which began, "I shot an arrow into the air. It fell to earth I know not where."

After completing the fifth grade our entire class was then transferred to the Washington School, a three-story brick building originally built in 1907 at a cost of $100,600. During the next year, it was to serve as a refuge for those residents rendered homeless by the Chisholm Fire of 1908. Originally constructed and used as the High School, in 1916 it was remodeled at a cost of $230,000 and was renamed the Washington School. The remodeled building had thirty-five classrooms including an auditorium capable of seating 750 people. The school was located on Second Avenue South between Spruce (Third) Street and Hemlock (Fourth) Street. The playground that was situated across Hemlock (Fourth) Street extended all the way to Poplar (Fifth) Street.

Moving from one grade level to another was always a source of some apprehension. Whereas we had always had only one teacher, except for the art, physical education and music supervisors who would visit our class at regular intervals, we were suddenly thrust into a three-teacher, rotating classroom arrangement. Though we were still assigned a primary homeroom, our fifth grade class from the Roosevelt School was joined by two fifth grade classes from the Washington School.

One of the sixth grade teachers taught English to all the classes, one taught history, and the third specialized in mathematics. Though there were no apparent academic advantages to the rotating class and teacher arrangement, it became quite obvious we were being prepared for the next step in the educational process—Junior High School.

Easing the transition to the Washington School and its rotating classroom and teacher routine was the fact that one of the teachers, Miss Rugna Gunderson, had been a classmate of our mother during her grade school days at Monroe Location.

Though we were again introduced to more poetry, the poem which stands out during our stay in the sixth grade is "Snowbound" by John Greenleaf Whittier. How appropriate that students living in northern Minnesota would be required to memorize a small portion of that famous poem. Who can ever forget that first verse?

> *The sun that brief December day*
> *Rose cheerless over hills of gray*
> *And, darkly circled, gave at noon*
> *A sadder light than waning moon.*
> *Slow tracing down the thickening sky*
> *Its mute and ominous prophecy,*
> *A portent seeming less than threat,*
> *It sank from sight before it set.*
> *A chill no coat, however stout,*
> *Of homespun stuff could quite shut out.*

If one is left with the impression that grade school was little more than a hard-core, never-ending, emphasis on mastering all phases of the English language, Mrs. Vaughan was probably more cognizant than many others that, "All work and no play makes Jack a dull boy."

Beginning in the fourth grade, several of our sessions with the music supervisor were designated as "Music Appreciation" time. It was during this period that we had our first exposure to classical music. Music was provided by recordings which were played on a Victrola, a large spring-activated phonograph, which was wheeled from room to room by the janitor under the close supervision of the music consultant. Not only were we expected to recognize the melody, but we also had to memorize the name of the composer and the country of his birth.

Classics included "In the Hall of the Mountain King" by the Norwegian composer Edvard Grieg as well as "Valse Trieste" by Jean Sibelius of Finland. Russia's contribution to our understanding of classical music included that portion of "The Nutcracker Suite" by Peter Tchaikovsky entitled, "The Dance of the Sugar Plum Fairy." The melody most of us appeared to be able to relate to was "The Song of the Volga Boatmen," a Russian folk tune arranged by the Russian composer Igor Stravinsky.

Considering the fact that most children of immigrant parents had never had any exposure to music other than the simple folk tunes as sung by their parents in the home or during festive events such as baptisms, birthdays, and weddings, classical music for many of us left much to be desired. Our music was simple folk music. By the time we were six to eight years of age, we had already memorized several verses of "Chervenna Rouzha" (Red Rose) and "Orano, Orano" (Plowing, Plowing), two Carpatho-Rusyn folk tunes.

Living in the midst of a Slavic neighborhood, we had no trouble mastering not only the music but also the lyrics to "Moja Dekla" (My Girlfriend) as well as "Kukavica" (Strange Bird). In fact we were even able to sing the chorus of those two Italian favorites: "Santa Lucia" (St. Lucy) and "O Marie" (Oh Mary). So classical music struck us as being way out.

Art appreciation provided us with our first exposure to some of the well-known art classics. Again, we were expected to be able to recognize the artwork and have some knowledge of the artist's background and country of origin.

In the Kosiak household, artwork in any form was limited to say the least. Little did we realize that the print of *The Last Supper* by Leonardo da Vinci, which had always hung on the wall above our kitchen table, was actually a copy of a classic painting. Displayed in the living room was a large framed picture of President Franklin D. Roosevelt, which remained there long after his death in 1945.

Because the family never subscribed to any magazines, Norman Rockwell's artwork, which was regularly featured on the covers of both *The Saturday Evening Post* and *Boys Life,* could only be appreciated during our visits to the local library. In our schools, Gilbert Stuart's portrait of George Washington was prominently displayed in virtually every classroom. We also got to discuss Emanual G. Leutze's *Crossing the Delaware*, a portrait depicting Washington's crossing of the Delaware River before attacking the British and Hessian troops the day after Christmas in 1776.

As part of "Art Appreciation," we soon came to recognize such classics as *Mona Lisa* painted by the Italian, Leonardo da Vinci, in 1506. *The Night Watch* by the Dutch artist Rembrandt van Ryn, *The Sower* by Jean-Francois Millet of France and *The Artist's Mother* by the American artist James Whistler were also studied.

That the Chisholm schools' attempt to enlighten our cultural lives was successful is demonstrated by the fact that most former students still vividly remember many of the works of art and music first presented to us more than a half-century ago.

# JUNIOR HIGH SCHOOL

Except for Johnny and Willy, we were all born and had lived all our lives directly across the street from the Chisholm Junior High School. However, the thought of going to school in that building was cause for some concern and anxiety. We were all aware of the fact that some students were known to flunk one of the grades, especially the eighth grade. To our knowledge, no one in grade school had ever been denied a promotion to the next higher class. Also of concern to us was the sheer size of the building, which covered an area equivalent to an entire city block. Although we lived across the street, few of us had ever been within the confines of the building except to attend athletic events in the gymnasium or a variety of programs presented in the auditorium.

Construction of the building, which literally straddled Third Avenue South between Hemlock (Fourth) Street and Poplar (Fifth) Street, was started in 1923. Partial occupancy began in 1924, and by 1925 the school was completely operational.

The three-story, H-shaped brick building faced to the north with the central core providing most of the classroom space. The west wing contained the gymnasium and swimming pool as well as a complete home economics department. The east wing of the building housed a state-of-the-art auditorium, including a balcony. The industrial arts department, which included a sheet-metal shop, a woodworking shop, a machine shop and an auto-mechanics shop, was also located in the east wing, as were the drafting shop, print shop and both the vocal and instrumental music departments.

To be sure, some of our initial anxiety was allayed somewhat by the fact that our entire sixth grade class from the Washington School was transferred practically intact to our homeroom in the Junior High School. Whatever consolation and comfort we may have derived from that situation was immediately counteracted by the massive influx of students from the Lincoln School, as well as the Monroe, Shenango, and Balkan schools.

In the early and mid-thirties, the people of Chisholm were a very homogeneous group. Basically, we all looked, acted and behaved pretty much alike and most of us were poor. So it wasn't the sudden influx of all these people from the north side of town that bothered us as it was their foreign-sounding names. Having been surrounded all our lives by persons of Slavic and Italian origin, we southsiders and location kids were suddenly deluged by students from the Lincoln School with names such as Anderson, Swanson, Peterson, Mattson, Williams, and Sullivan. After all, what were these people with such foreign-sounding names doing infringing on our territory? We had spent our entire lives on the south side and even the school was on our side of town.

However, after several weeks, we did become vaguely aware of the fact that the intermingling of children from both ends of town was potentially more of a problem for the northsiders than for the location and southside group. After all, any first grader who had mastered his flash cards could easily sound out names such as Swanson, Johnson, Anderson or even Ahola. On the other hand, even after several years of classroom exposure, the average ninth grader from the north side of town was still uncomfortable with the pronunciation of some Italian surnames such as Berarducci, Iannarelli, Pagliaccetti, Ciochetto, Franceschetti, or Detragiache. They didn't fare much better with Slavic surnames such as Perkovich, Smilanich, and Oreskovich—all southsiders. There were also the Monterottis, Kuriatnyks, and Namisniks from Monroe; Slaconiches and Rapkos from Shenango; Vukadinoviches, Dombrowskis, Simetkoskys, Beconoviches, and Kuharenkos from Lakeview. The north side, not to be outdone, offered such surnames as Gentilini, Zanoni, Kalafatich, and Pustoslemsek, all difficult to pronounce and impossible to spell.

Perhaps a somewhat greater problem than the family surnames was the wide variety of baptismal names, which were more often than not ethnically influenced to say the least. Our upbringing had, after all, taught us to never address any adults by their first names nor to address our peers by their surnames. Early exposure to such names while growing up in the location and southside neighborhoods resulted in general acceptance of the first names without question or concern. Though we had no problems pronouncing the names, we would have had considerable difficulty attempting to spell the names of some of our closest friends.

First generation children of immigrant Serbian, Italian and Finnish families appeared to have a monopoly on these strange-sounding names. The propensity for these ethnically rich baptismal names appeared to run in families, such as the family of Alphonso and Columba Valentini who had settled on Poplar (Fifth) Street just across the street from the Roosevelt School. According to son Frank, who was baptized Fransesco Florentino

119

Fortunato, the Valentinis appeared to adapt with some apprehension to the Americanization process as being actively promoted nationally and locally especially through the schools. The oldest son, Guiseppi, had his name changed to Joseph, Augustino became August while Marta, the only daughter, had her name changed to Mary. No attempt was made to Americanize the name of the third son, Valentine. Luigi became Louis, Quinto became Quentin and Giovanni became John. Attempts to Americanize the names Marbello and Fiorello were unsuccessful, while the youngest son's name was changed from Constantino to Constantine.[61]

Americanization of ethnic baptismal names of all the children of immigrant parents undoubtedly created a major problem for the school personnel. The problem was further complicated by the fact that not only were the children who were being given a name unfamiliar with the English language, but so were their parents. The entire procedure was not dissimilar from what the immigrant parents had experienced during their passage through Ellis Island, where unsympathetic immigration officers unfamiliar with the strange-sounding Italian, Slavic and Finnish names altered and actually provided names simply to the liking of the officer involved.

A child enrolling in the Chisholm school for the first time might leave home with the name of Guiseppi only to return home with the name Joseph. Goyko, when asked what he learned in his first day of school, would inform his parents that his name was really Gordon, not Goyko. Peka Paartinen did not fare much better. He excitedly ran all the way home after that first day of school to notify his Finnish immigrant parents that his name was really Peter not Peka. Though his teachers may have called him Peter, to his parents and his neighborhood friends, he was always Peka.

That this was not strictly a matter that concerned the children of immigrant families living on the south side of town was illustrated by the Lautizi, Zanoni and Gentilini families, who all lived on the north side of town. Whereas Ramaldo, the oldest child of Nazzareno and Fondino Lautizi, experienced no change in his baptismal name, the name of their second son Ferdinando was changed to Fred. The Lautizi girls fared about the same in that the oldest daughter Dionilla experienced no name change while Florica's name was changed to Florence, and Ferenziana became Phyllis.[62] Venancio Gentilini was known as Vincent Gentilini once he started school. Candido Zanoni was always Candido, while Gustavo Zanoni was always called Gustavo.

Other unusual Italian boys' names such as Premo, Secondo, Guido, and Umberto were never subjected to any Americanization changes. The same was true of young Italian girls whose names were Concetta, Leontina, and Giocondina.

Finnish boys' names such as Toivo, Eino, Konsto, and Risto were never altered while Wilho was changed to William, Jussie became John, and Olavi was changed to Oliver. Finnish girls whose names were Taimi, Impi, Lempi, or Mayme also escaped with their baptismal names intact.

Many children, especially those of Serbian heritage, confronted the schools with a myriad of unfamiliar names, many of which failed numerous attempts at Americanization. That this tendency appeared to be familial would again seem to demonstrate some resistance to the Americanization process by many of our immigrant parents.

Consequently, some Serbian children continued to carry their baptismal names throughout their entire school experiences. After all, what might one do to Americanize a name such as Nada, Nevanka, Milka, Bozilka, Borka, Grozdana, or Zvesdana? Draga, however, came to be known as Dorothy. Many of the boys' names also did not lend themselves to the Americanization process. Boys who were baptized Bronko, Merko, Bogdan, Dushan, Rade, Milo, and Slavko or even Zlatko never experienced a name change in their scholarly lifetime.

The Americanization of the immigrants' ethnic names prevailed throughout the pre-war years and was suddenly brought home to the Kosiak family when in 1942, I was asked by the senior class advisor how I would like my name listed on my graduation diploma. Somewhat surprised, I responded, "Mike is okay." I was even more surprised when the advisor replied, "You can't use Mike because Mike is not a name." After being called Mike for some twelve years of schooling, someone had determined that Mike was not really a name. The advisor suggested that using the name Michael would be more appropriate, and the folks had no objection. A quick trip to the Chisholm recorder's office resulted in a lifelong name change.

As one reflects on our early upbringing, one cannot fail to be impressed by the determination of our immigrant parents to maintain and preserve their ethnicity in spite of the never-ending pressures brought to bear by the community and the schools to Americanize as rapidly and completely as possible. Even with the schools' Americanizing of names, the proud traditions of these European settlers have prevailed over these past one hundred years as demonstrated by a wide range of organizations that still exist primarily to promote and preserve what remains of our European heritage.

As soon as we entered the Junior High School building, regimentation became the name of the game. The student walked, never ran, and always on the right side of the hall. Even when we were ninth graders, we would still pass from class to class walking two abreast, always on the right side of the hallway. Whispering while in transit was frowned upon— talking was absolutely prohibited.

The dress code was actually relaxed somewhat. Boys were no longer required to wear neckties. Rubber-toe boots and tennis shoes were still not allowed in the classroom. Girls wore slacks and snow pants under their skirts and dresses to and from school in cold weather, but these were always removed before going to class.

Academics presented no insurmountable challenges in that none of the family flunked out in the eighth grade. I did fail my Palmer Method writing course in the seventh grade, so that all through the eighth grade I had to go back to one of the seventh grade classes on a weekly basis in order to repeat the course. In all the twenty-some years that the Kosiaks collectively attended the Chisholm schools, we were never aware of any other child ever flunking the Palmer Method writing course.

In spite of the strict adherence to the English lesson plans as devised by Mrs. Vaughan, English never did appear to be a problem until we reached the eighth grade. Eighth grade English placed major emphasis on "Good Grammar" as used in "Good English."

It was in the eighth grade when we were suddenly introduced to the concept of "Diagramming," an activity to which most of us had never been exposed in the past. Hours of class work were expended on diagramming sentences concerning every subject matter known to man. We were barraged by terminology such as subject and predicate as well as noun, verb, adverb, adjective, not to mention participles and even dangling participles.

Statewide English examinations were conducted at least quarterly. Even the slightest evidence of erasure or rewriting was counted as a mistake. I reportedly established a rewrite record never equaled in the Chisholm schools in that while taking one of the State English Essentials Examinations, I not only rewrote over one word, I actually rewrote over an entire sentence. I was consoled when informed by my teacher that my rewriting the entire sentence resulted in the loss of only a single point, not one point for every word I had rewritten.

Industrial arts courses, covering the basics of woodwork, electricity, and sheet-metal work provided exposure to some equipment and procedures not found in the average home. Industrial arts was a required course in the seventh and eighth grade but optional in the ninth grade.

Home economics courses such as cooking and sewing were required seventh and eighth grade courses, while at the ninth grade level, home economics was an elective course. All levels of choral or instrumental music were encouraged, while swimming and physical education classes were conducted weekly at all class levels.

Other than the fact that the student's progress report was provided the parents only six times during the school year as compared to nine times while in the grades, the grading system was essentially unchanged except for the addition of one more grading category.

To the usual five separate letter grades, an additional classification of "Poor" utilizing the letter "P" was added. "P" (poor) was indicative of a classroom performance at or below the seventy-percent level or failure in the subject matter for the specific school period. However, the final grade was always arrived at by averaging out the performance of the entire school year. We're not sure as to how the final letter grade concerning the students' "Conduct" and "Effort" was determined. That grade probably was dependent primarily on the student's homeroom behavior.

Junior High School students were eligible for "Honor Roll" designation for the first time. Their standing and Honor Roll classification, which was recorded on the report card, was also published on a timely basis in both local weekly newspapers. My sisters almost always seemed to make A Honor Roll. Johnny and Willy alternated between A and B Honor Roll, and I always made Honorable Mention—about a C+ average.

Disciplinary measures, at times physically enforced by our principal, were responsible for keeping the Kosiak clan on a very level plane throughout our Junior High School years.

We did enjoy the luxury of being able to get to and from school in a matter of minutes in spite of the fact that we couldn't use the back doors to the school even in an emergency. In contrast, students living six or eight blocks north of Lake Street, or up to twelve blocks north of school, would have to traverse those distances four times each day, through rain, sleet, and snow in winter temperatures at times in the ten to twenty-degrees-below-zero range.

Extra-curricular activities while enrolled in the Junior High School were pretty seasonal. Most of the action was during the winter months when basketball was the number one sport. Teams that were formed primarily by grade level were somewhat dependent on the location of our homes. That is, there might be two or three teams from both the north and south sides] of town while students from Shenango, Monroe, and Balkan would each have one team. This arrangement prevailed at every grade level from the seventh through the ninth grade.

Coaches or advisers were some of the older students or even members of the varsity basketball team but never anyone's parents. The schools or the Chisholm Recreational Department provided the officials and scheduling was usually a simple round-robin arrangement to be repeated throughout the winter season. Although my brothers and I participated in these activities throughout our junior high careers, considerably more time was spent playing basketball in the back alley than was ever spent in the gym.

Completion of Junior High School was celebrated with a small graduation ceremony which was held in the auditorium, complete with musical accompaniment by the Junior High School Orchestra. No diplomas were issued, and our parents never did attend.

## SENIOR HIGH SCHOOL

Transition from the Junior to the Senior High School was less traumatic than going from grade school to the Junior High. We were already accustomed to the classroom and teacher rotation, and we had been advised through the grapevine that disciplinary measures were neither strict nor stringently enforced.

The Chisholm High School, a three-story brick structure is still located on Third Avenue South between Spruce (Third) Street and Hemlock (Fourth) Street. The west-facing building originally shared the entire block with the first High School, later designated as the Washington School. The High School playground occupies the entire block from Third to Fourth Avenue South and from Spruce (Third) Street to Hemlock (Fourth) Street.

The academic curriculum allowed for considerably more flexibility and course selection. All the basic foreign languages such as French, Spanish, and Latin were available.

English was again required all three years, with emphasis on composition and literature especially during the senior year. Though biology was required in the tenth grade, physics and chemistry were elective subjects available only in the junior and senior years.

Most of us followed the standard college-prep program: some math, some science and very limited foreign language. Mary Ann had two years of French and one year of Spanish, while Irene had two years of Latin. Considering the fact that none of us had any worldly plans, who needed another language?

Social and physiological changes resulting from the maturation process were more of a problem than the academic challenges in high school. The standard excuse for the boys' delayed social maturation was the fact that none of us, except Willy, owned a suit until a week or two before graduation. Suits were routinely ordered from the Richman Brothers of Cleveland, Ohio, and no date of delivery was ever guaranteed. Richman Brothers was a door-to-door, suit-selling operation in which the salesman came to the house with a book of stamp-sized cloth samples. Once the sale was completed, the salesman then took the appropriate measurements and forwarded the order to Cleveland with a suggested turnaround time of four to six weeks. Of course, because the salesman never returned, no alterations were ever possible.

Because I did not have a suit, I decided not to attend the athletic banquet in April of 1942. When the coach suggested that a sweater would be appropriate, I informed the coach that I still would not be attending because I did not own a sweater either.

My brown, double-breasted, wool graduation suit with vest, which arrived a week or two before graduation, cost Tato $17.50. For some reason, Willy got his suit in time for the junior prom. Incidentally, Willy wore the same suit to his medical school graduation seven years later. (Medical students in the forties did not receive their diplomas until they had successfully completed their one-year internship.)

As stated previously, academics presented no serious problems for our family. Mary Ann was elected to the National Honor Society in her senior year, while Irene was selected in both her junior and senior years.

In spite of the fact that the grading system remained unchanged from the "E" (excellent 94-100%) to "P" (poor less than 70%), the passing mark was still seventy-five. This meant that students with an "F" average were able to pass a course. Absenteeism and tardiness were still recorded, but conduct and effort were no longer evaluated or graded.

Although interscholastic athletic activities had traditionally played a major role in the Chisholm High School curriculum, the Kosiak family participation was rather limited. Although Johnny was always actively involved especially in the intramural basketball program at all grade levels, he made no attempt to participate at the varsity level. Willy played both B-squad and varsity basketball but left the varsity team in his senior year because of lack of playing time. I also participated in the basketball program, on the B-squad in my junior year and as a member of the varsity in my senior year.

Of considerable interest is the fact that the team Willy played for in 1940 advanced to the Minnesota State Tournament. We think Chisholm was the consolation champion that year. The team I played on two years later lost out in the district tournament in two overtime periods to Buhl, the school that went on to win the state basketball championship in 1942.

Of special interest on the subject of high school athletics was Willy's determination to be involved. Though he was born with a congenital heart defect, it never appeared to hinder his activity. However, Dr. A.W. Graham, our school doctor, decided that Willy would not be allowed to play varsity basketball in his senior year. With support from Tato and encouragement from Dr. Graham, Willy hitchhiked alone to Duluth to be evaluated by a cardiology consultant who determined that he could indeed participate in the basketball program. To this day, we're not sure who paid for the consultation.

Our educational careers in the Chisholm school system were concluded with impressive graduation ceremonies conducted in the Junior High School Auditorium. For the occasion, my brothers and I had all been fitted with suits, the first any of us had ever owned. The girls usually got new dresses and had the chance to wear high-heeled shoes to school for the first time. Entering the auditorium to the solemn strains of Schubert's "March Militaire" we were then privileged to listen to both the valedictory and salutatory comments by the outstanding students in our respective classes. (Irene gave the valedictory speech for her class.) After the commencement address by a well-known educator, we were presented our diplomas. We then departed our school experiences to the resounding beat of Verdi's "Triumphal March" from Aida.

So ended the scholarly, undergraduate pursuits of the entire Kosiak family.

Reflecting on our entire education in the Chisholm schools tends to remind us of that old refrain, "School days, school days, dear old Golden Rule days."

Although all the rules and regulations imposed on the students of the Chisholm schools may not have seemed golden, history has proved their effectiveness in providing the people of Chisholm during the first fifty years of the town's existence with one of the finest educational systems in all of America.

# 8

# *Educators*

JAMES P. VAUGHAN
February 22, 1882 – March 25, 1965

James Patrick Vaughan was born on February 22, 1882, in Eyota, Minnesota, a small town in Olmstead County. After graduating from high school, from 1898 to 1902 he attended Winona State Teachers College (later Winona State University). In 1905, after serving for three years as principal in the North Branch School District, he enrolled at the University of Wisconsin where, in 1907, he was awarded the degree of Bachelor of Philosophy. In May of 1907, Mr. Vaughan accepted the position of superintendent of the Chisholm School System where he served until retiring on July 31, 1948.[63]

Soon after his retirement, he and Mrs. Vaughan moved to Duluth where Mr. Vaughan served on the Board of Directors of the Alworth Memorial Scholarship Fund from its beginning on July 15, 1949. That Mr. Vaughan continued his interest in Chisholm graduates was demonstrated by the fact that of eleven students from St. Louis County chosen to receive scholarships that first year, two were from Chisholm. Sister Irene was the only high school senior selected that year—receiving $300 to attend Hibbing Junior College. Along with Alve Erickson, a 1947 graduate, they were the first of numerous Chisholm students who would benefit from the Alworth Scholarship Fund.

Mr. Vaughn died in Duluth on March 25, 1965. With his wife, Leathe, he is buried at the Calvary Cemetery in Rochester.[64]

# BUILDER

*One may see in such buildings... a new expression of the genius of American Democracy. (That is to say): that the institution which embodies the most characteristic expression of American democratic ideals be housed in homes expressive of the highest of American artistic ideals.*

—L.H. Weir

Only 250 people were living in Chisholm at the time it was incorporated on July 23, 1901. That year the first school building, a wood-frame structure, was built on the corner of what is now Central Avenue South and Hemlock (Fourth) Street. Known as Central School, it survived the fire of 1908 but was completely destroyed by fire on the night of January 7, 1912.

Prior to Mr. Vaughan's arrival, Chisholm was part of the Hibbing School District, which provided all facilities, personnel, and educational materials. In 1903, twenty-eight sections of land were set aside and organized as Common School District 45 of St. Louis County. In 1909, by voter referendum, the Chisholm schools were separated from Hibbing control and were designated as Independent School District 40. Voters also increased the size of the school board from three to six members. Chisholm's first school superintendent was J.F. Muench, who served for five years until 1907 when James P. Vaughan was appointed to the position.

School buildings in existence in 1907, in addition to the original Central School, included the Myers School, a two-room, wood-frame structure which was built in 1903 and enlarged to six rooms in 1906.

The Myers School was closed in 1933.

Myers Grade School, 1903-1933.

The Monroe Grade School, also a two-room, wood-frame structure, was first opened for classes in 1907. Additions to the school were effected in both 1910 and 1911. When completed in 1911, the school consisted of ten separate classrooms.

The Monroe School was closed in 1940.

Monroe Grade School, 1907-1940.
Courtesy of the Iron Range Research Center, Chisholm

Mr. Vaughan's arrival in Chisholm in 1907 coincided with the completion of the "Old High School" situated at the corner of Second Avenue South between Spruce (Third) and Hemlock (Fourth) Streets. The enrollment at the time of the opening was 584 pupils with fourteen teachers. The brick building, built at a cost of $100,000, survived the fire of 1908, and for the next year, it served as a refuge for residents rendered homeless by the disastrous Chisholm fire. In 1916-1917, after extensive remodeling costing some $200,000, the building was converted into a grade school to be known as Washington Grade School. Two wings of twelve classrooms and fireproof stairways were added to the building at that time.

Several major problems confronted Mr. Vaughan when he became superintendent of the Chisholm schools. The area's population had exploded from 250 in 1901 to 7,684 persons only nine years later, creating an urgent need for elementary schools in the various mining locations.

Old High School, 1907-1917
(Converted to Washington Grade School, 1917) (Courtesy of the Minnesota Historical Society)

Because the mining companies were responsible for a major portion of the school tax levy, maintaining good location schools was also good public relations policy. The well-educated mining engineers and administrators usually lived in the locations. They insisted on not only keeping the location schools but also providing them with excellent buildings and educational programs, both to attract workmen and for the benefit of their own children and their neighborhood's pride. Consequently, "School boards erected fine new buildings explicitly designed to serve as social centers from which Americanizing influences might reach directly into the workers' families."[65]

The location schools, as described by Bell, were also perceived as examples that introduced American values into immigrant homes. "Their polished hardwood floors, electric lights, telephones, running water and mysterious indoor toilets contrasted sharply with the ones from which the children came."[66]

"The location school was like a bridge for these immigrants," wrote George Chanak, remembering his childhood at Alice Addition near Hibbing.

132

*On one side was the little mining location, a world of our own. On the other side was the outside world, primarily town. Soon we would have to cross the bridge. For many, the crossing was but the first step in a long migration, which would end only at Los Angeles or New York, Chicago or Washington, D.C. But others must cross the bridge first in the opposite direction: visiting nurses, doctors, Americanization workers, and teachers, bearing the books and films, the medicine and the skills, which would slowly transform the lives of children and their parents as well.*[67]

Additional outlying schools constructed early in Mr. Vaughan's tenure included the Shenango School (1910) and the Balkan School (1911). There were sixty pupils and two teachers in the two-room, wood-frame Shenango School when it first opened in 1910. In 1926, while being remodeled, the building was destroyed by fire but was rebuilt and reopened the next year.

The Shenango Grade School was closed in 1940.

Shenango Grade School, 1910-1940. (Courtesy of the Minnesota Historical Society)

Built in 1911, the Balkan Grade School was initially a two-room, wood-frame structure which was enlarged in 1920. The school at that time included four classrooms, up-to-date plumbing, heating and lighting as well as living quarters for the staff.

The Balkan Grade School was closed in 1940.

Balkan Grade School, 1911-1940.

Although the total village population tended to level off soon after 1910, school enrollment almost tripled in the next ten years from 1,081 students in 1910 to 2,890 students in 1920. The explosive growth in the grade school population necessitated the building of an additional grade school. Since in 1910, all grade school students living in town attended classes at either the Central School or the High School (Washington), both on the south side of town, it was determined that the new school should be built north of Lake Street.

The Lincoln Grade School, located on Third Avenue North between Cedar (Fifth) and Willow (Seventh) Street, was built in 1911 at a cost of $115,000. Reported to be the first fireproof grade school in Minnesota,

500 students and twenty-five teachers were assigned to classes when it opened on January 8, 1912, just one day after the Central Grade School was totally destroyed by fire.

Lincoln School.    CHISHOLM, Minn.

Lincoln Grade School, 1911-1979.
Courtesy of the Iron Range Research Center, Chisholm

L.H. Weir, in his report submitted to the Chisholm School Board in 1915, described the Lincoln School as follows:

> *The Lincoln grade school is in no way inferior, except it is not built upon so elaborate a scale as the High School. The Lincoln building has been in use almost four years yet the construction work was so well done and the care of the building has been so perfect that one gets the impression from an inspection of it that it is an absolutely new building.*[68]

Coinciding with the rapid increase in system-wide enrollment was the even more rapid increase in the number and percentage of students requiring secondary-school services. Whereas in 1910 there were fewer than fifty students enrolled in the secondary grades out of a total enrollment of 1,081, by 1915 this number had nearly tripled to more than 130 students.

Chisholm High School, located at Third Avenue South, between Spruce (Third) and Hemlock (Fourth) streets, was completed in 1915.

Chisholm High School.
Courtesy of the Iron Range Research Center, Chisholm

L.H. Weir described the building as follows:

*The new High School is without a doubt, from the standpoint of exterior design, arrangement, equipment and evident high-grade workmanship shown in construction throughout one of the finest High School buildings in the country. These buildings are not fac-*

*tory or barn like structures. Nothing seems to be wanting in them from the standpoint of their efficient use in a material sense, and at the same time one is conscious everywhere and all the time, in going about in them, of a quality of beauty and quiet restfulness that must unconsciously influence for good the lives of the children who spend a few years within their walls. I believe this combination of art and utility in material environment is of great importance in the training of boys and girls.*

*One may see in such buildings as the above a new expression of the genius of American Democracy. [That is to say]: that the institution which embodies the most characteristic expression of American democratic ideals be housed in homes expressive of the highest of American artistic ideals.*[69]

Completion of the High School in 1915 was soon to be followed by extensive remodeling of the old High School and its conversion into the Washington Grade School. This remodeling project was completed in 1917.

Washington Grade School, 1917-1968.

The need for more classrooms for grade school students resulted in the building of the Roosevelt Grade School, located on First Avenue South between Hemlock (Fourth) and Poplar (Fifth) streets. The three-story brick building, erected at a cost of $300,000, opened in 1922 with an enrollment of 500 students.

Roosevelt Grade School, 1921-1979.

Superintendent Vaughan's final and undoubtedly most impressive structural accomplishment in Chisholm involved the planning, design, and construction of the Junior High School building. Contracts on the building were first awarded in 1923. Partial occupancy of the building, which cost $800,000, was possible by September of 1924. A comprehensive description of the school as published in the September 1925 issue of *The Minnesota Journal of Education* is as follows:

*In the Junior High School of Chisholm, Minnesota, dedicated in February 1925, is exemplified the prevailing tendency to combine*

138

Chisholm Junior High School, 1925.
Courtesy of the Iron Range Research Center, Chisholm

*efficiency with beauty. Even those accustomed to seeing this happy combination of the aesthetic and the utilitarian will be impressed by the effectiveness with which this double aim has been accomplished.*

*Tudor gothic in architecture, of soft-toned brick, it is an imposing structure nearly a block in length. It is built upon the unit plan which fits it for both school and community activities. Though each section has its outside entrance, they are all in direct communication. It closes, on three sides, a court whose brick walks and curving drive surround a central plot of flowerbeds.*

*The academic unit, which includes the general offices, classrooms, and library, occupies the three stories of the central section. The right is the "health" section, also opening upon the court. It includes the spacious, well-equipped gymnasium surrounded by roomy balconies for the accommodation of spectators; the carefully regulated showers, and dressing and locker rooms and the green and white tiled natatorium with its beautiful large pool. Across the central hall in the same section is the home economics department with completely modern sewing and cooking rooms, laundry and the cafeteria with its facilities for efficient service and its attractively painted furniture.*

*The left-hand section houses, in the rear part of the first floor, the industrial department with its numerous shops and display rooms for wood and metal work, and the print shop; on the second floor are the art rooms and the three music rooms which open into each other, and communicate, by means of stairways, with the auditorium, making easy access to stage and orchestra pit. The auditorium, Elizabethan in design, with a seating capacity of fifteen hundred, occupies the two stories of the front portion. In seating, lighting, and general arrangement, it is the peer of a metropolitan theater, while in artistry and simplicity of design, it surpasses most.*

*Upon viewing the Junior High School of Chisholm, one is particularly impressed by its perfection of detail. On the side of efficiency nothing has been overlooked, from the most economical general arrangement to the most satisfactory ventilation and heating systems and the arrangement of bulletin boards in the halls. On the side of beauty, from the harmonizing tones of the inlaid floors of the silent halls, the softly-gleaming finish of the library shelves, the groined arches of the gymnasium entrance and the colorful tiles and rich lamps of the foyer of the auditorium down to the classroom bookcases and even the iron work of the fire balconies, there is not an inharmonious note.*[70]

# EDUCATOR

*. . . it is these young men and women and others like them, who have had the advantages of the opportunities which the public schools afford, who constitute at its best both the history and the*

*prophecy of education in America. They are its product; they must be its justification.*

—J.P. Vaughan

At some time early in his career as Superintendent of Schools, Mr. Vaughan outlined his views on education in an undated report entitled, *Objectives in Education.*

*My thought is to consider as a major objective of education the inculcating in our boys and girls the character and conscience conditions of civilization that will make men and women of them — men and women with the qualities of mind and heart and body that will insure success in their personal relations with their fellows, and make them responsive to the rewards of social approval. We shall do this, not by the stressing of mere information nor by considering the school as a place merely to acquire academic knowledge, but by selecting socially significant problems of gradually increasing difficulty, assuring ourselves all the while that pupils persist, that they are helped at strategic times over difficult stages, and thus succeed in each successive task.*

*This habit of success in the face of difficulty, which is but the prelude to a habit of achievement in later life, is but another name for a strong will. No program of education is sound that leaves out effort and struggle with the joy of discovery and conquest. Have we not seen all too many examples of those who have never known the satisfaction that comes through surmounting obstacles that obstruct their paths and who in consequence become weak and vacillating and wayward? Of course, we shall not introduce hardship for its own sake, any more than we shall evade it, but rather shall we take advantage of the natural interactions between self and surroundings in which problems capitulate to purpose and the resultant satisfaction breeds the requisite enthusiasm for the next endeavor. The critical thing is to see that the result of the encounter benefits the individual, develops responsibility, trains in cooperation and helpfulness and teaches the efficacy of social approval.*[71]

Confronting Mr. Vaughan and all other educators of the Iron Range was the fact that according to the 1910 Federal Census, the percentage of foreign-born in the mining towns ranged from forty-eight percent in Ely to fifty-eight percent in Chisholm. This was more than double the proportion in other Minnesota cities with the exception of Duluth and South St. Paul that showed percentages of thirty-nine and thirty-eight percent respectively.

The primary barrier to the immigrant child's progress, which seemed most obvious, was his foreign language. The plan then adopted by all the Iron Range schools was to place all the children in kindergarten for at least a year before admitting them to regular first grade classes. Of interest is the fact that in many of the major cities of America, efforts to establish kindergartens in the public schools continued to encounter strong opposition.

Although the one-year experience at the kindergarten level did serve to introduce many of the children to the English language for the first time,

*At Chisholm however, J.P. Vaughan and the language teacher who later became his wife realized very early that in a community where a large minority of adults could speak English and a majority did not use it in their homes, more extensive measures were required. Mrs. Vaughan, who had studied under Francis W. Parker in Chicago, worked out very carefully an entirely new program of language instruction, stretching from the kindergarten through the twelfth grade. Every child in every grade beyond the first wrote something of his own composition in the English language every day.*

*Children in the first grade memorized nursery rhymes before they learned to read and write. Repeating these before the class gave them confidence in their ability to talk English. This led naturally to making up and telling stories of their own, based upon a simple picture which the teacher wrote down for them. Then followed, year by year, sentences, paragraphs, poems, essays and continuous experience in extemporaneous speech. Precise enunciation and correct grammar was an obsession in every classroom.*[72]

John Syrjamaki noted:

*From the earliest years the Range educators took a serious view of the particular difficulties which faced them. The predominant share of their students were second-generation immigrants, many of whom, in the years prior to 1920, arrived in the kindergarten or first grade knowing their mother tongue but little if any English. They represented, furthermore, a wide diversity of nationalities and cultures, making much more difficult the problem of dealing with them. The cultural standards in their homes were low, and no educational tradition existed in the lives of their parents. Having been nurtured in immigrant homes, the pupils had been better pre-pared to live as citizens in the land of their parents' birth than in the United States. The adults were not themselves adequately adjusted for life in the New World, and could not, therefore, furnish proper guidance to their children.*

*The Range educators fell upon the adoption of two policies by which to handle the situation which they faced: to practice com-plete non-discrimination between nationalities in their treatment of students, and to supply through the schools the cultural training which was lacking in the homes. In this first policy they have been pre-eminently successful. Even during the initial decades very infrequent cases of prejudice or hostility toward immigrant children occurred in the schools, despite the fact that antagonisms between the ethnic groups were prevalent in the communities. Their effort in the second instance, to furnish a cultural training to their students, has been one of the basic motivations in the enlargement and thor-oughness with which the schools and their educational activities have been administered.*

*In practice the policy of non-discrimination in the treatment of school children came to mean a virtual denial by the educators of the existence of diverse nationalities in the school population. They dealt with the pupils as if they were all native-born Americans of native-born parentage, and without any important cultural differ-ences among them.*[73]

Smith made note of the fact that:

*The children of immigrants generally, not just those from one country or culture, revealed immense enthusiasm for education. Given the favorable social and economic conditions such as those developed in Chisholm and the rest of the Iron Range, those children of Eastern and Southern European immigrants performed as well or better than the children of those parents who had come to America earlier.*

*More significant even than the record of individual students is that of families. Again and again when we inquired into the background of an outstanding individual, we found that brothers and sisters were also highly successful. This would seem to indicate that more than a spotting of individual excellence was taking place. Rather, the Range schools were generating the ambition, the means, and the know-how to get ahead in the community at large, and entire families were affected.*[74]

Smith also noted:

*The establishment of municipal junior colleges in Range towns was . . . an appropriate extension of the educational ladder. In 1916, when Hibbing announced plans to inaugurate a junior college, only sixteen other cities in the entire nation, six of these in Los Angeles County, California, could boast such an institution under municipal auspices. Yet during the next five years Eveleth, Virginia, Ely and Coleraine established one in their towns as well.*

*Students who could afford it were urged to go elsewhere to college; those who remained were, as Claude Alexander (Superintendent of Hibbing Schools, 1915-1924) put it, told that the work is to be made as difficult as the same work at the University and that laggards would be forced to drop out. "This course was not put in as a fad," Alexander added, "but to give opportunity for those who are not financially able to go away to school." What it provided, of course, was an important halfway house to college, entirely free of charge, to students who otherwise would never have dared to try.*[75]

Although Mr. Vaughan encouraged advanced training for many of the early graduates, he appeared to be especially supportive of the children of Finnish, Italian and Slavic families whose completion of college and graduate professional schools would serve as models, Horatio Alger style, for the rest.

That Vaughan's strategy was successful was evident when one compares a complete list of all the graduates from Chisholm High School for the years between 1908 and 1925 who went to college or advanced schooling. Whereas prior to 1917, students bearing Anglo-Saxon or Scandinavian names comprised a majority of those graduates attending college, by 1919, ". . . fifty-five percent of the graduates from Eastern and Southern European families went on to higher schools as compared with only thirty-six percent of the rest."[75]

On June 22, 1928, soon after completion of the new Junior High School, Superintendent Vaughan in a speech to the St. Louis County Historical Society noted:

*This material provision of school facilities parallels the constant increase in enrollment of students until the maximum of 3,688 was reached in 1926. This represents thirty-six percent of the total population of the district—almost twice the percentage found in the average community throughout the country. In addition, more than eleven hundred adults, the maximum attending evening school, swelled the total ten percent so that forty-six percent of the total population has been in attendance in the public schools at one time.*

*These evening schools were begun in 1909, largely with the purpose of opening the avenues of intelligence through an understanding of the language of our country to those newly come to our shores, and to familiarize them with our traditions and imbue them with American ideals.*

*The school curriculum has grown with the buildings and enrollment. The three R's are no longer sufficient for the training of young people to take their proper place in the New World, which thought, and science and industry are ever recreating.*

*In 1906 the first student was graduated from the High School, Miss Mildred Shane. One hundred thirty seniors completed the high school course in 1928. A large number of these young men and women will continue their education at universities and colleges to swell the numbers of previous classes in attendance at some thir-*

*ty institutions of higher learning and training throughout the land. And it is these young men and women and others like them, who have had the advantages of the opportunities which the public schools afford, who constitute at its best both the history and the prophecy of education in America. They are its product; they must be its justification. What they have wrought out in character and appreciation and will, often in the face of adversity, is imperishable, while brick and stone and mortar will crumble into dust. Their lives and the lives of all of these pioneers, who have planned for them or worked with them, will go on in the immortality of their deeds. Victor Hugo says, "The beautiful is often more useful than the useful," and so the intangible and the spiritual are more real and more enduring than the material itself. The true measure of the growth and development of education must be furnished by the lives and achievements of the oncoming generation.*[76]

## COMMUNITY LEADER

*The school was fast becoming the heart of the village . . . a center not only for academic instruction of the young, but for the recreational, cultural and social life of the adults as well.*

—L.H. Weir

In 1962, Timothy L. Smith noted the following concerning Superintendent Vaughan.

*Vaughan wrote in 1914 that whenever immigration reaches a "saturation point" in any community, "some consciously constituted agency must act as an instrument of civilization." The agency assuming this role, he continued, should preserve those elements of the immigrant's inheritance "such as reverence for authority, [and] love of art and music" which would help to "soften the materialism that tends to accompany our industrial progress." By this means also, he believed, "the break in home ties" that made for "lawlessness in the second generation" might be moderated. The conjunction of the idea of respect for authority and the love of art and music was not accidental; the image of the orchestra conductor closely fit the position*

146

*Vaughan consciously sought, and rapidly gained, in the life of his lit-tle immigrant town.*[77]

Smith also reported:

*L.H. Weir, executive secretary of the Playground and Recreation Association of America, spent the summer of 1915 surveying the social environment of the Virginia and Chisholm school systems, designing an extensive program of public recreation for each town. His long report to the Chisholm board began with praise for the "spirit of community service" which characterized the work of J.P.Vaughan and his teachers. "The school was fast becoming the heart of the village," he wrote, "a center not only for academic instruction of the young, but for the recreational, cultural and social life of adults as well." He saw great promise in the public interest in high school musical and dramatic programs, the six events in the annual lecture and concert series, extensive adult use of the new gymnasium, the social aspects of the night school and what was obviously one of the nation's finest systems of health care for children.*[78]

# HEALTH CARE

Medical care for children arose from the medical services provided by mining company doctors, as many of them were elected to the school boards. Because of the apparent inability of the most recent immigrant families to readily adjust to the increasingly restrictive sanitary conditions of the New World, in 1907 the Eveleth school contracted for the half-time services of a doctor. One year later, the Eveleth School Board approved the appointment of a visiting nurse.

Following these initial efforts to improve health, the schools determined that it was ineffective to provide health care and health education in schools without reaching into the homes.

Smith reported:

*At Chisholm, for example, in 1917, a full-time physician and nurse made over 5,000 routine inspections, gave every one of the 1,239*

147

*school children a complete physical examination, and made 1,474 calls at homes. They held daily clinics for children needing corrective exercises, fitted glasses at no cost, gave baths to unkempt youngsters "when necessary," and initiated the long famous "tooth brush drill," which for decades thereafter required every child to wash his teeth before going home each day. The school spent nearly $850.00 for medical and dental equipment that year, as compared with $82.00 for athletic supplies and $200.00 for band and orchestra instruments.*

*At Hibbing, both soup and soap were added to the program of educational salvation in 1916. Superintendent Claude Alexander became convinced that malnutrition retarded the mental development of children, and provided hot lunches in the city and at two location schools for those who did not have proper nourishment at home. "The teachers at almost every location school," he reported also, "are seeing that the pupils take baths and keep their clothes clean. The school furnishes towels and soap and the teachers do the work."*

*Meanwhile, the school doctor and three visiting nurses were busy treating both major and minor ailments, holding hygiene conferences with parents in the locations, and rounding up undernourished and anemic children for the "open-air" class which they believed would forestall tuberculosis. The equipment of the new junior and senior high school buildings with fine gymnasiums and swimming pools during this decade was more than an extravagant gesture. It signaled the beginning of a highly competent program of physical education and recreation, both in the schools and . . . in the communities as well.*[79]

## NIGHT SCHOOL

Night schools, which originated in Virginia before 1907, began as private endeavors supported by the mining companies. These were soon taken over by the public school system. In the fall of 1909, 175 adults enrolled in Chisholm for a seven-month term, two evenings a week. Whereas, originally the majority of students were men, by 1917 an almost equal number of women were enrolled. During the two decades, 1920 and 1930, women enrolled in the night school in ever-increasing numbers.

*At Chisholm in 1913-1914, 493 students attended an average of twenty-one nights each, many of them trudging two or three miles each way from location to school. . . . All towns had afternoon classes for night-shift workers, and in all large numbers of young people aged [sixteen to twenty-one] attended—in Chisholm, as many as one-fourth of the total enrollment. Some of the latter may have been completing high school courses interrupted by jobs or marriage, but many were recent arrivals from Europe, learning how to make a place for themselves in America.*[80]

It was during this period that our father, who in 1914 was twenty years old, availed himself of the benefits of Chisholm's night school program. His classroom attendance was probably marginal at best, for he referred to his educational experience as being "once in a while." We do know for certain that he never came close to completing the recommended seven-month English course. Perhaps part of the problem may have been due to the fact that classes were conducted in Chisholm, a half-hour's walk from Glen Location.

*The curriculum of the night schools tended to be divided into two parts: special instruction for the foreign-born with the purpose of assisting them to secure naturalization papers, and academic and industrial courses in adult education. Graded classes in English and citizenship were provided for the aliens to help them to meet the requirements for naturalization. . . . In the Chisholm night school in 1915-1916, instruction was given in the common school subjects, including civics, manual training, mechanical, machine, and architectural drawing, cooking, sewing, shorthand, typing, painting, agricultural, book-keeping, and physical education.*[81]

The desire of the immigrants to exercise their rights as Americans was reported by Smith as follows:

*The immigrant's interest in night schools stemmed partly from his desire to win the right to vote, while the educators were concerned that the student be equipped to exercise the right properly. . . . The federal law of 1906 required candidates [for citizenship] to speak English, but made no further educational demands. Its principal effect in the mining region was to restrict naturalization hearings for several years to the United States District Court at Duluth. This made the worker's acquisition of citizenship difficult . . . since he must pay train fare for his witnesses as well as himself to the county seat. But it also gave school superintendents in the Range towns time in which to develop a program of education for citizenship which went far beyond what the law required, and met many other social needs as well.*[82]

Many of the adults attending night school were illiterate even in their own language, so it was a major challenge to teach them to speak, read and write English. Relying on the specialized language program developed by Mrs. J.P. Vaughan, the night school principals settled on a strategy of teaching entirely in English, using conversation and imitation as well as objects and concrete experiences as a basis of communication, rather than trying to teach formal rules of grammar.

Smith described the course as follows:

*The English course required a minimum of two years, three nights a week, from early October to the end of April. Citizenship classes were open only to those who had achieved a working knowledge of English—sufficient to read a newspaper intelligently.*

*The immigrant had other reasons for seizing the opportunity to learn English, however. Mastery of the language would . . . help the newcomer get a better job, improve his relationships with his school-educated children, and hasten his acceptance in the community.*

*The superintendents were certain that widespread participation in night class was an important factor in uniting the interests of entire families in the public schools and in eliminating much of the estrangement between the generations that characterized immigrant life elsewhere in America.*[83]

Syrjamaki noted:

*. . . the adults, themselves attending classes in the public schools buildings, were slowly won over to the support of education for their own children. They came better to understand the American system of schools because many of their own instructors were those who taught the children during the day, and could make more intimate the life and activities involved in the process of education. No small numbers of teachers were persons interested in night school instruction, who consciously endeavored to be of value to the adults.*[84]

## COMMUNITY-WIDE RECREATION

*The development of community wide recreational programs under public school experience seems almost as important as the night school in knitting together the people of the Mesabi towns around a common devotion to education. The recreation movement grew nationally from this intent in health education and the playground and gymnasium activities of the summer and night schools.*

—T.L. Smith

Along with the schools of Eveleth and Virginia, J.P. Vaughan in 1915 contracted with L.H. Weir of the Recreation Association of America to assess each community's recreational needs.

Smith went on to report:

*At Chisholm in the early twenties, Fred J. Lipovetz, who had earned a graduate degree in physical education at Columbia directed during the summer a large staff of teachers and college students, most of them sons or daughters of immigrant miners, but one, at least, the daughter of a mining captain. . . . The average daily participation reached nearly 2,000 during the summer of 1925, or 20% of the population of the town, by far the highest percentage achieved by any summer recreation program in the state. Three other Range communities, Ely, Hibbing, and Virginia ranked in the top five.*[85]

## SPECIAL EDUCATION

*The Eveleth schools initiated summer sessions in 1909, declaring their purpose to be "to provide means for those who failed to pass in any subject" to make their deficiency up before the regular term opened in the fall. . . . Students with Anglo-Saxon names seem to have sought this help in as large number as those whose families were from Eastern and Southern Europe.*

*The programs of special education and the summer schools organized in the Range schools after 1910 also demonstrate how closely superintendents there kept abreast of new educational ideas. They reveal as well their determination to help the newcomers' children measure up, rather than to water the educational program down.*

*Nationwide concern for retardation among immigrant youngsters stemmed partly from a report of the Russell Sage Foundation on that subject and partly from the findings of the United States Immigration Commission published in 1911.*[86]

(The Russell Sage Foundation, incorporated in 1910, was an institution whose aim was "to remove the causes of poverty and allow people to earn enough to have sanitary homes, wholesome food and healthy children.")[87]

*The following year a national meeting of school superintendents called for a study of "exceptional children," a phrase which included those who were retarded, tubercular, or gifted. . . . Indeed, Hibbing, Duluth, and Minneapolis were the first three systems in the state to institute special education programs. After 1915, when the legislature made provision for state aid, the remaining Range towns joined Hibbing at the head of the parade. By 1922, the school districts located in St. Louis County employed thirty-four full-time teachers in special education classes, compared with twenty-five in Hennepin and twenty in Ramsey County, and only a scattering of individual teachers in other counties. Moreover, the Range towns sought much earlier than others to distinguish*

152

*between retardation arising from low mentality and that which was due to social or economic privation.*[88]

# TEACHER TRAINING

Superintendent Vaughan was most instrumental in the development of the post-graduate teacher-training program on the Iron Range. The state-subsidized program was developed as a means of relieving the shortage of qualified teachers in rural schools. Many of the early graduates were placed in the one-room schoolhouses located in St. Louis County.

Smith reported:

*The four Range schools which participated, Eveleth, Hibbing, Virginia and Chisholm, carefully selected as teacher candidates bright girls who could not afford to go directly from high school to college. Enthusiasm for school teaching among graduates of Range high schools seemed greater than usual. Perhaps this was due in part to the high status which teachers enjoyed in a community where the number of professions which could serve as models for the young was narrow. The image of service, however, rather than the salary must have been the compelling one; for despite large expenditures for other things, the mining towns never paid teachers more than a small percentage above the maximums elsewhere in the state.*[89]

# SUMMARY

Summarizing the impact of public education on the citizens of Chisholm and the Iron Range in the first half of the twentieth century, Smith noted:

*Thus it was that the European peasant, who had submitted in one decade to the disciplines of industrial labor embraced in the next the organization of his leisure. It was perhaps well that he learned both lessons within the span of one generation, and under the same teachers who were teaching them to his children. No deep moral or psychological conflict ever grew up in the region between the duty of toil and the love of play.*

*How broad the synthesis of public commitment to education became in this isolated region is evident, finally, from the series of great new high school buildings, which the Range towns erected in the latter part of the decade. Their ostensible purpose was to pro-vide the facilities necessary both for an expanding teen-age popu-lation and for the multiplying adult activities which took place with-in their walls. Viewed thus, the buildings signified nothing new. Schools on the Range had always been substantial; even in the earlier decade they were the largest and, next to the hotels, the best-appointed structures in town.*

*Indeed, temples these buildings were, shrines to the faith in edu-cation which had captured the allegiance of both rich and poor, new and old Americans. The tiny churches scattered about the vil-lage or nestling up against the school grounds seemed, by contrast with the cathedrals, which dominated European towns, forlorn reminders of a past that was forever gone. Gleaming in the sun-light, which bathed their hilltop campuses, cleaned and polished by the loving attention of custodians, to whom the superintendents had imparted their fierce zeal for cleanliness, these grand build-ings worked a subtle alchemy in the minds of newcomers. Two physical features stood out prominently in the Range communities: In the midst of all the school, and at town's edge the yawning pit. Only one bore promise for the future.*

*. . . So it was that men and women who had come by ones and twos from remote villages in the vast crescent stretching from Sweden's Lapland to Italy's toe, each with his own customs and dialect and few with more than a year or so of elementary school-ing, found with their children a new sense of belonging, a new hope of becoming, in the Minnesota wilderness. The lodestone which made living communities of these diverse peoples was not of the past but of the future. They could never be one in tradition. Only hope, a deeply shared hope that their children would have*

154

*the best that the nation afforded, could unite them. A far-sighted group of educators, supported heartily by the captains of the mines, nurtured this hope and made the public schools its focus. In them they built an educational ladder suited to the step and reach of the immigrant's children. And through them they taught the parents as well the language, the care of health, the civic ideals, and the "joie de vivre" which they wished to prevail in America.*

*They convinced the newcomers, as they were themselves convinced, that education was the key to the good life, the gateway to health, wealth and happiness. The priests and prophetesses of this faith, performing their rites daily amidst the splendor of their hilltop temples, were an aristocracy whose power over the minds of the workingmen proved greater than that which mining captains, merchants and bankers could muster. For this reason, and not because she was a lackey of capitalism, the teacher proved an effective deterrent to political radicalism as well. Her words were law, her will a synonym for "wisdom."*[90]

# 9

# Health Care

*The health of the people is really the foundation upon which all their happiness and all their powers as a state depend.*

—Disraeli

I n *Mesabi Communities: A Study of Their Development*, John Syrjamaki described the standard system of medicine that existed on the Iron Range prior to 1940.

> *A contract system of medicine was introduced upon the Range by the mining companies as early as 1892, and has continued to prevail to the present. Hospitals privately owned by doctors have contracted with the mining companies to provide medical care for their employees upon the basis of fees in proportion to the number of employees. Under this system a sum which has varied from $1.00 to $1.25 a month has been deducted from the pay check of each employee, and to this has been added another sum of about fifty cents, paid either by the company or an insurance company in its behalf. This fee has been paid to the hospital with which a contract has been made.*

> *Employees are entitled to receive under this arrangement medical treatment and free supplies not only for themselves but also for all members of their families. Home visits and treatment of patients in their homes has been included in the fee. Operations, child deliveries, and other cases requiring hospitalization, however, are charged for. Services must be secured at a definite hospital, but the patient is permitted choice of the doctors on its staff.*

156

*This system of contract medicine has tended to work, on the whole, satisfactorily. The immigrants have definitely profited from this easy availability of medical services. In many cases they have undoubtedly been prompted to seek the attention of a doctor by the realization that such service was free, inasmuch as their monthly hospital fee was deducted whether or not medical assistance had been given. Under other circumstances ailments might have gone untreated or cures attempted by self-medication. The hospitals have served the purpose, hence, of reducing almost from the start the use of homemade remedies or superstitious health practices which the foreign-born were accustomed to employ in their native homeland. Informants among the doctors and the immigrant groups testified to this fact. The quality of service given in the hospitals has generally been good, and some of the older doctors, who have made their careers on the Range, are regarded with genuine affection. There has never been any case of discrimination by the hospitals on the basis of the nationality of their patients.[91]*

Since the Kosiak family did not qualify for prepaid health care and could not afford visits to a doctor's office or hospital, there were few encounters with the medical establishment outside of school. Health care for the Kosiaks was either "Home Health Care" as diagnosed and treated by "Doctor" Julia Kosiak or "School Health Care" as provided by the medical and dental departments of the Chisholm schools.

## HOME HEALTH CARE

Treatment for minor wounds usually consisted of cleansing the wound, applying pressure if some bleeding was present, and then wrapping the wound with homemade bandages usually cut from a clean, discarded bed sheet or dishtowel. Since all of our bed sheets as well as dishtowels were made of flour sack material, the supply of bandages was unlimited.

Abrasions, contusions and superficial inflammations were managed with a variety of home remedies. Lard or our homemade butter was the treatment of choice for minor burns and abrasions. Commercial products usually sold door to door, such as Unguentine and Watkins Petro-

Carbosalve, were not used in our home because we couldn't afford them. In fact, the only commercial ointment available to us was Bag Balm, a petroleum-based product used for treatment of inflammation of a cow's udder but also very effective in providing temporary relief of superficial burns, including sunburn.

Vicks VapoRub was the treatment of choice for the persistent chest cold. For a sore throat it was gargling again and again with warm salt water. Aspirin was used to relieve the so-called "minor aches and pains," and very foul-smelling liniment was used in more resistant cases.

Cold, wet packs were used to relieve joint sprains and muscle strains. Snow was used in copious amounts for the management of frostbite, regardless of what part of the anatomy was involved. While our toes were most often affected when we skated or skied, our ears, our noses and our cheeks could sometimes be frostbitten after we simply walked home from school or from downtown. Although cough drops were not forbidden, they did cost money, and half a teaspoon of honey was usually just as effective.

Primarily through the sympathy and understanding of one of Tato's fellow countrymen, Steven Cherwyniak, a mining company employee, we were able to devise a plan to avoid both the billing and the payment for some of our medical care. My brothers and I would always register at the clinic as John, William or Mike Cherwyniak. Though the clerks at the registration desk may have been suspicious at times, we had no problems receiving care.

This scheme received its most severe test when while still in high school I suffered a rather deep laceration of my left wrist as I attempted to push open the front porch door, which just happened to be locked. Because Ma was concerned about tendon or nerve damage, the wound was dressed with a clean piece of cloth, and I was sent on my way to the clinic. To my surprise, the young lady at the reception desk was one of my classmates. When she was unable to find my name in the file, I told her to look under the name "Mike Cherwyniak." To complicate the situation, the doctor on call was Dr. P.H. Macfarlane, who also lived on Poplar Street just a block east of our home. Not only had I, along with some of my friends, babysat the two young Macfarlane sons on occasion, but Mrs. Macfarlane had been my third grade teacher at the Roosevelt School. Without asking any questions, Dr. Macfarlane cleansed, sutured and dressed the wound. The clinic never billed our family for that visit.

Fortunately, the Kosiak children's health care needs were limited throughout most of their childhood. The three major medical problems involved Willy, Johnny, and Irene. In the early thirties, during one of our swimming visits to Linden Pond, Willy ended up spending more time than recommended sunbathing on the banks of the pond. By the time he got home, his skin was bright red. Because of the unrelenting discomfort, both he and Ma spent a virtually sleepless night. Smearing the back with Bag Balm did not relieve the pain.

The next morning the situation had not improved, and by the afternoon the skin was beginning to blister. Continuing treatment consisted of the application of cold, wet packs and the ingestion of a lot of aspirin. By the third day, Willy's back was covered with large blisters, and the pain had not subsided. Finally, Ma called Dr. Macfarlane. The doctor added Burrows Solution to the packs and prescribed a somewhat stronger analgesic. In later years we learned that hospitalization ordinarily would have been recommended but, because the family had no health-care coverage, this was not possible. Needless to say, thanks to Dr. Macfarlane and Ma's round-the-clock nursing care, Willy survived what was potentially a life-threatening problem. We suspect that the house calls were made on a William Kosiak, not a William Cherwyniak.

Johnny required a tonsillectomy at about seven or eight years of age. After a hospital confinement of a few days, he was discharged home on an ice cream diet, which was recommended in order to limit the bleeding and to decrease pain and swelling. Since Johnny was only able to eat very small amounts of ice cream at one time and because the family did not own a refrigerator, Willy and I had a virtual field day, devouring more ice cream in a week than we had eaten in our entire lives.

Irene was ten years old when she required hospitalization. After the usual complaints of abdominal cramping, the diagnosis of acute appendicitis was made and she was admitted to the Chisholm Rood Hospital for surgery, which was performed by Dr. A.D. Klein. The confinement lasted about seven days at a room rate of five dollars per day. Since she was admitted as Irene Kosiak, Tato was responsible for the bill.

Because Irene's illness was not considered an excusable absence on her report card, she was therefore not eligible for the coveted Perfect Attendance Diploma awarded all children who had attended school every day during the entire year. Some consolation was gained from the fact that her teacher, Miss Louise Sartori, brought her a pair of slippers, the first pair Irene had ever owned.

For most of his life, Tato was afflicted with a generalized skin disorder, tentatively diagnosed as a form of neuro-dermatitis. Because his local physician had determined that the condition was probably work related, and because treatment at the Mesaba Clinic had not solved the problem, he was referred to the University of Minnesota Hospital for follow-up care.

In spite of the use of a variety of ointments, salves, lotions, and pills prescribed by the Dermatology Clinic, the condition showed little improvement. The irritation, which was worse in the winter when Tato wore long underwear, improved some during the summer months, and he did seem to get some relief with the use of an over-the-counter lotion called Zemo. Though the problem persisted even after his retirement, it never appeared to interfere with his way of life.

Ma's share of the health care costs for the Kosiak family was limited to physicians' services as provided for six normal home deliveries. We doubt that she ever sought or obtained any pre-natal care. We know that the charge for my delivery was only fifteen dollars. For Johnny and Willy, it was probably less than that, and for the three girls the delivery charges probably did not exceed twenty-five dollars each.

Ma's salvation concerning the health care she rendered her family for the thirty years when she had children in school was the ready availability of "second opinions" provided free of charge by Dr. Graham and the school's medical department.

Because of the daily toothbrush drills and the biannual dental examinations by Dr. W.A. Jordan, the school dentist, visits to the local dentists were limited. Only Johnny required orthodontic care.

## SCHOOL HEALTH CARE

For those Chisholm families who did not qualify for the pre-paid health care programs as provided by the mining companies and a few other employers, all primary health care was provided by the medical and dental departments of the Chisholm schools.

# DR. ARCHIBALD W. GRAHAM

*As late as 1945, acute appendicitis complicated by peritonitis almost always resulted in fatal consequences. For those families with no health care other than that provided by the Chisholm schools, initial diagnosis was frequently the responsibility of Dr. A.W. Graham.*

—M. Kosiak

Dr. Archibald W. Graham
"Moonlight" Graham
October 10, 1879-August 25, 1965

As with several of the other Iron Range communities, the Chisholm schools were fortunate to have the services of a full-time physician, Dr. Archibald W. Graham. Born in Fayetteville, North Carolina, on October 10, 1879, Dr. Graham graduated from the University of Maryland Medical School in 1905 after a short stint as a major league baseball player.[92] His baseball and his medical careers would later be featured in the movie, *Field of Dreams,* starring Kevin Costner. Burt Lancaster played the role of "Doc Graham."

Dr. Graham first came to Chisholm in 1909 where he practiced out of the old Rood Hospital until he assumed the role of school physician in 1917. Though he was a board-certified specialist in internal medicine, much of his post-graduate training also provided him with clinical expertise in the field of ophthalmology. As the Chisholm school's medical director, his practice would be classified as being primarily pediatric oriented. Dr. Graham's office was located on the second floor of the Washington School while each school had a nurse's office staffed by the school nurse who rotated to all the grade schools.

The two original functions of the school physician and nurse were the detection of physical defects and the control of communicable diseases. In later years, more emphasis was placed on health education and mental health.

The initial selection of children requiring special medical attention was usually the responsibility of the teacher. From daily observation of her classes, she would refer those pupils who failed to do the work of which they were capable, those who developed social and psychological problems of adjustment and those who appeared ill or who were frequently absent from school.

Physical defects of which the parents had not been aware might be detected on the annual school examination. The four most common defects were dental problems, abnormalities of vision and hearing, and malnutrition. Because almost twenty percent of all school children have defective vision, routine testing in the schools frequently revealed cases of impaired vision which were totally unsuspected by both the child and parents. The Snellen Chart, prominently displayed on the wall of the nurse's office in each school, generally provided a fairly effective method of detecting most visual disturbances. The ordinary test for hearing, the whispered voice, was used by both Dr. Graham and the school nurse for detecting any gross hearing deficits.

In addition to performing routine, annual health examinations, Dr. Graham also supervised a variety of preventive measures such as vaccinations and inoculations. Diphtheria inoculations, small pox vaccinations, and Mantoux testing for tuberculosis were provided all children, while the typhoid fever vaccination was available for children scheduled to go to summer camp. Dr. Graham also performed some minor surgery such as the incision and drainage of carbuncles and small abscesses—usually after a period of simple hot packing, which was done at home.

Prevention of infection at every level was of utmost importance because until the middle forties, antibiotics such as penicillin were not part of any physician's armamentarium. Mercurochrome, a deep red, mercury-based compound, was the antiseptic of choice. Superficial wounds were liberally bathed in the solution while swabbing the tonsils with Mercurochrome was accepted care in the treatment of acute tonsillitis. (Recalling the bitter taste of the mercurochrome, one might postulate that its effectiveness in the treatment of tonsillitis was the fact that any organisms residing on the inflamed tonsillar tissue would surely succumb simply because of the bitterness of the antiseptic.)

Dr. Graham or his nurse treated strains, sprains, contusions, and abrasions as well as minor lacerations. Serious lacerations, many of which did not occur on school property, acute appendicitis, and bone fractures were always referred immediately to the physicians at the Mesaba Clinic. Diagnostic problems including such conditions as measles, mumps, chicken pox, and even scarlet fever all came under Dr. Graham's domain. Most of these medical problems could be managed in the home, and quarantine measures were strictly enforced. If one member of the family was afflicted with any of a number of contagious diseases including pink eye (conjunctivitis), all grade-school siblings were required to stay home from school for at least two weeks. On occasion, especially in severe cases of chicken pox, Dr. Graham would actually go into the home to follow-up the student.

Because of the potentially tragic complications of scarlet fever, which could progress to rheumatic fever and damage the heart and kidneys, the doctor followed these children with daily home visits. Many were confined to the Detention Hospital, Chisholm's contagion hospital at that time. As the primary treating physician, Dr. Graham continued to make bedside rounds on a daily basis.

Lest one were to get the impression that Dr. Graham's medical practice was any less challenging than that of today's practitioners, one is reminded of the fact that in the 1920s, '30s, and '40s, children and adolescents were being afflicted with a never-ending list of serious and even life-threatening diseases. Rheumatic fever was the most serious chronic childhood disease from the 1920s to the 1940s, causing more deaths among children and adolescents five to nineteen years of age than any other disease.[93] Even during World War II, more than 100,000 young men were ineligible for military service because of rheumatic heart disease, and an additional 40,000 suffered either their initial attack or a recurrence of the disease while stationed at various training centers.

The most serious complication of rheumatic fever is rheumatic carditis, an inflammation of the heart, which often leads to permanent disability and even death. Acquired heart disease in children aged five to fourteen is usually caused by rheumatic fever. The disease is more prevalent in northern sections of the central states and appears to be more common in families of lower income level.

Chisholm's geographic location and the fact that a majority of the school children were from poor immigrant families surely must have provided Dr. Graham with a large number of children who were potential candidates for rheumatic fever. Clinical surveys as conducted in the Chisholm schools often led to the early detection of minor cardiac defects, which had developed unnoticed by the parents and the child.

Tuberculosis was the fourth leading cause of death in children ages ten to fourteen in the middle '30s and early '40s. Although the disease was nearly eradicated prior to the influx of millions of immigrants after World War II, Mantoux testing of school children was critical to the early diagnosis and management of this devastating disease.[94]

As late as 1945, appendicitis was still the fifth leading cause of death in the children ages ten to fourteen.[95] Before the advent of antibiotics, appendicitis complicated by peritonitis (infection of the abdominal cavity) caused by a perforated appendix was almost invariably fatal. Perforation generally occurs earlier in children than in adults, and there is also a greater tendency for the infection to spread. Since diffuse peritonitis consistently follows perforation, delayed diagnosis almost always resulted in fatal consequences. For those families with no health care other than that provided by the Chisholm schools, initial diagnosis was frequently the responsibility of Dr. Graham and his nurse.

That acute appendicitis was indeed a serious medical matter was impressed upon the Kosiak family following the sudden death of a seven-year-old neighborhood boy because of peritonitis resulting from a ruptured appendix.

As the result of his extensive post-graduate training, Dr. Graham also possessed expertise in the field of ophthalmology. Consequently his office in the Washington School contained all of the state-of-the-art equipment necessary for a comprehensive eye examination including the prescription and fitting of eyeglasses. Teachers referred many students to Dr. Graham because of learning difficulties, which the teacher suspected might have been due to visual problems.

Because Dr. Graham's salary was obviously not in keeping with the salaries of those physicians employed by the Mesaba Clinic, he was allowed to supplement his salary by providing ophthalmologic care for the adult population of Chisholm and much of the Iron Range. Until his retirement from the practice of medicine in 1961, Dr. Graham continued to fit our father with eyeglasses.

That Dr. Graham was more than a small-town school doctor was demonstrated by his classic study of children's blood pressure, which was

Dr. A.W. Graham
(Bi-annual Clinical Evaluation), 1940.

published in the *American Journal of Diseases of Children* in April 1945. In collaboration with Drs. E.A. Hines and R.P. Gage of the Mayo Clinic, Dr. Graham demonstrated for the first time, ". . . a linear increase in blood pressure, both systolic and diastolic, with each year of age. . . . Systolic blood pressure ranged from 92 mm. at the age of five years to 122 mm. at the age of sixteen years. The corresponding diastolic pressure ranged from 52 to 62 mm."[96]

There is no question that the medical care Dr. Graham provided the students of Chisholm was of the highest quality available. While reflecting on his forty-four-year tour of duty as the chief medical officer, one cannot help being impressed by his many contributions to the well-being of all the citizens of Chisholm. Dr. Graham's gentle demeanor and compassion, which were so essential in establishing a comfortable and long-lasting doctor-patient relationship, had an especially consoling effect on the immigrant parents.

Dr. Graham was our doctor, the only doctor who, along with his nurse, routinely provided almost all of the medical care for the Kosiak kids and medical reassurance to our mother as she managed our multiple medical problems throughout our entire childhood.

On August 25, 1965, Dr. Graham died at the Chisholm Memorial Hospital. With his wife, Alicia, he is buried at the Calvary Cemetery in Rochester, Minnesota.

## DR. WILLIAM A. JORDAN

*. . . it is important to realize that clean teeth and a clean mouth are just as essential to personal hygiene as a clean face and body.*
—Dr. W.A. Jordan

Although the Chisholm schools had organized a School Health Department as early as 1917 with the employment of a full-time physician as well as a school nurse, it was not until 1926 that the schools engaged the services of a full-time dental hygienist. In 1930, she was replaced by a full-time dentist, Dr. William A. Jordan.

Dr. Jordan was born on August 21, 1901, in Cleveland, Ohio. One year later, the family moved to Chisholm where Dr. Jordan grew up, graduating from the Chisholm High School with the class of 1919. He then

Dr. William A. Jordan
August 21, 1901-December 10, 1995

continued his education at Marquette and Northwestern Universities receiving his DDS (Doctor of Dental Science) from Northwestern University in 1924. He would later continue his formal education by earn-

167

ing a Masters Degree in Public Health from the University of Michigan in 1945.[97]

After his graduation from dental school, Dr. Jordan returned to Chisholm where he entered into the private practice of dentistry. In 1930, he accepted the appointment as the dentist for the Chisholm schools, where the imminent need for a school dental program was supported by surveys, which indicated:

> . . .*up to ninety-five percent of the pupils had remedial dental defects. . . . The problem was particularly acute in the pioneer days of our own mining community of some nine thousand people, representing approximately thirty national origins, with varying concepts of health and living standards and with very limited economic resources with which to provide medical and dental care. Extractions were the rule . . . all on the written authorization of the parents.*[98]

Dr. Jordan described the dental program as provided the Chisholm schools as:

> *Dental care, except for emergencies, is limited to the elementary schools, pre-kindergarten through the sixth grade and is restricted to the filling of decayed, deciduous teeth and first molars, prophylaxis and any necessary extractions . . . all on written authorization of parents . . .*[99]

The four main aspects of the Chisholm schools' dental program included dental examinations, prescribed dental care, dental health education, and research. According to Dr. A.W. Jordan, the school dental program was designed to:

> . . . *protect the child against the hazards of oral and dental disease through early and continued care beginning with the pre-kindergarten child, while educating him to an appreciation of this care to general health and life efficiency . . . to make sure that the child early in life learns the importance of regular trips to the dentist, acquires a toothbrush habit, and understands the proper place of foods in building a sound body and sound teeth.*[100]

In addition to the dental care he provided, Dr. Jordan continued the nationally recognized, daily toothbrushing drills, first instituted in 1917. Every student from the first through the fifth grade at every school in the Chisholm school system participated in the Toothbrush Drill as described in Chapter 6—"Our Schools." Dr. Jordan justified the costs and time required to carry on the program by stating, "While brushing the teeth may not prevent cavities, it is important to realize that clean teeth and a clean mouth are just as essential to personal hygiene as a clean face and body."

That Dr. Jordan was not only an outstanding pediatric dentist but also one who attempted to endear himself to his grade school clientele is demonstrated in a report he submitted to the Chisholm School Board in 1936.

> . . . I find the reaction of the children to dental work, on the whole, very good. The kindergarten students react wonderfully well considering the age and size. Many of these little tots are making their first visit to a dentist. Short appointments are more successful, as little ones tire easily. I think children react better in groups. The timid seem to bolster their courage, while the ill tempered will calm down. Children do not like to be criticized in front of other children and will, therefore, be better behaved. The child that comes to the dental office with other children or alone is a much better patient than the one that has the parents with him. The parents mean well, but it is not helping the child any to have them hovering over the chair and commenting on how terrible it is to have a tooth extracted or telling the youngster how they will be right there and help them suffer all the pain. Children like to be talked to and thought of as grown-ups. They want to act for themselves.
>
> To create some incentive to have the work done, we offer gold star certificates, or some little health book or pin to the child with perfect teeth, or to the ones who have all the necessary work completed by the school dentist or their family dentist. These little honors, as you might call them, worked the impossible.[101]

Speaking before the Minnesota State Dental Association in April of 1946 concerning Chisholm's school dental program, Superintendent Vaughan first commented on the general health of America's youth.

169

*. . . medical rejections in World War II were so numerous as to justify national concern.*

*This was also true in the field of dental health, where rejections of young men because of poor teeth . . . were so numerous as to compel a downward revision of standards for acceptance, and the inauguration of a program of correction in service. It has been estimated that the Army Dental Corps rehabilitated with prosthetic appliances more than a million and a half men who could not have qualified otherwise, while making available and maintaining many thousands more by other types of corrective work. This was a great contribution by the profession in an effort to patch up the results of 20 to 30 years of neglect.*[102]

Without the dental care provided by Dr. Jordan, large numbers of Chisholm graduates would surely have become part of that group of World War II recruits requiring extensive, expensive dental care—those recruits who, Mr. Vaughan in 1946 reported, were the victims of . . . "20 to 30 years of (dental) neglect."

On October 19, 1944, Dr. Jordan resigned from his position with the Chisholm schools in order to seek a Masters Degree in Public Health from the University of Michigan. After his graduation in 1945, he accepted the position of Director of the Dental Division of the Minnesota Public Health Department.

It was in this capacity that he became involved in extensive dental research concerning the effect of the topical application of fluoride to the teeth. He also actively campaigned statewide promoting the fluoridation of community water supplies as a means of improving dental care.

The Chisholm schools in 1944-1945, in cooperation with the State Division of Dental Health, were one of the few schools in the nation involved in assessing the effectiveness of the topical application of sodium fluoride for the prevention of dental caries. Follow-up after three applications of sodium fluoride showed a forty percent decrease in the number of cavities in deciduous teeth and a twenty percent decrease in the incidence of cavities involving permanent teeth.

Dr. William A. Jordan, who was a faculty member of both the University of Minnesota College of Dentistry and the College of Public Health, died in Minneapolis on December 10, 1995. With his wife

Winnifred and their son, Thomas Barry, he is buried at Lakewood Cemetery in Minneapolis.[103]

# 10

# Food and Staples

Although bread is often called the staff of life, for the Kosiak family the true staff of life was flour, the main ingredient not only in the bread we ate but also in most of the main dishes that were on the daily menu. Flour was the main staple in our family's diet, followed by potatoes and cabbage.

Flour is made by grinding wheat or other cereal grains. Its chief use is in making bread, which has been one of mankind's most important foods for thousands of years. The grinding of grain goes back to prehistoric man. Scientists have found grinding stones in France that date back 25,000 years. Similar stones dating back almost 10,000 years have also been found in the United States. The milling process advanced from flat stones that people rubbed together by hand to revolving stones powered at first by animals and slaves and later by water, windmills, and steam engines.[104]

One can only speculate regarding the milling process that was used when our parents lived in the old country. Since the first high-pressure steam engines were not developed until the late 1700s and early 1800s, it is doubtful that such machinery was available in the rural areas of East-Central Europe. Our ancestors must have spent much time and effort making flour for their daily bread.

In Chisholm, however, flour was plentiful and relatively inexpensive. The flour bin Tato had built in the pantry could hold 100 pounds of flour. Through the years, up to the early forties, at least once a month we had a 100-pound sack of flour delivered to our home.

Flour was used in a variety of ways in the Kosiak household, but especially in bread making. At least twice a week, Ma baked seven to eight loaves of bread in the oven of the wood range. Bread was served at every meal, breakfast, lunch, and dinner. Tato took sandwiches to work every day in his lunch pail. Whether toasted and spread with homemade jelly or jam, or simply covered with butter when butter was available, bread was on the menu. Bread smeared liberally with ketchup was a snack-time favorite as was fresh bread dipped into warm bacon grease. No one, at any time, questioned the nutritional value of bread. Bread was cheap, tasty and very filling; best of all, it was always available.

Although the making of bread may have consumed the bulk of the monthly allotment of flour, flour was also the basic ingredient in the ethnic foods we fondly remember and sometimes crave, each one consisting of a basic dough made by mixing flour with egg, warm water and a little salt. During Lent, vegetable oil replaced the egg. The dough could be broken off, rolled and cut into different shapes, sliced, filled and folded, and each different form had a name of its own.

*Halushki, babailki, steranka, rizanka,* and *perohi* were all cooked in boiling water until they rose to the top. They were then drained and served hot with butter or warm cooking oil.

*Halushki* were made by rolling out the dough to approximately one-eighth inch in thickness on a tablecloth lightly dusted with flour. The dough was then cut into small squares measuring about two by two inches. After cooking, these were served plain, with mashed potatoes or with a mixture of slowly fried sauerkraut and onions. The *halushki* might also be combined with chopped, sweet cabbage, which had been boiled until tender.

*Babailki* were made by separating one-inch pieces from the basic dough and rolling them into pencil shapes, about two or three inches in length. These we called "rollies."

*Steranka* were still another nutritional presentation of the dough. Pieces of the dough were pinched off the ball of basic dough; in fact, as children we called them "pinchies." After cooking and draining, they were then returned to the pan, covered with milk and reheated before serving.

*Rizanka* were homemade noodles. The rolled-out dough was folded over loosely before being cut transversely into quarter-inch strips. After cooking, the noodles were usually flavored with butter or covered with gravy from the last pork chop meal.

*Perohi,* a family favorite, were a peasant delicacy especially in the Russian community. Once the dough was rolled out and cut into three- to four-inch squares, a tablespoon of filling was placed in the center of each piece. The dough was then folded into a triangle and the edges were pressed firmly together. Sealing the edges was critical so that they didn't separate and lose the filling while cooking. Most often the filling was simply cooked mashed potatoes, fried sauerkraut, a combination of the two, or cottage cheese. For our Christmas Eve supper, *perohi* were filled with prunes.

Other culinary delicacies created by our mother included what she called her "jiffy cake." The basic ingredients were flour, baking powder, one egg, salt, sugar, shortening (not butter) and milk. The end product was slightly yellow in color, a little coarse in texture but delicious to the taste.

Ma also used simple sweet dough to make raised doughnuts, especially during times when large quantities of lard were available for frying. After the dough had been rolled out, the top of a cup or glass was used to cut out the doughnut. We didn't have a doughnut cutter. All the doughnuts were fried in pure lard and the end product was usually lightly sugared.

For Christmas and other holidays Ma would make *potica,* a Slavic delicacy. *Potica* is walnut-filled bread which also includes liberal amounts of honey, sugar, butter and milk. The dough is stretched out very thin and the honey and ground-walnut filling is spread over the dough before it is rolled up and placed into pans for baking. Because we always thought Ma skimped on the walnuts due to their cost, we called her product "The Missing-Nut *Potica.*" Years later, we discovered that the recipe she used was exactly as printed in the *Slovenian Women's Union Cookbook,* published in 1963.[105] However, we doubt that she used the amount of walnuts suggested in the recipe.

Although bread or flour products in various forms constituted the bulk of our diet, homegrown products such as potatoes and sauerkraut ran a close second and third. Potatoes were without question our second most plentiful source of nutrition. Unlike flour, which had to be purchased, we were able to provide almost all of our potato needs, even when we only had the small garden on the south side of Chisholm. It was necessary to buy potatoes only on rare occasions, in late spring or early summer.

It can be stated with absolute certainty that potatoes were a part of our daily menu every day of the year. We never had potatoes for breakfast, but they were frequently served for lunch, especially on weekends, and almost always for supper. Potatoes could be prepared in a variety of ways, most of them not very interesting or enticing. Ketchup was absolutely essential for the ingestion of Ma's American-fried potatoes. Baked potatoes required either butter or sour cream.

Mashed potatoes just weren't mashed potatoes without liberal helpings of gravy. There were times when Ma might fry a single pork chop just for the gravy. If two pork chops were available, Tato would get one of the pork chops while the children would share the other one. There were no complaints as long as the supply of gravy was unlimited. We were reminded of the importance of gravy by Willy who, in later years, often commented on the fact that he was twenty-one years old before he realized that pork chops were actually for eating, not merely for the making of gravy.

A simple variation of the potato was the potato dumpling, another family favorite. The potatoes were first grated and drained. Flour and a single egg would then be added to the grated potatoes. The mixture was then dropped, a tablespoon at a time, into boiling water. The dumplings were thoroughly cooked when they floated to the surface of the water. They were then served in a bowl with butter and chopped, fried cabbage. On occasion the dumplings could also be served with fried sauerkraut.

Cabbage, usually in the form of sauerkraut, was the third most important staple in the family's diet. Even when we still owned the farm, we were unable to grow all the cabbage necessary for our family needs. More than eighty percent of the cabbage grown on our farm was turned into sauerkraut, which is simply shredded cabbage fermented in brine until it sours.

Shredding the cabbage into a forty-gallon wooden barrel usually took two evenings. The cabbage cutter, an apparatus used to slice the cabbage, was borrowed from a relative. Because the blades were razor sharp, only Tato or Uncle Mike was permitted to operate this equipment.

Salt was liberally applied at regular intervals, and the shredded cabbage was packed down using a round wooden block six or eight inches in diameter, which was attached to a metal rod. Once the cutting and packing had been completed, a round piece of wood, weighted down by a ten to fifteen-pound stone, was placed over the shredded cabbage. After several weeks, the sauerkraut was ready to be eaten.

Sauerkraut could be prepared in many ways and could even be eaten raw, right out of the barrel. It could be fried or it could be combined with mashed potatoes. However, at least once a week, it was prepared as soup called *kapusta*. *Kapusta* is made by slowly cooking in water, sauerkraut that has been rinsed in water and drained to reduce the salt content. The end product is then thickened by the addition of a small amount of oatmeal and an evenly browned mixture of sautéed onions and flour. Cooked navy beans and cut-up potatoes as well as small slices of Polish sausage can also be added if desired. Ma always made a large container of *kapusta*, enough to last for several days.

Cabbages that were not cut up for sauerkraut were used to make *holubka*, also called "pigs-in-the-blanket." The cabbage leaves were first parboiled in hot water to soften them and enhance their flexibility. Then each leaf was wrapped around a mixture of ground meat, rice, egg, and onion, appropriately seasoned. The individual rolls were packed closely into a large pot and then cooked slowly on the stove. Since *holubka* were a meal in themselves, only some homemade bread was needed to complete the meal.

Another special food was *studenina* (jellied pigs' feet). The meat was simmered for several hours with onion and spices, cooled and refrigerated overnight. Before we had a refrigerator, the front porch served the purpose. *Studenina* was a Sunday morning treat during the winter months.

Perhaps the most nourishing and comforting food was *hamula*, which had to be our mother's original creation. *Hamula,* a thick, creamy soup containing no meat or vegetables, was routinely served to any family member who was not feeling well. Years later, when Willy was in the hospital, he said he would surely feel better if only he could have some *hamula.*

Before leaving our mother and her wood-stove cooking skills, mention must be made of her scrambled egg recipe. One summer, when Irene was still in college, she was hired by a Twin City family to work at their lakeside compound near Park Rapids. One of Irene's duties was to prepare breakfast for the elderly woman in whose home she stayed. After several encounters with Irene's delicious scrambled eggs, the lady said, "Irene, you must get that recipe for scrambled eggs from your mother." Irene excitedly called home the next day, requesting the famous scrambled egg recipe, to which Ma responded, "There is no recipe. You just beat the eggs with a fork, add a little salt and milk and then pour it all into the frying pan." This is exactly what Irene had been doing. Probably because the woman was elderly, she forgot about her request for the scrambled egg recipe and Irene was asked to return the next summer.

The fact that the major portion of our nutritional needs was provided by the three basic food staples of flour, potatoes, and cabbage is a testimonial to the ingenuity and never-ending labor of our mother.

# 11

# *Our Religion and Holidays*

*Wherever they live, religion has remained for the Carpatho-Rusyns the most important aspect of their lives.*

—P.R.Magocsi

St. Nicholas Russian Orthodox Church, Chisholm, Minnesota.

C hristianity was first brought to the Carpathians during the second half of the ninth century. Popular legends supported by scholarly writings suggest that Carpatho-Rusyns received Christianity in the early 860s from the Apostles to the Slavs, Cyril and Methodius, two monks from the Byzantine Empire.[106]

As with their language and culture, Orthodox Carpatho-Rusyn churches share elements of both the Eastern and Western Christian worlds. The split in the Christian Church between East and West is generally marked at 1054, when the Roman pope excommunicated the Patriarch of Constantinople. But it had started much earlier and extended centuries afterward. Much of the division lay in the distance between Rome and Constantinople—physically, culturally and in language. While the downfall of Rome came in 485, Byzantium continued to flourish widening the East-West gulf. Second, when Charlemagne was crowned Emperor of the Holy Roman Empire in 800, the pope essentially cast his lot with the West, leaving the Eastern Patriarchies behind. When the Christian Church was divided after 1054, many Carpatho-Rusyns remained within the Eastern Orthodox sphere under the authority of the Patriarch of Constantinople.

Religious affiliation helped to distinguish Orthodox Carpatho-Rusyns from their Slovak, Hungarian and Polish neighbors who were either Roman Catholic or Protestant. As Eastern Christians, the Orthodox Carpatho-Rusyns used Church Slavonic instead of Latin as the language in religious services, received both leavened bread and wine at Communion and allowed priests to marry. They also followed the Julian calendar, resulting in the fact that Christmas was celebrated on January 7th, some thirteen days later than on the western Gregorian calendar.

The Orthodox Carpatho-Rusyns were distinguished as well from fellow Eastern Christians by certain practices and rituals borrowed from their Latin-rite neighbors, but in particular by their liturgical music. That music, still in use today, consists primarily of congregational and cantorial singing—no organ or other instrument is permitted. Based on traditional East Slavonic chants and influenced by local folk melodies, the music is known simply as Carpathian plain chant. The use of Church Slavonic especially in America, has decreased markedly in the past fifty years.

*The renowned missionaries to the Slavs, Cyril and Methodius, had devised a modification of the Greek alphabet suited to the tongue of the Slavicized Bulgars of the Danube. Instead of requiring the Russian clergy to learn Greek, the necessary ritual books were translated for their benefit into Old Church Slavonic.*[107]

The essence of Orthodoxy is in the liturgy, first developed in the fifth century by St. John Chrysostom, a revered figure in the Eastern Church. That liturgy is still used today and links the modern worshipers with the earliest days of Christianity. Boasting a liturgy from the fifth century and a reverence for the apostolic fathers, Orthodoxy continues to attract converts who question the modern changes found in many different churches including those denominations who bill themselves as New Testament-based.[108] "It's amazing the number of young people who are coming into the Orthodox Church. The people are attracted to the church because of its strong emphasis on tradition and family. People want structure and discipline in their lives."[109]

In the late sixteenth century, attempts were made by the various state governments and the local aristocracy to bring the Orthodox Carpatho-Rusyns closer to the official Roman Catholic religion of the state in which they lived at that time. The result was the creation, between 1596 and 1646, of a Uniate Church—that is, an Eastern Christian Church in union with Rome. The Uniates were allowed to retain their Eastern rites and traditions, but they had to recognize the Pope of Rome, not the Patriarch of Constantinople as the ultimate head of their church. Hence, from the seventeenth century, Carpatho-Rusyns were either Orthodox or Uniates. The Uniates in 1772 were renamed Greek Catholics.

Although in practice there is not much difference between the Orthodox and Greek Catholic religious service (Divine Liturgy), even today, many Carpatho-Rusyn villages have both a Greek Catholic and an Orthodox Church.

Tato's older half-brother Frank and brother Max always worshiped at the Greek Catholic Church while living in America. His other older half-brother Aleck who settled in Rauch, a rural area about fifty miles north of Chisholm, was a charter member of the Sts. Peter and Paul Russian Orthodox Church of Rauch, where he worshipped until his death in 1925. He is buried in the small parish cemetery, which is located just north of the church on the east side of Minnesota Highway 65.

Although brother Steve was married in the Russian Orthodox Church in Chisholm, upon moving to the Pinconning, Michigan area, he became affiliated with the Greek Catholic Church. Tato as well as brothers Mike and Peter remained life-long members of the Russian Orthodox Church in Chisholm. Ma's family, the Billos, were members of the Greek Catholic Church in America as they had been in Europe.

Our earliest religious training started in the home. As far back as we can remember, Tato always said "Grace" and made the sign of the cross before every meal. Although our parents were bilingual, all religious functions were conducted in Church Slavonic so that "The Lord's Prayer" (*Oche Nash*) was first memorized and always recited in Church Slavonic.

Due to administrative and congregational problems, there were periods of time during our youth when the Chisholm church did not have an in-house priest. During those periods, which often lasted more than a year, all religious activity was confined to the home, especially during the major religious holidays of Christmas and Easter.

Because in the Orthodox faith, Confirmation occurs at the time of Baptism, the traditional catechism classes and training were not a part of our early religious upbringing. However, over a period of several years, whenever a priest was employed by the congregation, "Church School" was conducted three or four days a week over a period of four to six weeks during the summer vacation. Formal religious training was only a small part of the curriculum. Most of the time was spent learning *po nashemu,* the Carpatho-Rusyn language as spoken by our parents. Using the Cyrillic alphabet, we also developed a smattering of fluency in reading and writing. Unfortunately, except for Mary Ann, the girls in our family never were exposed to this training.

Church attendance on Sundays was expected of all of us from the grades into at least early high school. We have already alluded to the standard Sunday service, which always lasted at least two hours. There were no pews in the church. The men and boys stood on the right side facing the altar, while the women and girls occupied the left side facing the altar.

All services were conducted exclusively in Church Slavonic. The music consisted primarily of congregational and cantorial singing. In spite of the length of the service and the strain imposed by prolonged periods of standing and kneeling in what during the winter was a less than marginally heated building, the church service was generally an interesting experience.

Contributing to the general mystique were several factors: the cantorial-chanting dialogue between the priest and the congregation along with the choir in Church Slavonic, a language we children did not understand; the colorful priestly vestments, which varied with virtually every special holiday; the numerous icons, religious pictures and beautiful stained glass windows; the myriad of lighted candles; and the ever-present, pungent smell of incense that permeated the atmosphere increasing in intensity as the service progressed. Adding to the enjoyment of the church service, especially during the major holidays, was the incorporation of centuries-old carols and hymns always rendered with enthusiasm and volume, though frequently more than slightly off-key.

But what left its greatest impression on us as young worshipers, first generation children of European immigrants, was the obvious deep-seated, unquestioning religious fervor as demonstrated by all the parishioners in attendance. For "Our People" this was their religion.

Religious involvement for our family was more than just attending the church services on Sundays. Tato was also always actively involved in church maintenance. In fact, during one summer he not only painted the church steeples by himself but he also designed and constructed all the necessary scaffolding. For many years, he was on the church council and from 1954 to 1966 he served as president. In 1966 he was elected Honorary President, an honor he cherished all the remaining years of his life.

Ma's contributions were equally as great but not always as obvious. She on many occasions prepared the leavened bread that was distributed to all parishioners at the end of the church service. Her greatest contribution, however, occurred during the year that the Russian priest lived at our house. In addition to providing for her own family of five children at that time, she also did all the cooking, cleaning, and washing for the priest. No monetary compensation, as far as any of us know, was ever forthcoming from either the priest or the church congregation.

Although Mary Ann sang in the church choir in her late teens, I was the one who was most frequently involved in church activities. For several years in my early teens, I functioned as an altar boy. The job involved assisting the priest, lighting candles, keeping the incense burning in the sensor and serving *prosphors* or leavened altar bread at the end of the service.

I also received many hours of private tutoring from the in-house priest in an effort to better master my reading of the Church-Slavonic language. For my efforts I was rewarded with the opportunity to function as reader during several of the major church celebrations including a funeral or two. I did acknowledge the fact that though I was a fairly accomplished reader, I never did really understand more than a word or two of what I was reading.

As with all good Russian Orthodox families at that time, we always suspected that our parents would have been overjoyed to have had one of their sons become a priest. But that was not to be.

# EASTER

Just as Easter was considered the most important religious celebration for all the Christians, so it was for the Kosiak family. Unlike other religious events, Easter was a more prolonged religious process, beginning with the Great Lent seven weeks earlier. The Eastern and Western church both specify that Easter should be on the Sunday following the first full moon after the vernal equinox. Eastern churches, however, add the provision that it must be after the start of the Jewish Passover, resulting in the Orthodox Easter always being celebrated after Easter in the Western church except in the years when the holiday falls on the same date in both churches.

Lenten penance, as practiced by most of our non-Orthodox friends, covered a wide range of material goods and activities ranging from staying away from Saturday matinees to giving up chewing gum. In our family, penance was served primarily through dietary restrictions. Animal products of any type, especially meats, were absolutely forbidden especially on Lenten Fridays. This did not impose any great hardship on our family because meat at any time of the year was a rather scarce commodity. The daily menu during the Lenten season included a breakfast of graham or saltine crackers crumbled into a cup of sugar-sweetened, milk-whitened coffee. Because we all walked home for lunch during the school year, potatoes, sauerkraut, and large helpings of bread supplied our nutritional needs. Supper was usually just more of the same.

To be sure, we were allowed the use of limited amounts of butter, and milk was also allowed for whitening and weakening the coffee, which was our usual breakfast beverage even when we were young children. Although Tato was, on occasion, rewarded with a meat sandwich in his lunch pail, this was not a family secret in that one of us would have to go to the corner grocery store to buy the meat and then one of us was always needed to carry the lunch pail to the fire station. Absolutely no meat was ever prepared or eaten on any Friday during Lent.

Although we undoubtedly breached the dietary restrictions on multiple occasions early in the Lenten season, penance was more stringently enforced as the Holy Week approached. Only the use of milk in our coffee was allowed; there was no butter and not even the thought of meat in any size, shape, or form.

Palm Sunday seemed to be the second most important religious holiday on the Kosiak calendar. In lieu of palms, the Orthodox Church would dispense pussy-willow branches. Since Tato was one of only a handful of congregation members to own a vehicle and because the willow trees grew in outlying swampy areas, we would take a short trip to pick up the celebratory branches.

Palm Sunday service invariably exceeded the usual two-hour Sunday service, but at least the church was several degrees warmer than at Christmas. The blessing and dispensing of the pussy-willow branches usually concluded the service.

Ma was busy during most of Easter week preparing special food for the Easter basket. She baked a round loaf of bread called a *Paska* and made a cheese called "*hrutka*." She showed us how to make simple decorations on the hard-cooked eggs using the end of a common pin dipped into melted wax. The eggs were then dyed in brewed tea or the juices of beets or onions. The eggs, bread and cheese, along with sausages, a ground mixture of horseradish and beets, a small pork roast and butter were placed on a cloth in the green wicker basket set on the dining-room table. The priest came to our home on Saturday and blessed the food, which represented the end of the Lenten fast period and which provided the major portion of our Easter dinner.

Easter Sunday church service, which was embellished with several seasonal hymns, always lasted more than the traditional two hours. Even as young children, we could appreciate a somewhat enlightened atmosphere. The congregation as well as the choir appeared to be singing with more enthusiasm and volume especially during the traditional *Christos Voscres* (Christ Is Risen). The prolonged periods of standing or kneeling during the Easter Sunday service did not seem as uncomfortable or tiring.

Easter dinner commenced with Tato leading the Slavonic rendition of 'The Lord's Prayer." One can imagine the enthusiasm with which the Easter dinner was attacked, considering the long period of time during which these foods were considered taboo. Family guests always included Uncle Mike, Uncle Harry Billo, as well as Uncle Bill and Aunt Eva Smolensky.

In addition to the much-anticipated food, Tato usually saw fit to supply the adult friends and relatives with a small keg of beer while the children enjoyed two cases of locally bottled pop. After dinner we might take a short trip to visit Grandpa and Grandma Billo, who lived in Monroe Location. On occasion, due to the generosity of Uncle Harry or the Smolenskys, we would be given the one thin dime needed to attend the local theater matinee.

# CHRISTMAS

Christmas in the Kosiak household was the greatest and happiest holiday of the year. Since we were of the Orthodox faith, we celebrated Christmas on January 7th rather than December 25th.

The pre-Christmas season was considerably shorter than it is today. Rarely was there any form of advertising until a week or two before Christmas, and then only by means of black-and-white print advertising in the local newspapers. Television was non-existent, and few people had radios. The Montgomery Ward and Sears Roebuck catalogs were the primary source of information as to what toys were available.

An editorial in the January 1, 2001, edition of the *Minneapolis Star Tribune* entitled, "Once a kingdom of Christmas dreams," captured the anticipation and joy with which we perused these catalogs.

*. . . you could always count on Montgomery Ward. Its big catalogs came with the change of the seasons, and it was from them that many school clothes, coats, and boots were ordered, along with sheds and fencing and just about anything a household needed.*

*The best, though, was the Christmas catalog that arrived in the mail each autumn. It was smaller than the general catalog, but still boasted a couple of hundred pages. And what pages they were, filled front to back with the most incredible toys a child could want. Possession of the toy catalog was a sought-after status in many households, and more than one fracas erupted when siblings could not agree on who would get it when. Over many weeks, the book would become dog-eared and torn as young people looked at bicycles and dolls, cowboy outfits and chemistry sets and microscopes and cooking sets and erector sets. There were so many things.*

*Over time, each child would settle on the items most highly prized. Rarely did they get many of them, but somehow that did not matter; it was almost understood, and superfluous to the fall dreaming the catalog stimulated. The point wasn't to have the items in the catalog, but to dream of how it would be if you did. Most of the time, that was enough. For many years, Montgomery Ward provided quite a few youngsters with a wholesome, fun way to pass fall days and evenings. Critics might find this too materialistic, but that misses the point: Dreaming is a part of childhood; Wards' Christmas catalog was a wonderful tool for setting those dreams free.*[110]

The schools were the source of most of the pre-Christmas activity. Much time was spent singing carols and preparing the Christmas program with a strong religious flavor. These types of programs would not be allowed in the public schools today. Each classroom was provided with a fresh-cut evergreen tree to be decorated by the students. The story of Christmas was told and retold every year throughout our grade school years with an enacting and reenacting of the Nativity at virtually every class level. Santa Claus visited the schools, and the High School Band came to each school for a short concert of Christmas carols. On the last day of school before Christmas, each child received a popcorn ball and a small box of hard candy. At least in our family, we all brought the candy and popcorn balls home to be placed under the tree on Christmas morning.

Two weeks of vacation from school was a standard part of the holiday season. While a majority of the people in town celebrated on the 25th of December, we never had a Christmas tree in the house until New Year's Day. Although most of the neighbors had already discarded their trees, Tato absolutely insisted on a freshly cut tree.

Tato provided the trees when we were very young, but as we grew older, we boys were given the responsibility of bringing in a tree. Getting a tree was a fairly simple matter involving a walk of a mile or so from our home. The balsam tree was usually the tree of choice because it tended to retain its needles for a longer period of time. Rather than selecting a smaller tree with an imperfect form, invariably we would find a large tree with a well-shaped top. After felling the large tree, we then cut off the top section and dragged it home.

The tree stand was of simple construction—pieces of a one-by-four-inch pine, nailed together in the form of a cross with four one-by-two-inch diagonal supports positioned to stabilize the trunk of the tree. There was no way to water the tree, so the trees tended to dry out very rapidly, becoming a potential fire hazard. The tree was usually discarded immediately after the Orthodox New Year, on January 14th.

Our Christmas tree always stood along the north wall of the living room. Trimming the tree was truly a family affair. While Ma was initially responsible for positioning and securing the lights, this duty was taken over by the children in later years. Once the lights were in place, two strands of well-worn, commercial garland were placed on the tree—running from top to bottom. One strand circled the tree in a clockwise direction while the other strand was positioned in a counter-clockwise direction.

Ma again took charge as she carefully attached a dozen or more very fragile, colorful Christmas tree ornaments. These same ornaments had decorated the tree year after year as long as any of us could remember. Once the ornaments were in place, tree trimming again became a total family affair. Fine strips of silver foil tinsel were carefully draped over the tree branches, giving the tree an appearance of being covered with icicles. In fact, we always referred to the tinsel as "icicles."

(During the war, the Allied bombers dropped large quantities of silver foil from their aircraft in an attempt to disrupt Japanese radar that was used to direct anti-aircraft guns.)

Although applying the tinsel was a time-consuming procedure, removing and salvaging it when the tree came down was far more tedious and frustrating. Each individual strand was carefully removed, smoothed out and replaced in the original commercial container to be used and reused for several more years. Only broken strands, less than three or four inches in length, could be honorably retired from service.

Tato usually seemed to be more in the Christmas spirit than Ma, probably because Christmas in the Kosiak household required the preparation of large amounts and varieties of food. For many years, especially when we were of grade school age, Tato insisted that we learn several centuries-old Russian Christmas carols. Each year he would sit us down on several occasions before Christmas and have us sing. The fact that Mary Ann, Irene, and I can still sing most of these carols in Russian illustrates the intensity of these childhood sessions.

Tato's Christmas religious fervor was best demonstrated on at least two occasions when he transformed the entire main floor of our home, except for the kitchen, into a manger covered with several inches of hay. All this was done in spite of the presence of the wood-burning kitchen stove and our coal-burning furnace.

Christmas in our home was truly a religious happening embellished with a variety of homemade foods. Christmas Eve supper (*Sviatey Vecher*) was the highlight of the holiday season. On the afternoon of Christmas Eve, we brought hay in from the barn and put it on the table under the tablecloth to signify the hay in the manger.

After lighting the single candle, which signified the Star of Bethlehem and Christ as The Light of the World, the family stood and recited in Church Slavonic "The Lord's Prayer" (*Oche Nash*). The twelve dishes of the traditional Christmas Eve supper, which are supposed to be eaten in sequence from bitter to sweet, represent the twelve apostles. The foods included cabbage soup (*kapusta*), garlic, herring, potatoes, beans, and mushrooms. We also had rice, cooked prunes, bread with honey drizzled over it, whole yellow peas, and *perohi* with prune, sauerkraut or potato filling. Of course, we also had our bottle of pop. There were no meat, milk or cheese dishes.

During the Depression, family income was meager at best, and seasonal commercialism was virtually nonexistent. Christmas was the season of food and drink. Except for fruits such as apples and oranges, all the food was prepared from basic ingredients.

Although Tato was not a drinking man, he did appreciate an occasional glass of beer. At Christmas and Easter he would reward himself with a small, wooden, six-gallon keg of beer. Because the beer was under pressure, more often than not, tapping the keg resulted in a shower of beer, which reached as high as the ceiling at times.

For the children, two cases of pop were ordered from the local bottling company. The locally made pop included such flavors as lime, orange, strawberry, and cream soda. There was no Coke or Pepsi to drink in those days. The pop usually disappeared after the first day because most of us hid our allotment to be enjoyed at a later date. Hard liquor (moonshine) was used sparingly, only when some of the old timers or the church carolers came over to extend season's greetings.

Christmas morning was the only time during the entire winter when, after getting out of bed, we did not head directly for the warm kitchen. Tato, if he weren't working, or Ma would always be there to greet us, "*Christos Razhdaetsia*" (Christ Is Born) to which we would reply "*Slaviti Yeho*" (Adore Him). The tree lights were always turned on by the time we got there, and at no time was there a lack of space around the tree for gifts or packages. Most of the articles were not even wrapped. After all, colorful wrapping just didn't seem to enhance the appearance of winter underwear, long-sleeve shirts, or knit mittens for the boys and winter underwear, long stockings, or matching home-knit scarves and tassel caps for the girls. There was never any of the Montgomery Ward or Sears Robuck merchandise we had come to dream about for weeks before Christmas. There was the pair of skates one year and a pair of skis a few years later. Always, there was a hand-written letter from Santa Claus pleading hardship to justify the fact that there were no toys under the tree.

Besides much-needed clothing, under the tree for each child was a bowl containing the hard candy and the popcorn ball we had brought home from school three weeks earlier. Each bowl also contained a handful of peanuts, a small orange and, of course, money—always one thin dime. Beginning in the late 1930s, Uncle Harry Billo and Uncle Bill and Aunt Eva Smolensky provided several gifts, especially for the girls.

After breakfast, it was time to go to church. The service, which included the singing of several carols, was more festive than usual and always lasted more than two hours, during which time we stood or kneeled on the cold hardwood floor. The adults always stood near the walls so they could lean when tired, but the younger folks were relegated to the center of the church.

After dinner, if Christmas occurred on Saturday or Sunday, we would spend our dime at the local theater matinee. If Christmas fell on a weekday, we would stay home relishing the fact that we had an extra day away from school.

Christmas afternoon was the day that the priest and church carolers visited all the homes of the parish families. The priest conferred a blessing on the home and the family while the carolers sang a series of traditional, centuries-old Christmas carols. Caroling was a moneymaking enterprise for the church, with donations frequently exceeding the total Sunday service collections of the previous several months. Families also were expected to liberally dispense beverages (moonshine) for the carolers, which was probably a powerful incentive for persons to volunteer for the job.

The Chisholm congregation also ministered to the Russian Orthodox Church in Rauch, a small farming community located about fifty miles north of town. Therefore, an annual caroling expedition was usually conducted the weekend after Christmas (January 7th) or sometime in mid-January. Because of the cold weather, the poor conditions of the road, the almost total lack of any other traffic and the lack of a spare tire, one can appreciate the potentially hazardous nature of the trip. In spite of the fact that a vehicle breakdown might result in an overnight stay along the road, emergency supplies such as flashlights and blankets were never even considered. The annual pilgrimage was conducted with considerable risk to the participants. Perhaps the fact that a priest accompanied us provided a false sense of security.

Tato provided transportation of the main participants, at first in his 1928 four-door Hudson and later in his brand new 1937 Chrysler Royal. Next to Tato in the front seat were the local priest and I. Three senior carolers, selected for the amplitude rather than quality of their voices, occupied the rear seat.

The first order of business on arriving in Rauch was to conduct an abbreviated Christmas service at the small wood-frame church, which was heated by a wood-burning, potbelly stove. After the service, the entourage was always invited to one of the farm homes for a Christmas dinner. A variety of foods was usually served, but the main dish was always chicken. Frequent toasts, with liberal amounts of homemade moonshine raised the spirit as well as the decibel level of the carolers. Once the meal was completed, the Chisholm carolers began their rounds accompanied by a second vehicle of local carolers who, by then, were obviously in a partying mood. Visiting the ten to fifteen families in the parish lasted into the early evening and usually included at least one more formal Christmas chicken dinner and, of course, more toasting.

Our family has always maintained that the reason I was included on those trips was not to assist the priest but rather to keep an eye on Tato. The fact that all the trips ended successfully and safely is surely a testimonial to my vigilance.

# 12

# *National Holidays and Travel*

Thanksgiving, Memorial Day, and the Fourth of July were the major public holidays celebrated by our family. Labor Day was important only because it was followed by the start of the new school year. Armistice Day was observed exclusively in the classroom, and the schools were closed on Washington's and Lincoln's birthdays whenever they occurred during the school week. There was never a spring break, but schools were always closed in observance of Good Friday.

## THANKSGIVING

Thanksgiving in the early and mid-thirties was considered one of the finest holidays of the year. It was celebrated more as it was meant to be, with close family gatherings and simple foods, some of which were homegrown and all of which were home prepared. For the student, Thanksgiving also meant a two-day vacation.

Thanksgiving at that time was not considered a major holiday, especially from a commercial standpoint. Surely, it was not the beginning of the Christmas shopping season. Promotion of the Thanksgiving holiday celebration rested almost exclusively with the public school system. At every grade level, the first Thanksgiving in Plymouth was thoroughly discussed, acted and reenacted, to the extent that any child from the third grade could probably recite verbatim the entire menu of that first feast:

turkey and dressing, mashed potatoes and gravy, cranberry sauce, and of course, pumpkin pie.

The degree to which this standard menu was engraved in the minds of the children was demonstrated during the "Show and Tell" sessions which took place at school the following Monday. When asked by the teacher, "What did your family have for Thanksgiving?" the standard response was "Oh, we had turkey and dressing, mashed potatoes and gravy, cranberry sauce, and pumpkin pie." All this in spite of the fact that most families could not afford turkey. Turkeys were actually a very rare commodity in the early thirties. If a family could afford a turkey, it was purchased live, kept at home a few days for fattening, then sacrificed before cooking.

Consequently, chicken was usually the main course for Thanksgiving dinner. In fact, our Grandmother Billo always referred to Thanksgiving simply as "Chicken Day." Our neighbors of Slavic heritage would usually feature pork chops, ham, or roast beef, mashed potatoes and gravy as well as pumpkin pie.

Although for years chicken had been the fowl of choice in our family, on two or three occasions Tato brought home a live goose, which for a week or so was allowed to roam freely throughout our basement. Anyone familiar with the habits of the Canadian geese that spend their summers in our parks and golf courses can imagine what the basement floor looked like by Thanksgiving Day. The goose was sacrificed the day before Thanksgiving with Tato functioning as the executioner. Plucking the feathers and down as well as dressing the bird was Ma's responsibility.

Uncle Harry Billo is responsible for introducing the Thanksgiving turkey to our family. His employer, the Oliver Iron Mining Company, conducted an annual turkey raffle during which a turkey was awarded to each winner. We later learned that no one was a loser in that everyone who attended the function went home with a turkey. Uncle Harry would bring the turkey to our house where Ma would dress the bird and make the dressing. Aunt Eva Smolensky would bake several pies for the dinner. The guest list on Thanksgiving usually included Uncle Mike Kosiak, Tato's older brother who lived with us, Grandma Billo, Uncle Harry, and our aunt and uncle, Eva and Bill Smolensky.

Since Thanksgiving was not a religious holiday, Tato did not feel privileged to accord himself a keg of beer. Consequently, there was no pop for the children either. Activity after the dinner depended upon one's age.

Because all of the public buildings, including the library, were closed on that day, recreational activities were relegated to the outdoors. The older family members usually sat around and socialized. Because there was no television, there were no college or professional football games and of course there was no watching the Macy's Parade.

## MEMORIAL DAY

Memorial Day was and still is an official holiday in most states. Though once observed on May 30, since 1971 the date was changed to the last Monday in May. With the exception of Louisiana, all states observing Memorial Day adopted the change. Memorial Day was also known as Decoration Day.

Congress recognizes Waterloo, New York, as the official birthplace of Memorial Day, since the custom of placing flowers on the graves of the war dead began in that city on May 5, 1866. In 1868, General John A. Logan, then president of the Grand Army of the Republic, declared that May 30 would be a day to decorate with "flowers the graves of comrades who died in defense of their country during the late rebellion."[111]

After World War I, the day was set aside to honor the dead of all American wars, and the custom was extended to pay homage to deceased relatives and friends, both military and civilian. The most solemn ceremony conducted on Memorial Day is the placing of a wreath at the Tomb of the Unknowns located in Arlington National Cemetery.

Until 1915, Chisholm's observation of Memorial Day was limited to simple decoration of soldiers' graves along with a memorial service at the cemetery. According to the *Chisholm Tribune Herald* of May 28, 1915, "Spanish-American War Veterans will have charge of the first observation of Memorial Day in Chisholm."[112] The June 4, 1915, edition reported that in addition to the Commercial Band, the parade included Spanish-American War Veterans, Boy Scouts, and school children.

The following year, 1916, the Memorial Day parade was described as, "the largest and most elaborate in the history of the Village." More than 2,400 children representing the High School as well as Lincoln, Monroe, and Meyers schools participated in the parade.[113]

The beginning of World War I in the summer of 1914 was followed by the rapid mobilization of American forces, especially in 1915 after the

German sinking of the *Lusitania* with the loss of 128 American lives. Patriotism in America was slowly rising and reached a fever pitch with America's entry into the war on April 6, 1917.

Soon after our entry into the war, the *Chisholm Tribune Herald* on May 4, 1917, reported on the "Loyalty Demonstration Parade" of April 29, 1917.

> *Although skies were overcast and a drizzling rain fell throughout the entire day, Chisholm ignored most adverse weather conditions Sunday afternoon and 7,000 persons marched in a loyalty demon-stration, which was the largest parade ever held in the Village. . . . The divisions were large and four bands were not sufficient to fur-nish the music necessary. Young America was well represented. Two thousand children from the Village schools marched with the step of veterans, each one holding aloft a miniature flag. The chil-dren of each grade marched in a body with their teacher at the head of the section. The parade stretched out over a mile and a half in length and as the parade was leaving the school grounds, the head of the procession was turning onto Third Avenue, just three blocks in the rear.*[114]

The line of march that day began on Third Avenue South and Spruce (Third) Street, proceeded down Spruce Street to Second Avenue, then south to Oak (Sixth) Street, east to First Avenue, north to Birch (Second) Street, east to Central Avenue, north to Lake Street, up Lake Street to Third Avenue and then down Third Avenue back to the High School. Bands participating in that parade included the Hibbing City Band, the Chisholm Commercial Band, the High School Band, and the Chisholm National Band.

Although Memorial Day celebrations were somewhat subdued dur-ing World War I, school children participated every year. Concerning the first post-World War I Memorial Day Program, the *Chisholm Tribune Herald* of May 30, 1919, reported the following: "Monster parade and impressive services at the Cemetery will mark Chisholm's observance of the first Memorial Day to follow the Great World War."[115]

Ceremonies at the cemetery included the decoration of veterans' graves, a rifle salute, and the sounding of "Taps." The parade began at 10:00 A.M. Participants in the parade included Civil War, Spanish-

American and World War I veterans, as well as the High School Band and school children.

Involvement of several hundred grade school children in the Memorial Day celebrations continued well into the post-World War II era. Preparations always began about two or three weeks before Memorial Day. Practice sessions for the Roosevelt School classes were held along cordoned-off Hemlock (Fourth) Street, from Central to First Avenue South. The children lined up by class, six to eight students abreast. The teacher counted cadence—"left-right, left-right"—as we proceeded down the street.

On occasion the High School Band might lead the practice session. On those occasions, practice included all the Roosevelt School classes from the third through the sixth grade. In addition to stressing proper cadence and keeping the rows of children as straight as possible, special emphasis and training was necessary to execute the corner turns. "Pivot, pivot, pivot," teachers kept reminding the marchers as they rounded each corner. During the dress rehearsal a day or two before the Big Day, each child was provided with and instructed in the proper way to carry a small American flag. The dress code for Memorial Day was quite strict: all the girls wore white dresses, white stockings, and black shoes; the boys wore white shirts with bow ties, dark trousers and leather shoes.

Final formation on the day of the parade took place on Spruce (Third) Street, between Second and Third Avenue South next to the High School. The marchers proceeded down Spruce Street to Central Avenue, north to Lake Street, up Lake Street to Third Avenue and then back to the High School. The High School Band preceded students from the Monroe and Shenango locations, as well as the Roosevelt and Washington schools. Beginning in the early 1930s, the Lincoln School and Balkan School children were led by the Lincoln Grade School Marching Band, the highlight of the Memorial Day parade. Various veterans' organizations as well as the American Legion Drum and Bugle Corps and the Chisholm Municipal Band also participated in the parade.

Since the end of World War I, Memorial Day has on occasion also been referred to as "Poppy Day." The poppy, which blossomed over many of the battlefields of France, became the symbol of the tragedy of war and the renewal of life. Poppy Week, the week before Memorial Day, traditionally honored the men and women who had served in the United States armed services. Receipts from the sale of small, red, artificial poppies are used to assist in the care of disabled veterans. The Veterans of Foreign Wars conducted the first nationwide sale of poppies in 1922.[116]

Tato, a World War I veteran, was a member in good standing of the Chisholm Veterans of Foreign Wars. Therefore, our family was always supplied with some twenty-five to thirty poppies to sell in the neighborhood. This task always fell to either Mary Ann or Irene, once they got to the fifth or sixth grade. Along with Ma, they would go from door to door throughout the neighborhood. Even though the asking price was either five or ten cents, sales were never very good.

Because in the 1930s and early 1940s our entire immediate family, including our grandparents and all our aunts and uncles, was living and well, our family was never involved in any of the activities at the cemetery.

## FOURTH OF JULY

As far as my brothers and sisters and I were concerned, the Fourth of July celebration was the most important public holiday of the year. Because the sale of fireworks was still legal, the ability to purchase fireworks as well as an ice cream cone or two was of prime importance.

Johnny, Willy, and I were involved in a variety of group activities designed to generate the desired income. The best way to earn money was to collect and sell scrap metal. Scrap copper as found especially in old pans and copper boilers, as well as in discarded electrical wiring with the insulation removed, paid as much as six to ten cents a pound. Four cents or so was paid for a pound of scrap aluminum or brass. Zinc, as found in canning-jar covers, might pay as much as a cent a pound, while scrap iron and dry, clean rags were worth only a half-cent per pound.

Most of these materials were obtained by scrounging up and down the back alleys (garbage cans were not in use in those days). Scrap iron was usually picked up at or near any of the mines that were not functioning during the Depression. However, the mining companies always had their own police force, so, when looking for scrap iron on the mining company property, we had to be on constant lookout for the police. Just the sight of a police officer, even at a distance, would cause one to drop the iron and run.

I can still remember quite vividly when Willy and I, along with several friends, were picking up angle irons from the Glen Pit mining property just south of Chisholm. Angle irons are pieces of steel about twenty-four inches in length which are used to connect two sections of railroad track. One angle iron is positioned on the inside of the joined track section while another one is situated on the outside. The joint is then stabilized by means of large bolts that pass through both angle irons as well as through the adjoining rails.

Having located several spare angle irons at the bottom of the Glen Pit, we then struggled up the side of the pit, each lugging a twelve-pound angle iron. Upon reaching the top, we were suddenly confronted by an Oliver Iron Mining Company police officer, who had obviously spotted us earlier and had watched us drag ourselves and the weights out of the pit. We had no place to run. The officer instructed us to carry the angle irons back down into the pit and put them in the exact area from which they had been taken. After disposing of our loot, we then climbed the side of the pit again and walked past the officer, who was still waiting. We then proceeded home empty-handed.

Although this was neither the first nor the last time we were confronted by the mining company police, the incident was especially galling for several reasons. First, the policeman had waited for us to haul the heavy irons out of the pit before presenting himself. Second, the combined value of all the angle irons would have been less than fifty cents, to be divided among me, Willy, and three of our friends.

Another less-than-successful financial endeavor involved a log-peeling experience. Farm fencing required the use of cedar logs or poles, upon which were strung three or four strands of barbed wire. Because the longevity of these cedar posts was greatly enhanced if the bark was removed from the log, there was always a demand for log peelers at the McKusick's Sawmill located about one mile north of Chisholm.

I was just out of the fifth grade, Willy had completed the seventh grade, and Johnny was going into his sophomore year when the three of us, each armed with a draw knife and a lunch provided by Ma, set out walking one summer day to McKusick's Sawmill. Because the going rate of pay was three cents per peeled log regardless of size, by the time we arrived at the sawmill the older fellows had already corralled most of the smaller logs. My total production that day was three mid-sized logs, earning myself nine cents. Willy and Johnny did somewhat better. All that after a two-mile walk and eight hours of hard, hot work.

Fourth of July civic activities included a variety of races and free ice cream for all who showed up for the event. Since we boys were not known

197

for our athletic prowess, only Irene and Mary Ann ever participated in the competitive events. The afternoons were usually spent at home using fireworks to dispatch a variety of objects. The targets, always in the back alleys, ranged from small fruit and vegetable cans to the ubiquitous manure piles into which were inserted the larger fireworks, cherry bombs. A short fuse in the cherry bomb usually resulted in a quick trip home to wash up.

The evening consisted of more fireworks, for those who had not already exhausted their supply, and a street dance which was held downtown. This was also the one night of the year when the nine o'clock curfew was not strictly enforced, much to the enjoyment of all the children.

The Fourth of July also signaled the start of the watermelon season. At that time watermelons sold for about one-half to one cent per pound, and one was required to purchase an entire watermelon. Because there were neither refrigerated trucks to transport the watermelons nor home iceboxes in which to store them the watermelon season was very short-lived.

## LABOR DAY

Labor Day, a federal holiday since 1894, was important only in that it signified the beginning of the new school year the next day.

## VETERANS DAY
## (ARMISTICE DAY)

November 11th was first proclaimed a holiday in 1919. Originally called Armistice Day, the holiday commemorated the signing on November 11, 1918, of the armistice that brought an end to World War I. Armistice Day was of little importance to the young child in that there was school as usual. However, in school we were all required at eleven minutes past eleven o'clock in the morning to stand for one minute in complete silence while facing the East, toward the battlefields of Europe. Appropriate school activities were conducted, reminding us of the significance of this holiday.

On June 1, 1954, President Dwight D. Eisenhower signed an Act of Congress changing the name of the holiday to Veterans Day "to honor veterans on the eleventh day of November of each year—a day dedicated to world peace." New legislation enacted in 1968 changed the date of the federal holiday to the fourth Monday in October, effective in 1971.

Beginning in 1978, because of the historic and patriotic significance of November 11, Public Law 94-97, enacted on September 20, 1975, returned the annual observation of Veterans Day to the original date of November 11.[117]

## THE ST. LOUIS COUNTY FAIR

Although we considered the Fourth of July the most important public celebration during the summer months, the St. Louis County Fair ranked a close second. The fair was usually held during the second week of August at the County Fair Grounds in Hibbing, on the site of the present-day Hibbing Community College. Once the Fourth of July festivities were completed, we all started to save or attempt to raise some spending money for the fair.

The fair had something for everybody, young or old. In addition to the usual animal and farm produce displays, there were automobile and horse races as well as a midway featuring all types of games of chance and carnival rides. Admission to the fairgrounds was nominal by today's standards: ten cents for a child, twenty-five cents for an adult; but who had ten cents to spare? One also had to get to and from Hibbing, a distance of about seven miles from Chisholm.

One year, when Johnny was about twelve years old, Willy, ten, and I was eight, the folks gave each of us a generous donation of twenty-five cents to spend at the fair. Since the admission was ten cents, that left fifteen cents for each of us "to have a good time." Because we didn't have enough money to get into the grandstand to watch the car races, we spent a lot of time going through the animal barns and just walking around the midway. Since only ten cents was available to go on a ride, the last five cents was used to buy some nourishment around suppertime.

Since Tato was working the three-to-eleven, second shift, we spent much of the time that afternoon to no avail looking for a neighbor who might give us a ride home. Finally, at about eight o'clock or so, we decided that maybe we should be on our way home. For anyone without a vehicle, hitchhiking was the transport method of choice. So we started out hitchhiking to Chisholm.

One would think that some sympathetic driver would have stopped to pick us up. On the other hand, most of them must have thought, "What are those kids doing out on the highway at this time of night?" It was getting darker by the minute. Even if there were pay phones in those days, we were out of money, and Tato was working anyway. So we started out for Chisholm, walking down the highway. The farther we got from the Hibbing city limits, the faster the traffic seemed to move, and no one even appeared to slow down.

It was already quite dark before we crossed over the Mitchell Bridge, about two miles east of Hibbing. Once we reached Kitzville, a small location about three miles east of Hibbing, we decided to take a shortcut through the mines, which were situated south of Chisholm. The Godfrey Mine road was not surfaced and of course there were no lights along the road. The only traffic was during the shift change at the mine, and that would not be taking place until around eleven o'clock. The lights at the Godfrey Mine served as a beacon as we trudged along the dark, dirt road swatting pesky mosquitoes.

Because the Godfrey Mine was an underground mine, the only miners on the surface were either on the stockpile or in the dry-house. Even though the area was well lit, we proceeded past the mine without being sighted or interrupted. We then continued down the dirt road, past the Leonard Mine head frame to the Wellington Mine. On approaching the Wellington, we were in our familiar cattle-grazing territory, and even though it was pitch dark, we felt more comfortable and safe.

From the Wellington Mine head frame, we then followed the Duluth, Mesabi and Iron Range Railroad tracks back into town, arriving home just before Tato got home from work. Although Ma had never alerted him concerning our prolonged absence, the family was obviously elated, especially Ma.

Before leaving the county fair, I must relate another fair-going incident. As noted, we considered the fair to be one of the major events of our summer vacation. As we got older, hitchhiking to the fair was the preferred form of travel, and over the years this took place without any incidents. Because there was an admission charge, even for students, the entire fair complex, which was surrounded by fencing, was also patrolled by Hibbing police. However, since the fairgrounds covered an area of at least forty acres, police patrols along the fencing were limited at times. In spite of the fact that the top of the hurricane-type fence contained multiple sharp, barbed projections, one could, with luck, get over the top of the fence with a gentle lift or push from a friend—and save the ten cent admission change.

Unfortunately, one day Johnny ran short of luck and failed miserably in an attempt to scale the fence in spite of help from some of his friends. In the process of falling from the top of the fence, the palm of his hand came into contact with one of the barbs, resulting in a rather deep and long laceration. Fortunately, Johnny's friends who did the pushing realized the serious nature of the injury and immediately notified a Hibbing police officer on duty in the area. A police car transported Johnny to the emergency room of the Hibbing hospital where the wound was sutured and dressed.

Of some interest is the fact that neither the police nor the hospital personnel contacted our folks, even though Johnny was a minor and we did have a telephone. Since the accident happened on a Sunday afternoon, we suspect that the folks may have been out visiting their friends or our grandparents, so no one was at home.

However, all the family was home when the Hibbing police delivered Johnny to our front door. Johnny reportedly was more apprehensive about his reception at home than he was about the condition of his hand. Since Tato had no health insurance for the family, we never did find out who picked up the tab for the emergency room visit. Perhaps the St. Louis County Fair Board was billed for the services.

# TRAVEL

In today's world, the word "travel" conjures up a variety of vacation destinations: Disney World, Scottsdale, San Diego, or a Caribbean cruise in the winter; Yellowstone Park, Washington, D.C., a Canadian fishing trip or maybe even a trip to Europe in the summer.

In the early thirties, travel usually meant trudging on foot from one place to another: to school, to church, to the library or to the store to pick up some groceries. Very few people owned automobiles, and the leisurely Sunday drive just did not exist.

Although our family owned a car, it was usually a second-hand model with high mileage and well-worn tires. Travel meant going to Monroe Location to visit the Grandparents Billo on summer afternoons, a distance of one mile each way. Otherwise drives were limited to the family garden and later to the family farm located in Great Scott Township. We also used the car to haul hay, firewood, and manure. Never did we go for a pleasurable joyride.

That we were homebodies was demonstrated by the fact that none of the children had ever traveled as far as Duluth before the age of ten or twelve, even though Duluth was less than eighty miles from Chisholm.

None of my brothers or I had ever been as far west as Keewatin until we were involved in high school sports. Once a year in the summer, we traveled as far as Ely to visit Uncle Peter and Aunt Eva. Since Tato was not a fishing buff, we never traveled north to any of the lakes except for one occasion when the family traveled to McCarthy Beach on Big Sturgeon Lake for a picnic.

The limitations on travel in the thirties were due to a variety of factors. Except for Uncle Peter who lived in Ely with his family, all our relatives lived in the immediate Iron Range area. The vehicles Tato owned were probably not the most reliable. Flat tires and mechanical unreliability were the primary factors restricting the frequency and range of vehicular travel. The tires on Tato's cars were usually more than simply well-worn, and spare tires were unheard-of. Experiencing a flat tire meant jacking up the car, removing the rim and the tire, separating the tire from the rim and then extracting the inner tube. A blown-out inner tube usually meant Tato walking or hitchhiking home to get another inner tube. For minor leaks that might be caused by a nail, the leak had to be found and that area of the tube had to be roughened or abraded before a patch could be glued over the puncture site. The tube was then inserted into the tire before being inflated using a hand pump.

In spite of the general uncertainties associated with travel, the entire Kosiak clan, as well as Uncle Bill and Aunt Eva Smolensky, began an extensive motor trip during the summer of 1932. One-year-old Irene was left at home with Grandpa and Grandma Billo. Tato at that time was driving a 1928, gray-colored, eight-cylinder Hudson. In 1932, Johnny was twelve years old, Willy was ten, I was eight, and Mary Ann was five. Considering that the Hudson had a stick shift, we still marvel at not only how we all fit into the car, but also more importantly how we all survived the two-week trip.

All clothing was stashed in the car's trunk along with the usual assortment of tools: wrenches, hammers, screwdrivers, a car-jack as well as inner tube repair supplies and a hand pump. Ma prepared a substantial two-day lunch for eight people, and we were off. Down Highway 53, through Duluth and Superior and into upper Wisconsin, we proceeded at what must have been an average rate of speed of between forty and forty-five miles an hour. We decided to spend our first night on the road at a small hotel in Ashland, Wisconsin.

We children had never spent a night in any place other than our home, much less in a hotel in a strange town. In a room with two double beds, the three boys slept in one bed while Mary Ann slept with the folks. The Smolenskys had a room of their own. The need to use the toilet situated in a small bathroom at the end of the hall was very disconcerting especially for us children. Tato accompanied us boys down the hall when necessary, while Ma went with Mary Ann. Located on a dresser was a pitcher full of water and a large bowl—all that was available for washing.

Crossing the Mackinac Straits by ferry was an unforgettable experience. The trip probably reminded Ma of her trip to America as a ten-year-old child, whereas Tato had been to Europe and back by ship during World War I.

In Pinconning, Michigan, for the first time we got to meet two of Tato's brothers as well as many of our first cousins. Accommodations were excellent, as was the food. We also were exposed for the first time to large-scale farming.

Our visit to Detroit was rather uneventful until such time as the folks decided to take a side trip to Windsor, Canada. The problem was encountered on our return into the United States. Because the smuggling of beer and liquor into America was apparently a frequent occurrence and because prohibition was still the law of the land, all persons crossing the border into the United States were subjected to close scrutiny. Perhaps of even greater significance was the fact that, though both Tato and Ma were American citizens, neither possessed a passport and their citizenship papers were at home.

Once the customs officials determined that our parents were not native-born Americans, they were removed from the car and taken into custody without any explanation. Both Ma and Tato were escorted separately into the customs office. One can imagine the fear we experienced following the removal of our parents for no obvious reason.

For what seemed like an eternity, we were left in the car with no communication with our parents and no explanation from the customs officials as they performed a comprehensive examination of the vehicle, including the trunk. The entire procedure was as exasperating and irritating to our parents as it was frightening to us. Eventually the customs officials determined that our parents were citizens, and we were allowed to continue.

After leaving Detroit the next day, our first stop was Gary, Indiana. Although Gary's steel industry was also a victim of the Depression, we at least got to drive by the giant but inactive steel mills. Our greatest surprise took place when we visited one of the local junior high schools, which was available during the hot summers for bathing purposes. In the early 1930s there were no black people in Chisholm. To our amazement, except for Tato and us three boys, 100 percent of the bathers that day were black. Needless to say, there was not much communicating with our fellow bathers.

On the way to Milwaukee, we stopped in at the Field Museum in Chicago, where we spent several eye-opening hours. What impressed us the most was the large number of mummies on display. Never having seen any building more than four or five stories in height, except what we had seen in Detroit, the sight of the Chicago skyline was overwhelming. In fact, Tato stopped the car along Lake Shore Drive on several occasions and allowed us to get out for a better view.

In Milwaukee, we stayed at the homes of two of our first cousins, daughters of Uncle Mike Kosiak, who was living with us at our home in Chisholm at the time. Two incidents that occurred in Milwaukee were remembered for a long time. The first occurred during an evening meal prepared by our cousin. The dinner presentation was considerably more formal than what we were accustomed to in our home in Chisholm. We had never even seen, much less used stemware, especially fancy glasses filled with a clear liquid and an ice cube. Without exception we thought that the stemware was a sophisticated means of dispensing some form of soft drink. Though we all would have appreciated some liquid during the course of the meal, we all held off, saving the "soft drink" as a sort of dessert. When we sampled the treat and found that it was plain water, we were very disappointed. Why would anyone dispense water in such a fancy piece of glassware? Because in our home, the kitchen sink was located within ten or fifteen feet of the kitchen table, water was never served during the meal. Although our host may not have been aware of our disappointment, the matter was discussed on multiple occasions all the rest of the way home.

The second incident, which took place on our visit the next day to the Wisconsin State Fair, was the source of a period of short-lived but extreme anxiety. Attempting to shepherd four young children around state fairgrounds is no mean feat even under the best of conditions. Considering the fact that we had already been on the road for two weeks, traveling eight people in a very crowded automobile, sleeping in strange beds and eating a variety of foods, the task was monumental. Understandably there had been some fraying of the nerves.

As we plowed through the crowds, we suddenly realized that Mary Ann was missing. She was nowhere to be seen. Ma reined in the three remaining children while Tato and our cousins started to backtrack. After what seemed like an eternity, but before any fair officials could be notified, down the street came Mary Ann, screaming and crying. After rounding up the family, we left. That was the end of the Wisconsin State Fair. The next day, we started back home, non-stop all the way.

The boys did most of the out-of-town traveling after this family trip. In 1938, after the sudden death of our Uncle Steve, Willy and a friend of his hitchhiked to Pinconning, Michigan, where they spent much of the summer helping our cousin Peter, who was fifteen years old at the time, run the farm.

Johnny was considerably more adventurous. In 1940 he and fellow Chisholmite Dick Logefeil embarked on a prolonged hitchhiking trip, bumming their way to the West Coast. Decades later, Dick described the details of the trip in a personal letter to all of Johnny's children:

*The first day we breezed along and got to Fargo with no trouble. The second day progress was slower. We got to Bismarck [North Dakota], and then across the river [Missouri River] to a little town called Mandan. There, trouble started. We couldn't get a ride. It started to rain. It got dark. We were cold, wet, hungry and tired. We had slept under a bridge on cardboard and covered with cardboard. The next morning, still cold, wet and hungry we had a meeting and discussed the situation. We considered going back home since the going on a bum wasn't turning out to be as much fun as we had thought it would. We knew our friends would never quit razzing us. We talked some more and came to the conclusion that people were reluctant to pick up two healthy looking, athletic guys. We decided we had to separate. We got out our maps and agreed*

205

*to meet at the post office of a town about 150 miles away. This worked fine and shortly we were each picked up separately and met at the designated town.*[118]

They arrived at Seattle after only four days on the road. Dick continues his account of their progress from Seattle to San Francisco:

*Along this stretch we discovered how handy used-car lots were as a place to sleep. We'd crawl into the back seats of those boxy old Hudsons or the like and conk out. We'd clean up in a gas station the next day and be on our way.*

After spending ten days with friends in the San Francisco area, the travelers started for home. Dick describes the trip home including a "lay-over" in Vernal, Utah, some seventy-five miles east of Salt Lake City.

*We couldn't get out of there. We were there for three days. We tried everything we could think of. At the end of the first day, one of the locals told us that if we went to see the sheriff and agreed to sweep the streets, we could get a free meal. We did that. We saw the sheriff; he gave us each a big push broom and told us which street he wanted swept. Then he said, "Here's a meal ticket for a meal at Mom's Café. I won't be here when you're done so I'll give it to you now." We spent the night in the local jail—the Radisson it was not. We were the only guests. It was really miserable. Just a cot with a mattress and of course no sheets or blankets. We slept in our clothes.*

The world travelers left Vernal and backtracked to Salt Lake City before resuming their trip home. Soon after, they became separated and Dick returned to Chisholm one day earlier than Johnny. Concerning the benefits of the trip, Dick reported:

*We compared notes but our big adventure was over. We had learned a lot about our country, about human nature and had had a lot of fun.*

# 13

# *The Depression and World War II*

*If one were to attempt to ascribe any benefits which the people of Chisholm and the entire Range may have realized from the Depression, it was the fact that the bleak outlook for employment may have encouraged many young adults and recent high school graduates to seek advanced education especially at one of the five junior colleges located on the Iron Range.*

—M Kosiak

T he Great Depression had virtually no immediate effect on our family's way of life. Although Tato was unemployed when the family bought the house on Poplar Street, he was not unemployed for long.

The story is told that after Dr. E.H. Nelson had come to the house to assist in my delivery, he asked Tato, "John, how are you planning to pay for this delivery?" Incidentally the charge for a home delivery in those days was $15. When Tato replied that he was unemployed, Dr. Nelson, who was a member of the Fire Department Commission at the time, asked him if he'd be interested in working for the fire department. Needless to say, Tato accepted the offer. Except for a period of two years between 1926 and 1928, he served in the department continuously until his retirement on February 1, 1960, a period of almost thirty-five years.

Although the pay was not comparable to that of the men employed by the mining companies, the work was steady, not seasonal as it was in the mines. Because being a firefighter was usually not the most strenuous form of work, Tato always had an abundance of energy available for projects around the home. As noted, these energies were directed toward a variety of efforts aimed primarily at supplementing the food supply (cows and a garden) and keeping the woodbin full.

Just a few words about Tato's job at the fire department. Talk about steady work. Tato always worked seven days a week and, even after many years, he was entitled to only one week of vacation each year. In addition, he was also on call twenty-four hours a day. Whenever the fire department responded to a call, every off-duty firefighter was expected to report immediately to the fire station to provide back-up support, day or night.

If the firefighter could not be contacted by phone, he would be alerted by the fire alarm whistle, which was always sounded whenever the fire engine left the station. Even when we were on the farm, our ears were continuously tuned for the fire whistle, which was barely audible at best. This was the signal for Tato to jump into his truck and return to the fire station as rapidly as possible.

Tato's salary during the Depression was not much different from the salaries of those men employed constructing the new causeway across Longyear Lake or those working on W.P.A. projects building the Memorial Park. In January, 1932, Tato's monthly salary was $135.00. At that time he was working an eight-hour shift, seven days a week. The hourly pay for 224 hours of work was just over $.60 an hour. Workers on the new bridge project were paid $.50 an hour, $3.00 for every six-hour shift or $45.00 for working two weeks.

On February 9, 1933, Tato's salary was reduced to $121 per month while men working on the Memorial Park under the C.W.A. grant were paid $100 per month for a forty-hour week. Tato's hourly pay at that time was just over $.50 per hour as compared to the C.W.A. workers who were earning 62½ cents per hour. Tato's last pay cut during the Depression took place on March 31, 1938, when his pay was reduced from $121.00 to $116.60 per month or slightly less than $.50 per hour. At that time, common labor on the Memorial Park Project was paid $119.60 each month or $.74 per hour for a forty-hour work week.

Because most of our immigrant neighbors were also capable gardeners, woodsmen, and even hunters, as very young persons we were not aware of any serious food or fuel deprivations. Our schoolmates continued to attend school regularly. Our school clothes were clean and warm, and we still continued to look pretty much alike.

Instances when we children came to realize that hunger did affect others happened when poorly dressed men, or bums as we called them, came to our house asking for food. What impressed us more than anything was the fact that Ma always insisted that they share a meal with the family. There was never an overabundance of meat on the table, but there were always liberal amounts of potatoes, gravy, sauerkraut, and, of course, plenty of bread and milk. Though Ma undoubtedly was aware that these strangers were the source of considerable family anxiety, she continued this practice for several years. When pointedly asked, "Ma, why do you invite these people into our house?" she would invariably respond, "How do you know? It might have been God."

Following the election of President Franklin D. Roosevelt in 1932, a variety of federal work projects was initiated. The most extensive of these programs was the W.P.A. (Works Project Administration), which was founded in 1935. Jobs were provided building roads, bridges, parks, and highways. The program also created work for artists, writers, actors, and musicians. In Chisholm, most of the effort was expended in the creation of the Memorial Park complex. The minimum wage at that time was only about $.50 an hour, so the monthly wage for a laborer was about $80.00.

In 1933, the Civilian Conservation Corp (C.C.C.) program was also instituted.[119] Young adults were employed in various conservation activities under a modified military supervision program. The men were housed in military-type barracks in the general area of their primary activity. Two C.C.C. companies were situated in the immediate surrounding area, one at Big Sturgeon Lake just north of Chisholm and one at Luna Lake, also about twenty miles north of Chisholm. For their work, which involved planting trees, building roads, clearing brush and drainage ditches, the young men were paid $25.00 a month plus board, room and clothing. Of the $25.00 salary, $20.00 was sent to the home of each man. The simple fact that the C.C.C. program was even instituted was an indication of the serious lack of employment possibilities for the young adult.

The mines were virtually closed except for the part-time work provided some of their veteran employees. Because the Depression was nation-wide, the job possibilities were no better in the large industrial centers than they were on the Iron Range. Consequently, most of the young adults, male and female, did not leave town but continued to live at home with their parents and younger siblings.

Helping our neighbors to plant or harvest the crops, bring in the hay or assist with woodcutting, would usually be rewarded with a generous, large-sized glass of homemade root beer (cool only if the family owned an icebox) or a generous helping of walnut *potica* or apple *strudel*, especially from our Slavic neighbors.

The standard reward for assisting in the delivery of a quarter ton of winemaking grapes was several large bunches of grapes to be shared by all the carriers. (Wine-making was legal even during Prohibition but only for personal use.) Whatever grapes were provided the carriers were then carefully transported to Vuicich's corner where under the glow of the street light, the feasting continued until all the grapes were gone.

Although there was no market for the potatoes, corn, and the cabbages we had raised on the farm, there was always a limited market for wild produce: blueberries, strawberries, and raspberries. A quart of cleaned blueberries could be sold for $.10 or more while a quart of cleaned wild strawberries or raspberries was always worth at least $.25. Dr. Graham was one of the few cash-paying customers who lived in our neighborhood. However, he absolutely insisted that all the berries be cleaned. Dried hazel and hickory nuts as well as choke and pin cherries had only limited market value.

The Kosiaks never entered into the wild berry and nut business because all wild produce that was not eaten immediately found its way into Ma's jelly and jam warehouse to be used at a later date.

Very few jobs delivering newspapers were available because the three out-of-town newspapers, the *Hibbing Daily Tribune* as well as both Duluth papers, the morning *Tribune* and the evening *Herald*, had only limited circulation especially on the south side of town.

Mary Ann and Irene, during the war years, shared a *Duluth News Tribune* route, which extended several blocks into the near north side of town. They would first have to walk six blocks to Chestnut (First) Street North, to begin delivering their newspapers before returning home to get ready for school.

The Kosiak children, not to be outdone by our more enterprising neighbors, simply fell into a job that was not only conducted on a strictly cash basis but included a fair amount of suspense, intrigue, and excitement. No special training or equipment was required, and the amount of energy expended was minimal. Above all, the work was illegal, against the law, and we knew it. Our job was "running" whiskey.

Primarily through the efforts of the Woman's Christian Temperance Union (organized in 1874) and the Anti-Saloon League (organized in Ohio in 1893), by July 1, 1919, thirty-one states were "dry" or had voted for statewide prohibition of alcohol.[120] During World War I, the prohibition leaders strengthened their cause through the food-control bill. On July 1, 1919, under the wartime act, no more intoxicants could be sold and no saloon in America could operate legally. Amendment 18 to the

Constitution, prohibiting both the sale and possession of alcohol anywhere in the entire country, went into effect on January 16, 1920.

When Prohibition ended the legal production of whiskey, individual
entrepreneurs took up the slack. Their homemade whiskey was called
"moonshine." Moonshiners in our neighborhood produced a pure distillate
with an alcohol concentration of at least eighty percent. This was a potent
but very desirable alcoholic beverage, which was in great demand by many
of the immigrant population. Several small neighborhood "distilleries" were
operational during prohibition. Although Tato was known to take a drink on
occasion, our family functioned primarily as "moonshine runners."

As in most ethnic groups, the word got around that moonshine was
available in our general neighborhood. So as not to draw suspicion to the
moonshiner's house or to any adults who might go there, the Kosiak kids
functioned as undercover moonshine runners.

So-called customers would come calling, always entering through
the back door of our home. Generally the individual, always a gentleman,
would come alone.

Over the several years that we functioned as moonshine runners,
we soon got to know the clientele well, and there never was any question
as to the reason for their "social call." Perhaps one of the reasons we were
able to function so efficiently was because we had a telephone, required
because of Tato's work at the fire department. The moonshiner also had
a phone—the only other phone on the block—and he didn't work for the
fire department. Once the purpose of the visit had been established, the
scheduled contact took less than five minutes. Ma would call the distiller
to alert him that a sale was imminent. One of the boys, or occasionally
Mary Ann, was handed a small brown-paper bag containing a covered
one-pint Mason jar and a fifty-cent piece to pay for the merchandise.

The route we followed was always through the back alley. We never
walked on the sidewalk. We had been instructed on numerous occasions
as to the hazards of the operation and the emergency measures that
might be followed.

First of all, "You go alone. No buddies; tell them they can't go
along." Second, "Conceal the bag and bottle as well as possible." In the
winter this was no problem in that we could hide the Mason jar under our
coats. Summers were something of a problem, but we hid the bag as best
we could. Third, "If you see any strangers or cars in the alley, just exit into
a neighbor's yard." Fourth, "Always look up and down the alley before

entering the merchant's backyard." Finally, "Don't hesitate at the porch door of the merchant. Just walk onto the porch and knock on the back door. Be sure to look around before entering the porch."

Once we got into the house, things got more interesting. The merchant first subjected us to a visual "going over" and then checked the windows, front and back, before disappearing into the basement with the little brown bag.

For what seemed like an eternity, we'd just stand there waiting. We were never asked to sit down. We never saw any of the rest of the family although we knew all the children and the wife. Finally, the basement door would open slowly, and the merchant would come out and carefully hand us "the goods." After he took another quick glance out the front and back windows, we were allowed to leave. The cash payment had taken place at the time the brown bag was first exchanged, and now the only words spoken were, "Be careful."

The trip home was considerably more exciting. We were carrying a very valuable product contained in a fragile glass jar. One slip, stumble or fall would result in a few very unhappy people. The same precautions taken on our trip to the distiller's home became of even greater importance. "Be alert, keep your eyes open. If a stranger even looks at you, drop the bottle and run." Since the alley was surfaced with more rocks than dirt, the evidence would surely have been immediately destroyed.

On arriving home, we were rewarded for our law-breaking efforts. Although there were no standard tipping or commission percentages, ten percent, or five cents, was the usual tip. Not much, but also not bad for a rather adventurous journey.

During Prohibition, agents of the Internal Revenue Service called revenuers (we called them "Revenoors") were always on the lookout for distilleries of any type, and arrests were fairly common. Guilty persons received significant fines and various periods of prison confinement, sometimes even at the Federal Penitentiary in Leavenworth, Kansas.

That the Kosiaks were not the only family involved in these illicit activities was documented in *A Peak into the Past,* a packet of memoirs of current and former Chisholm residents published in a booklet during the Chisholm All-Class Reunion of 1997.[121]

A Chisholm resident reported that as a child living in Glen Location she was frequently called upon to deliver jugs of moonshine to her father's customers in Chisholm. She would first place the jug into a baby buggy, cover the merchandise with a blanket and push the buggy all the way into town—a distance of at least two miles—over the old wooden Glen sidewalk.

In 1932 both the Republican and Democratic parties included in their party platforms a proposal to have the question of the repeal of Amendment 18 submitted to the people. When Utah, on December 5, 1933, became the thirty-sixth state to ratify the 21st Amendment, liquor became legal again. Prohibition ended because the nation's most influential people, as well as the general public, acknowledged that it had failed. Prohibition had actually increased lawlessness, drinking and alcohol abuse. By 1936, all but eight states again permitted the sale of liquor. In Minnesota, ratification of the 21st Amendment repealing prohibition took place on September 12, 1933.[122]

As the Depression was waning in the late thirties, the city and county would provide the citizens with three and five-day work slips paying $5.00 a day in wages. This practice was continued into the early postwar era with most of this hiring done during the Christmas holidays, much to the joy of vacationing college students.

If one were to attempt to ascribe any benefits which the people of Chisholm and the entire Range may have realized from the Depression, it was the fact that the bleak outlook for employment may have encouraged many young adults and recent high school graduates to seek advanced education, especially at one of the five junior colleges situated on the Iron Range. Tuition charges at Hibbing Junior College for students who were residents of Hibbing were nominal. Tuition costs for non-resident students from Chisholm, Keewatin, Nashwauk, and Buhl were only slightly higher. Free bus service to and from Hibbing was provided twice daily from Chisholm, including the Shenango, Fraser and Monroe locations. A school car was even provided in the late afternoon, especially for those Chisholm students competing for the Junior College football, track, and basketball teams.

After both Johnny and Willy completed their high school education at the height of the Depression, continued education was the only realistic option. Their enrollment at Hibbing Junior College was the start of a prolonged Kosiak family involvement, beginning with Johnny's enrollment in the fall of 1938 and ending when Eve finished her Junior College education in the spring of 1956.

# THE WAR YEARS

*They also serve who only stand and wait.*

—John Milton.

World War II killed more persons, cost more money, damaged more property, affected more people and probably caused more far-reaching changes than any other war in history. The number of people killed, wounded or missing between September 1939 and September 1945 can never be calculated. More than ten million allied servicemen and nearly six million military men from the Axis countries died in the war. The three main causes of World War II were the problems left unresolved by World War I, the widespread rise of dictatorships, and the desire of Germany, Italy, and Japan for more territory.[123]

Although historians do not agree on the exact date when World War II began, many consider the German invasion of Poland on September 1, 1939, as the beginning of the war. Two days later, Britain and France declared war on Germany. On May 10, 1940, Belgium and the Netherlands were invaded, and on June 22, 1940, France surrendered to Germany.

Japan's expansionist activities had commenced in the early 1930s with the invasion of Manchuria on September 19, 1931. The invasion of China began on July 7, 1937, and on September 22, 1940, Japanese troops pushed into French Indonesia. Finally, on December 7, 1941, the Japanese attacked Pearl Harbor. One day later, on December 8, 1941, the United States declared war on Japan and on December 11, 1941, the United States declared war on Germany and Italy.

Even after the invasion of Poland and the declaration of war by both France and England in September of 1939, the people in America were somewhat isolated and uninformed. Some of this may have been due to the fact that many Americans were staunch isolationists, refusing to allow America to become involved at any level except to serve as a source of supplies for the Allied forces.

Information provided the American public continued to be less than marginal even during Germany's almost unimpeded march through western Europe. America's primary source of information was the radio. Coincident with the onset of The Battle of Britain, which was Hitler's attempt to subdue Britain through air power alone, was the introduction to the American radio public of Edward R. Murrow who was chief of the CBS European Bureau. His calm and courageous reporting captured America's and the world's attention during the German Blitzkrieg of Great Britain in 1940 and 1941.[124]

Many of Murrow's broadcasts during the Battle of Britain were punctuated by the sounds of air-raid sirens and bomb explosions. Even the CBS offices in London and the BBC studios from which Murrow made his broadcasts experienced direct bomb damage.

On several occasions, in order to provide the American radio public with an eye-witness account as to what the people of Britain were experiencing, the broadcasts were made ftom the roof of the BBC Studio. Murrow began all his reports with, "This is London," a phrase which was to become his hallmark. Until he returned to America at the conclusion of the war in 1945, the Edward R. Murrow program remained an evening ritual in the Kosiak household.

President Franklin D. Roosevelt, in one of his "fireside chats" had suggested early on that every family have in their possession a large world map so that progress of the war could be followed in some detail. Sometime in 1942, Tato did purchase a large world map, which was mounted on the dining room wall. Primarily through information provided on the Edward R. Murrow program as well as information from the newspapers, some attempt was made to stay abreast of the progress of the war.

On September 16, 1940, the United States Selective Training and Service Act (The Draft) became law.[125] All men age twenty-one to sixty years of age were required to register with their local draft boards and become available for induction into the services. Each registrant was assigned a draft number following which a national lottery, held in Washington, D.C., determined the order of call-up for screening and ultimate induction. Initially the call to active duty was determined strictly by one's assigned lottery number whereas, as the war progressed, call-up appeared to be based on age alone.

The period of service was initially set for one year, but in August 1941, it was extended to eighteen months. When the United States entered World War II, the age limits were expanded to eighteen and sixty-five years, though only those twenty to forty-five were liable for actual combat service. Exemptions were reduced, and the period of service was extended to include the duration of the war plus six months. By 1942, eighteen-year-old inductees were declared suitable for combat duty.

Each community had its own draft board, which was involved primarily in determining a registrant's draft status when called to duty. The draft board had the authority to defer registrants for various reasons such as those persons in crucial defense industries, those who were married with several young dependents, those with obvious physical or emotional impairments, and those persons who were responsible for family and parental support. Because neither Johnny nor Willy was twenty-one years old in September 1940, neither was required to register for the Draft at that time.

Within months after the enactment of the Selective Service Act, conscription of some of the young men in Chisholm was begun. Initially, the draft proceeded rather slowly, but each month some fifteen to twenty young men left home. Inductees continued to report for active duty in gradually increasing numbers throughout all of 1940 and 1941.

That the United States had begun to exhibit some urgency in this process was demonstrated by the almost immediate call to active duty of various Army and Navy Reserve units. Along with at least a dozen other young men from Chisholm and several other Range towns, our uncle Harry Billo, a member of the Naval Reserve, was called to active duty on Christmas Day, 1940. The simple fact that all these young men, many of whom were husbands and parents, must leave home on Christmas Day was an eye-opening experience to say the least.

A rude awakening occurred on December 7, 1941, with the bombing of Pearl Harbor and the declaration of war the next day. In typical American style, most of us shrugged off the attack with the feeling that, "They'll be sorry. We'll take care of them in a couple of months."

What left an unforgettable impression on our family at that time was the fact that, on December 8, 1941, while listening to President Franklin Roosevelt give his "Date which will live in infamy" speech, Tato started to cry. None of us had ever seen him cry. He had been in World War I some twenty-five years earlier and knew first hand of the potential hazards and hardships of war. He was also the father of three sons, all of military age.

Because of numerous military setbacks experienced early in the war (Pearl Harbor, the Japanese capture of the Philippines, and our defeat in the Naval Battle of the Java Sea) a high degree of anxiety began to permeate the entire country, including Chisholm and the entire Range. This was especially true among those families whose children were on active duty. This anxiety was markedly accentuated after the announcement of Chisholm's first wartime casualty when, in early March 1942, the parents of Leonard Prusak, a twenty-seven-year-old infantry-man, were informed of his death which had occurred on the Philippine Islands on January 18, 1942. Two months later, Chisholm was informed of its second war casualty. John Braiovich, a young, twenty-one-year-old seaman was reported missing in action and presumed dead following the sinking of his ship on May 8, 1942, in the Battle of the Coral Sea.

Wartime rationing was one of the earliest consequences of war affecting all the people of Chisholm. Once America entered the war, the military had first priority on all materials and supplies. Civilian needs took a back seat to the thousands of ships, tanks, and airplanes rolling off the ways and assembly lines of the great war industries.

Government-controlled rationing and price control began in December, 1941, after the Japanese attack on Pearl Harbor.[126] The Office of Price Administration (OPA) was created, together with subsidiary local boards staffed by volunteers. Automobile tires led the list of items rationed, which by war's end included automobiles, typewriters, bicycles, stoves, leather and rubber footwear, coffee, sugar, canned and processed foods, meats, fats, gasoline, fuel oil for home heating, and coal. Most Americans accepted rationing as necessary, although violations did occur, and a black market or illegal trade existed in some items.

Rubber, a critical war material, was the first item rationed followed by the rationing of gasoline. Beginning in 1942, sugar was the first food item to be rationed. The rationing of coffee began in November, 1942, but it was taken off the ration list in July, 1943.

The mechanics of rationing involved the use of certificates, coupons, or stamps. Local boards issued certificates for items infrequently needed such as tires. Books containing ration coupons were issued for commodities frequently purchased, such as gasoline or sugar. Books of ration stamps covered various categories of food. Red stamps for example could be used for meat, fish, cheese, and dairy products. Blue stamps were exchanged for vegetables, canned fruits, and similar products. The consumers would surrender a certain number of coupons for each rationed item they bought. If all the allotted coupons or stamps were used before the ration period ended, further purchases for rationed items were not possible until the next period.

War Ration Book One was issued in May of 1942 through the local schools, and three more books were issued over the next several years. Each red or blue coupon was worth a certain number of points. Each month, every American was allowed sixty-four red points for the purchase of meat, butter and fats and forty-eight blue points to be used for purchasing processed foods such as ketchup. At the store, grocers tagged food by price and by points. A pound of pork chops might cost $.38 and eight red points, depending on the cut and how much pork was available.

The rationing of gasoline for domestic use was primarily the result of the severe shortage of rubber. To preserve existing tires on America's automobiles, in March of 1942 government officials proposed gas rationing and a thirty-five-mile-per-hour speed limit. It was May before gasoline rationing went into effect and by December of 1942, became nationwide. Gasoline rationing closed parks and tourist attractions and halted America's love affair with the automobile.

Gasoline rations varied with need. Most people qualified for an "A" sticker—four (later three) gallons of gasoline a week—enough to go shopping or visit the doctor, but no Sunday drives. Commuters such as defense workers or those working in the mines were provided a "B" sticker that entitled them to a larger gasoline allowance.

Because Tato was apparently classified as a "farmer," he was awarded a "C" stamp. The Kosiak family was provided with enough gasoline for the daily summertime round trip to the farm in Great Scott Township, a distance of about ten miles. Awarding of the "C" gasoline stamp appears to have been justified in view of the fact that Tato also required the need of a pickup truck to pursue his farming efforts. "T" stamps were available for physicians and other emergency personnel allowing almost unlimited mileage.

Rationing and governmental price controls imposed no special problems on our household. Except for sugar, rationing did not affect the family's dietary needs. Because Ma had no special interest in pastry baking, the rationed sugar supply was usually adequate for the family's needs, except during the summer and fall canning seasons. The problem was resolved to some extent by attempting to limit sugar consumption during the rest of the year or by borrowing stamps from Grandma Billo .

The price controls imposed on the public also had no effect on our family. Fresh cow's milk, delivered daily door to door 365 days a year, still sold for five cents a quart. The family's financial situation did not improve appreciably even after Tato began working part-time for the Paige and Hill Corporation, a company involved in the production of wooden shipping-pallets.

By the fall of 1942, Johnny was already in the army, and Willy was in Minneapolis attending the University. Willy required only limited financial support because, as a motorman for the old streetcar system all the years he was in college, he literally worked his way through school. He also worked for his meals at Pioneer Hall, one of the University dormitories.

Supplementing food rations became a national pastime. Nation-wide, more than twenty million families planted backyard "Victory Gardens," which in 1943 reportedly yielded one-third of the total U.S. vegetable crop.[127] The Kosiaks at that time, were more than "Victory Gardeners"; we were small-time farmers.

Salvage drives played an important role in the home-front activities. In 1942 President Roosevelt reminded the public of the urgent need for old tires, garden hoses and rubber gloves. Within a month, civilians had collected 450,000 tons of used rubber, much of which was recycled and remolded.

Because the glycerin in fat was an ingredient used to make explosives, by 1943 bonus rationing points could be earned by returning bacon grease and other kitchen fats to collecting stations. Two red ration points would be awarded for every pound of used animal fat turned in for recycling. Paper drives, under the direction of the school systems, were conducted at regular intervals with each child encouraged to bring in waste paper, magazines, and cardboard.

In September of 1943, the Chisholm schools, in cooperation with the Junior Chamber of Commerce, conducted a jewelry salvage campaign. According to the Chamber, "Old jewelry was the necessary medium of exchange for those members of the Armed Forces stationed in the South Pacific in order that they might barter with the natives." Items that were collected included necklaces, bracelets, rings, earrings, and pins. By October 27, 1943, in the Chisholm schools alone, 11,137 items had been collected.[128] Although both Uncle Harry Billo and I had served extensively in the South Pacific area, neither one of us could ever remember being supplied with such trinkets.

Of greatest importance were the numerous "War Bond" drives conducted on almost a semi-annual basis during the war. Between the official drives, students were encouraged to save their money for the purchase of War Stamps and War Bonds.

Pupils were encouraged to make use of public institutions such as the banks, the post office, and other establishments for the purchase of stamps and bonds. On occasion, teachers might accompany their pupils to the post office. Surveys were conducted in each classroom at the end of the month and the results were tabulated for each school in the District. For the 1943-1944 school year, Chisholm school children reportedly purchased $8,793 worth of stamps and $22,000 worth of War Bonds.

Irene recalls the formation of a "Defense Club," which consisted of her and five of her girlfriends. All the members were very patriotic and would meet regularly every two weeks. Savings stamps could be purchased at the school or at the post office in denominations of ten or twenty-five cents. These stamps would then be inserted into a small booklet, which when full could be turned in at the post office or bank for a twenty-five dollar War Bond, which cost $17.50. The girls' efforts were reported to their classroom on a regular basis. Irene also reported that none of the members ever acquired enough stamps to purchase a single War Bond.

One of the fallouts of the gas rationing that directly concerned the Chisholm schools was the ruling of the Office of Defense Transportation effective April 1, 1943. As of that date, all noontime school-bus transportation to the locations was discontinued. Because these students could no longer be transported to their homes at lunchtime, the hot lunch program in all the schools was expanded.

In the grades each child was provided with a free hot dish daily, fruit or fruit juice when available, and occasionally a dessert. A half-pint of milk, provided by the Food Distribution Administration of the United States Department of Agriculture, could be purchased for one cent.

"Pupils in Junior or Senior High School may bring sandwiches from home or they may purchase their entire lunch at the nominal charge of nine cents." Almost twenty-six percent (25.9%) of all Chisholm school children in 1943-1944 were participating in the hot lunch program.

The greatest impact of the war years on our family, in addition to waiting for letters from Uncle Harry and the boys, was a realignment of responsibilities within the home and on the farm. As noted previously, in addition to his regular work at the fire station and the operation of the farm, Tato took a part-time job with the Paige and Hill Corporation. The plant was located on the south side of Oak (Sixth) Street between Central and First Avenue South, less than three blocks from our home.

Ma continued to remain primarily involved in homemaking, within the limits of the national food rationing and child care. Eve was only six years old when I left for the Air Corps in June of 1943. By the beginning of the war, Ma already had an electric stove, so the wood harvesting of the previous years was no longer necessary.

Because by the summer of 1943 all the boys had already left home, the operation of the farm was now more dependent on the efforts of the girls, especially Mary Ann and Irene. We've already mentioned Mary Ann's task of driving Ma to and from the farm twice each day from early May to late October, before and after school, just to get the cows milked. During planting and harvesting of the crops, as well as during the haying season, Mary Ann and Irene were regular workers at the farm. When not driving, Mary Ann was often charged with simply staying at home while keeping an eye on Eve.

Even though Irene was not old enough to have a driver's license, this did not interfere with her operating the truck as well as the hay-mower and hayrake during the haying season. Tato would operate the truck while Irene would operate the mower and the rake, a task which involved a fair amount of dexterity and considerable strength, especially when attempting to raise the rake or the cutting blade on the mower. The work also entailed a fair amount of risk primarily due to the fact that the field was quite uneven, and the operator was not strapped into the seat, not to mention the fact that Tato was usually in a hurry and was not always looking into the rear-view mirror. As noted previously, planting, harvesting and haying were strictly a total family affair, and harvesting might entail some time lost from school.

"They also serve who only stand and wait." So it was that the entire Kosiak family did indeed serve their country during the war.

# Epilogue: The Kosiaks

## The John and Julia Billo Kosiak Family, 1940
Johnny, Willy, Mike, Mary Ann, and Irene
Tato, Eve, and Ma

### John Kosiak
Chisholm High School, 1938
Hibbing Junior College, 2 yrs.
University of Minnesota
College of Medicine, 1950

### William Kosiak
Chisholm High School, 1940
Hibbing Junior College, 2 yrs.
University of Minnesota
College of Medicine, 1946

### Michael Kosiak
Chisholm High School, 1942
Hibbing Junior College, 2 yrs.
University of Minnesota
College of Medicine, 1954

### Mary Ann Kosiak
Chisholm High School, 1945
Hibbing Junior College, 2 yrs.
University of Minnesota
College of Education, 1949

### Irene Kosiak
Chisholm High School, 1949
Hibbing Junior College, 2 yrs.
University of Minnesota
College of Medicine, 1956

### Eva Kosiak
Chisholm High School, 1955
Hibbing Junior College, 2 yrs.
University of Minnesota
College of Education, 1960

# *Pictorial Index*

# Endnotes

Chapter 1

[1]Francis Dvornik, *The Slavs: Their Early History and Civilization* (Boston: American Academy of Arts and Sciences, 1956), pp. 13-14.

[2]John Goman, *Galician Rusins on the Iron Range* (Minneapolis: Robart Service Desktop Publishing, 1990), p. 1.

[3]Paul R. Magocsi., *Our People: Carpatho-Rusyns and Their Descendants in North America,* 4th ed. (New York, Ontario: University of Toronto Press Incorporated, 1944), pp. 12-13.

[4]*Tracing the Family's Footsteps to a New Life—They Came to America Part 1.* (Online) Available <http://www.depworld.com/ghout/ftimgranl.htm> (January 9, 2001).

[5]Congressional Record, *Reports of the Immigration Commission. Vol. 37,* "Steerage Conditions. Importations and Harboring of Women for Immoral Purposes," (Government Printing Office, 1911).

[6]*Passage Across the Atlantic, Ellis Island History.* (Online) Available at <http://www.ellisisland.com/passage/html> (January 9, 2001).

[7]Pamela Reeves, *Ellis Island: Gateway to the American Dream* (New York: Barnes and Noble Books, 1998), pp. 51-75.

[8]John S. Pardee and Dwight E. Woodbridge, eds. *History of Duluth and St. Louis County, Vol 2* (Chicago: C.F. Cooper, 1910), p. 722.

[9]C. Whit Pfeiffer, *From Bohunks to Finns: The Scale of Life Among the Ore Strippings of the Northwest,* Survey 36:9 (April 16, 1916).

[10]Helen D. Ramage, *A Mining Location, My Roots,* Undated Memoir.

[11]U.S. Government Census, *Report, 1910,* p. 185.

[12]Theodore Vuicich, *Memories,* Golden Jubilee Souvenir Book, St. Vasilije of Ostrog Serbian Orthodox Church, Chisholm, Minnesota,

229

Unpublished Memoir, 1960, Translated by Mrs. Nick Lagather.

[13]Ramage, H., no pagination.

[14]Goman, J., p. 36.

[15]Magocsi, P.R., p. 12.

[16]John Syrjamaki, *Mesabi Communities: A Study of Their Development* (Ph.D. dissertation, Yale University, 1940), p. 235.

[17]Syrjamaki, J., p. 237

[18]Vuicich, T., no pagination.

[19]*World Book Encyclopedia*, Vol. 20, 1971 s.v. "World War I."

[20]*World Book Encyclopedia*, Vol. 19, 1971 s.v. "Villa Pancho."

[21]Magocsi, P.R., p. 48.

[22]Goman, J., p. 52.

[23]U.S. Government Census, *Report, 1920*, p. 200.

[24]*Chisholm City Directory* (R.L. Polk & Co., Duluth, Minnesota, 1922), p. 86.


Chapter 2

[25]Syrjamaki, J., p. 1.

[26]George R. Stuntz, *Mound Builders,* Read before Minnesota Academy of Natural Science, January 6, 1895, St. Louis County Historical Society, Duluth, Minnesota.

[27]Lewis H. Merritt, *Autobiographic Notes*, Typescript Collection, 1917, St. Louis County Historical Society, Duluth, Minnesota.

[28]Horace V. Winchell, "The Mesabi Iron Range in Minnesota 1892," Extracted from the *Twentieth Annual Report. Minnesota Geological Survey*, St. Louis County Historical Society, Duluth, Minnesota.

[29]Edmund J. Longyear, *Mesabi Pioneer. Reminiscences of Edmund J. Longyear*, Minnesota Historical Society, St. Paul, Minnesota, 1951, p. 14.

[30]Edward Davis, *Pioneering with Taconite*, Minnesota Historical Society, St. Paul, Minnesota, 1964, pp. 89-90.

[31]Syrjamaki, J., pp. 135, 137.

[32]Ibid., pp. 12-13.

[33]*Arrowhead Country. The W.P.A. Guide to the Minnesota Arrowhead*, Works Progress Administration, 1941, Minnesota Historical Society, St. Paul, Minnesota, p. 94.

[34]*Historical Souvenir Edition (Virginia Enterprise*, Virginia,

Minnesota, September 1909).

[35]Walter Van Brunt, *Duluth and St. Louis County Minnesota: Their Story and People* (Chicago and New York: American Historical Society, 1921), p. 500.

[36]*A Brief Sketch of Chisholm's History, Industrial Life, Government and Educational Facilities*, Chisholm Commercial Club, 1915, Minnesota Historical Society, St. Paul, Minnesota, pp. 1-21.

[37]Van Brunt, W., p. 504.

[38]*Chisholm Tribune Herald*, September 1, 1919.

[39]*Chisholm: The Geographical Center of the World's Greatest Iron Mining Region*, Chisholm Commercial Club, 1925, Unpublished Reprint in James P. Vaughan Papers 1904-1963, Box 1, Folder 3.

[40]*Chisholm Tribune Herald*, November 5, 1931.

[41]*Chisholm Tribune Herald*, November 11, 1931.

[42]*Chisholm Tribune Herald*, February 22, 1932.

[43]*World Book Encyclopedia*, Vol. 14, 1971, s.v. "New Deal."

[44]Ibid.

[45]Ibid.


Chapter 3

[46]*Assessed True and Full Value, 307 West Poplar Street, 1930*, Assessor's Office, Chisholm, Minnesota.


Chapter 5

[47]*Chisholm Tribune Herald*, August 30, 1934.

[48]*World Book Encyclopedia*, vol. 2, 1971, s.v. "Bangs Disease."

[49]*World Book Encyclopedia*, vol. 16, 1971, s.v. "Rabbits."


Chapter 6

[50]*Chisholm Tribune Herald*, April 20, 1933

[51]Van Brunt, W., p. 505.

[52]L.H. Weir, *Plans and Suggestions upon the Organization of a*

*System of Employment of the Free Time of the People of Chisholm, Minnesota,* Unpublished Reprint in James P. Vaughan Papers, 1904-1963, Box 2, Folder 15.

[53]*Hibbing Daily Tribune,* March 6, 2001.

[54]*Chisholm Tribune Herald,* July 21, 1938.

[55]*Chisholm Tribune Herald,* January 20, 1918.

[56]Joseph S. Komidar, *As It Was: Family: Town and Growing Up,* Personal Memoir, Unpublished, 1996.

Chapter 7

[57]*The Ranger* (Chisholm High School Annual, 1922).

[58]Timothy L. Smith, *School and Community: The Quest for Equal Opportunity, 1920-1921,* Immigration Historical Research Center, Elmer L. Anderson Library, University of Minnesota, Minneapolis, Minnesota, p. 3.

[59]Vaughan Papers, Box 2, Folder 5.

[60]Vaughan Papers, Box 2, Folder 7.

[61]Frank Valentini, Personal Communication, 2001.

[50]*A Peek into the Past. Memories of Chisholm* (All-Class Reunion Booklet, Chisholm, Minnesota, 1997), p. 29.

Chapter 8

[63]Theodore Christianson, *Minnesota—A History of the State and Its People,* (Chicago and New York: American Historical Society, 1934), p. 429.

[64]*Chisholm Tribune Press,* March 30, 1965, p. 2.

[65]Vaughan Papers, Box 2, Folder 15.

[66]William J. Bell, *Bell Papers,* Unscripted speech manuscript, May 1927, Minnesota Historical Society, St. Paul, Minnesota.

[67]George Chanak, *Farewell to Poverty and Happiness,* Multi-graphed reminiscence, Hibbing, Minnesota, 1962, p. 7, in Smith T.L., p. 10.

[68]Vaughan Papers, Box 2, Folder 15.

[69]Ibid.

[70]*The Minnesota Journal of Education*, September 1925, Minnesota Historical Society, St. Paul, Minnesota.

[71]James P. Vaughan, *Objectives in Education*, Undated address in Vaughan Papers, Box 1, Folder 3.

[72]Smith, T.L., p. 2.

[73]Syrjamaki, J., pp. 386, 387.

[74]Smith, T.L., p. 23.

[75]Ibid, pp. 20, 21.

[76]Vaughan Papers, Box 1, Folder 3.

[77]Smith, T.L., p. 5.

[78]Ibid., p. 1.

[79]Ibid, pp. 25, 26.

[80]Ibid, pp. 31, 32.

[81]Syrjamaki, J., p. 379.

[82]Smith, T.L., p. 28.

[83]Ibid, pp. 29, 30.

[84]Syrjamaki, J., p. 30.

[85]Smith, T.L., pp. 36, 37.

[86]Ibid, pp. 5, 6.

[87]*World Book Encyclopedia*, vol. 20, 1971, s.v. "The Russell Sage Foundation."

[88]Smith, T.L., p. 6.

[89]Ibid, pp. 16, 17.

[90]Ibid, pp. 37-41.

Chapter 9

[91]Syrjamaki, J., pp. 232, 233.

[92]*Chisholm Free Press*, August 26, 1965.

[93]Ann C. Kuttner, *Rheumatic Fever* (Mitchell-Nelson Textbook of Pediatrics, 1952), pp. 179-182.

[94]Robert A. Lyon, *Prevention of Disease* (Mitchell-Nelson Textbook of Pediatrics, 1952), pp. 157-174.

[95]Rudolph N. Schullinger, *Observations of the Mortality from Acute Appendicitis at a University Hospital, 1916 to 1946*, Ann. of Surgery, 1947, 126:448-471.

[96]Archibald W. Graham, E.A. Hines and R.P. Gage, "Blood Pressures in Children Between the Ages of Five and Sixteen Years." *American*

*Journal of Diseases of Children*, April 1945, 69:203-207.

[97]*Chisholm Tribune Press*, January 4, 1996.

[98]William A. Jordan, Undated Report, in Vaughan Papers, Box 12, Folder 2.

[99]Ibid.

[100]Ibid.

[101]Ibid.

[102]James P. Vaughan, *A Practical School Dental Program*, Speech to Minnesota State Dental Association, April 1946, James P. Vaughan Papers, 1904-1963, Box 1, Folder 2.

[103]*Chisholm Tribune Press*, January 4, 1996.

Chapter 10

[104]*World Book Encyclopedia*, vol. 7, 1971, s.v. "Flour."

[105]*Woman's Glory - The Kitchen,* Slovenian Women's Union of America (Benedictine Press, Chicago, Illinois, 1962), p. 27.

Chapter 11

[106]Paul R. Magocsi, *Carpatho-Rusyns Pamphlet* (Carpatho-Rusyn Research Center, Inc., Orwell, Vermont, 1995).

[107]Jessie D. Clarkson, *A History of Russia* (New York: Random House, 1969), p. 36.

[108]Graydon Royce, "Christianity's Ancient Face," *Minneapolis Star Tribune* (June 29, 2000), B5.

[109]Yvonne Betowt, "Orthodox Church Finds New Members in Latin America," *Minneapolis Star Tribune* (June 29, 2000), B8.

[110]"Once a Kingdom for Christmas Dreams," Editorial, *Minneapolis Star Tribune* (January 1, 2001), AI0.

Chapter 12

[111]*World Book Encyclopedia*, Vol. 11, 1971, s.v. "Memorial Day."

[112]*Chisholm Tribune Herald*, May 28, 1915.

[113]*Chisholm Tribune Herald*, June 2, 1916.

[114]*Chisholm Tribune Herald*, May 4, 1917.

[115]*Chisholm Tribune Herald*, May 30, 1919.

[116]*World Book Encyclopedia*, Vol. 11, 1971, s.v. "Memorial Day."

[117]*World Book Encyclopedia*, Vol. 20, 1971, s.v. "Veterans Day."

[118]Richard Logefeil, Personal Communication, 1998.

## Chapter 13

[119]*World Book Encyclopedia*, vol. 14, 1971, s.v. "New Deal."

[120]*World Book Encyclopedia*, vol. 15, 1971, s.v. "Prohibition."

[121]*A Peek into the Past, Memories of Chisholm* (All Class Reunion Booklet, Chisholm, Minnesota, 1997), p. 32.

[122]*Chisholm Tribune Herald*, September 20, 1933.

[123]*World Book Encyclopedia*, vol. 20, 1971, s.v. "World War II."

[124]"Edward R. Murrow," (Online ) Available <http://statelibrary.dcr.state.nc.us/nc/bio/literary/murrow.html> (January 9, 2001).

[125]*World Book Encyclopedia*, vol. 5, 1971, s.v. "Draft, Military."

[126]*Encyclopedia Americana*, vol. 20, 1981, s.v. "Rationing."

[127]Silvia Whitman, *V. Is for Victory: The American Home Front During World War II* (Lerner Publications Minneapolis, 1992).

[128]Vaughan Papers, Box 2, Folder 14.